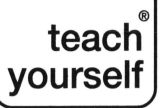

teach yourself

beginner's greek

teach
yourself ®

beginner's greek
aristarhos matsukas

For over 60 years, more than 50 million people have learnt over 750 subjects the **teach yourself** way, with impressive results.

be where you want to be
with **teach yourself**

For UK order enquiries: please contact Bookpoint Ltd, 130 Milton Park, Abingdon, Oxon, OX14 4SB. Telephone: +44 (0) 1235 827720. Fax: +44 (0) 1235 400454. Lines are open 09.00–17.00, Monday to Saturday, with a 24-hour message answering service. Details about our titles and how to order are available at www.teachyourself.co.uk

For USA order enquiries: please contact McGraw-Hill Customer Services, PO Box 545, Blacklick, OH 43004-0545, USA. Telephone: 1-800-722-4726. Fax: 1-614-755-5645.

For Canada order enquiries: please contact McGraw-Hill Ryerson Ltd, 300 Water St, Whitby, Ontario, L1N 9B6, Canada. Telephone: 905 430 5000. Fax: 905 430 5020.

Long renowned as the authoritative source for self-guided learning – with more than 50 million copies sold worldwide – the **teach yourself** series includes over 500 titles in the fields of languages, crafts, hobbies, business, computing and education.

British Library Cataloguing in Publication Data: a catalogue record for this title is available from the British Library.

Library of Congress Catalog Card Number: on file.

First published in UK 2001 by Hodder Education, 338 Euston Road, London, NW1 3BH.

First published in US 2001 by The McGraw-Hill Companies, Inc.

This edition published 2003.

The **teach yourself** name is a registered trade mark of Hodder Headline.

Typeset by Transet Limited, Coventry, England.
Printed in Great Britain for Hodder Education, a division of Hodder Headline, 338 Euston Road, London, NW1 3BH, by Cox & Wyman Ltd, Reading, Berkshire.

The publisher has used its best endeavours to ensure that the URLs for external websites referred to in this book are correct and active at the time of going to press. However, the publisher and the author have no responsibility for the websites and can make no guarantee that a site will remain live or that the content will remain relevant, decent or appropriate.

Hodder Headline's policy is to use papers that are natural, renewable and recyclable products and made from wood grown in sustainable forests. The logging and manufacturing processes are expected to conform to the environmental regulations of the country of origin.

Impression number   10 9
Year   2009 2008 2007 2006

contents

Acknowledgements

Several people have contributed directly or indirectly to the writing of this book. Special thanks go to: Sue Hart, Rebecca Green and Ginny Catmur, my editors at Hodder & Stoughton; my colleagues Sonia Krantonelli, Daniel Gorney and Christine Easthope at the British Hellenic College for comments, corrections, and encouragement; one of my most unique students Karl Kirchner for questioning and discussing everything with me; my daughter Arianna for giving me inspiration and my wife Joanna for putting this inspiration in perspective.

introduction

About the course

Teach Yourself Beginner's Greek is the right course for you if you are a complete beginner or if you are starting again. It is a self-study course which will help you understand and speak Greek well enough to function effectively in basic everyday situations. There is an opportunity for you to find out about the Greek writing system if you want to be able to recognize public signs and notices. The course will also offer you an insight into aspects of Greek life and culture.

Before you know the Greek alphabet

Contrary to popular opinion, Greek is not a difficult language to speak, particularly at beginner's level. The **Pronunciation guide** in this introductory section along with **pronunciation tips** in each unit, and the section about the Greek alphabet at the end of this course, will make most points about pronunciation clear. Where Greek offers a more serious challenge to the learner is in reading and writing the language. This book uses the standard Greek alphabet alongside an informal transliteration system, so that the learner can start to understand and speak the language without the obstacle of the new script. We call it an informal transliteration system because various ways have been devised to represent Greek sounds using a western alphabet but no standard form has ever been established. The transliteration system used in this book is a close phonetic representation of Greek words transcribing their sounds into English script. Transliteration does have its shortcomings but its value, especially assisting reading at early stages, has been generally accepted. The transliteration system has been used throughout the book. It is put before the Greek in Units 1 to 10. From Unit 11 onwards there is a shift to using the Greek script first, so that you get used to working with it.

Transliteration versus Greek script?

Transliteration cannot replace the Greek script. It cannot even be found in a written form of any kind including books, signs or public notices. It simply helps learners to overcome the challenge of a new script in the early stages, as already stated above. The book makes use of both transliteration and Greek script in most instances. Where this is not the case and transliteration stands alone it is because listening comprehension or vocabulary building is tested without focusing on spelling in Greek script.

Many of the exercises at the end of each unit use only the transliteration, and not Greek script. This is done to ensure that beginners can practise initial phrases and vocabulary, without being hindered by the new alphabet. If you are interested in practising the Greek script further, look out for *Teach Yourself Beginner's Greek Script*.

How the course works

The book is divided into two main parts. Units 1 to 7 introduce you to the basic structures and grammatical points you'll need in everyday situations. Units 8 to 15 expand on that and give you more opportunity to reproduce language or to try creating new language yourself, practising more and consolidating what you have learnt so far. This is one of the reasons why the learner, after having completed Unit 8, is advised to start revising previous units. Many of the learning tips and suggestions make clear how to proceed and how to revise previous units. All units should be studied in order, as each builds on the previous one and it is suggested that you do not omit a unit. You can always consult the **Key words and phrases** section of an unfamiliar unit if the need arises, but you should get back to the unit you are studying as soon as you can.

A few words about the recordings

This book can be successfully studied without its accompanying recordings. However, it is highly advisable to use them since they will help you a great deal to pronounce Greek correctly, acquire a more authentic accent, and distinguish sounds, something extremely vital at this early stage. Many learners sometimes complain about not being able to speak a language, even after some considerable effort, but it has been widely accepted that the more we hear a language and try to tune into its sounds and rhythms the more we can speak it in practice. The recorded dialogues and exercises will also offer you plenty of practice in understanding and responding to basic Greek. Bear in mind that although we can always ask native speakers to repeat something for us, we can play the recordings back and forth without hesitation, as many times as needed, to hear something or distinguish a sound. Readers without the recordings will find that there are some exercises that cannot be done with the book alone, but in such cases the material is always covered by other activities in the specific unit or in the **Revision tests**.

Introducing the main characters

There is a story line running throughout the book. It is actually the story of '24 hours in the life of John and Mary Easthope'. Unit 1 starts with their arrival at Athens airport one morning and Unit 15 ends with an enjoyable dinner they have that very evening! Of course, your time with this book will obviously last a little longer!

The following characters appear in some, or all, of the units: **John Easthope** is an architect from Australia married to **Mary Easthope**, a writer of children's books from the United States. They have two children and they reside permanently in London. They are visiting their friends **[ángelos]** Άγγελος and **[elpíTHa]** Ελπίδα **[papás]** Παπάς, who live in Athens with their two children **[andónis]** Αντώνης and **[yioryía]** Γιωργία. John and Mary have visited Greece on several occasions in the past and their command of Greek is really impressive. They have encounters throughout the units with some other characters including **[ána]** Άννα at the airport, a passerby in the street, a bank clerk, a travel agent and a waiter.

About Units 1 to 15

All sections mentioned below appear in all units. Each unit starts by telling you what you are going to learn in that unit.

Learning tips give you advice on everything from how to master vocabulary to how to improve your listening and speaking skills. **Learning tips** appear throughout the units, particularly with regard to grammar aspects that need special attention, but they are always present in the first part of each unit called **Before you start** and they advise you where and how to proceed, what to watch out for or what to focus on.

Before you start This is the section following the outline of key points you are going to learn in the specific unit. You should not skip this section as it tells you how to proceed. You will find various tips on how to study, learn and speak Greek in a fun and easy way.

Key words and phrases   Here the most important words and phrases of each unit are listed. Try to learn most of them by heart. You need to go over this section more than once to become familiar with the new vocabulary. Apply the learning tips and suggestions regarding learning new vocabulary in this book and focus on learning habits that work best for you. Some of the key words are also on the recording to help you with pronunciation.

Pronunciation tips   This is a section that works in parallel with the **Pronunciation guide** in the beginning of this book and the Greek alphabet in the back of the book. It also helps you understand, step by step, the transliteration system used throughout the book. This section makes use of authentic visual material such as signs, adverts, cards, etc. associated with the sounds presented in each unit. That way, more associations between sound and spelling can be gradually established and you can make more sense of the Greek script.

▶ [THiálogos] Διάλογος *Dialogue*   Units 1 to 10 include two dialogues each. Units 11 to 15 have three dialogues in every unit. The dialogues (and word lists) will show you how the new vocabulary is used in context. If you have the recordings, listen to the new dialogues at least two to three times with the book closed. Then listen again, trying to read along. You can pause whenever needed. Don't worry if you cannot follow at the speed of the recording or if you cannot understand everything all at once. Then, using the pause button, break the dialogue into manageable chunks and try repeating each phrase out loud. This will help you gain a more authentic accent and confidence in speaking Greek.

If you do not have the recordings, use a ruler or bookmark to cover part of the dialogue so you can concentrate on a small piece at a time. The most important thing in either case is to speak out loud! It's good to hear yourself in this new learning experience.

Language rules   This section provides you with the nuts and bolts of the language. It explains the main grammatical structures in the units and gives plenty of examples. Some rules are examined and explained further in subsequent units in order to give you a clearer picture of some points when you have learnt more and are ready for them. Bear in mind though that this is not a grammar-oriented course, so some notes might be regarded as over-simplified or not fully explained. It's good if we can say some useful things in a new language even if we don't know all the rules behind them! The **Grammar summary** at the end of the book will provide more explanation for you.

i There are short notes in this section that give you an insight into different aspects of Greek society and culture and are usually linked to the situations you are learning about in each unit.

Practice makes perfect Each activity in this section will help you practise what you studied and learnt in all previous sections. For some exercises you need to listen to the recordings. It is not essential to have the recordings in order to complete the course and most activities do not depend on them. However, if you have the recordings it will make your learning much easier and more varied.

Mini test This section gives you the opportunity to test yourself on what you have learnt in a specific unit.

At the back of the book

The following sections are included at the back of the book:

Revision tests At the end of Units 5, 10 and 15 you can take a revision test, which will test you on the materials covered in the units. All three revision tests are at the back of the book following Unit 15. If tests are not your strong point you can omit the revision tests altogether or take them at a later stage!

The Greek alphabet This section goes unit by unit and lists the sounds you have already met with spelling associations and examples of words. This section can be used in parallel with the **Pronunciation tips** section in each unit. It expands the information found there and offers more notes and explanations to learners interested in the Greek script.

Grammar summary This grammar summary is intended mainly to act as a reference for readers who want to know more about the structure of the language in terms of what is covered in the book. It is by no means a complete grammar, although sometimes materials in this section do not form part of the course itself and are included for the learners who wish to progress a little further, or see a fuller picture of an aspect of Greek grammar.

Key to the exercises and **Key to the revision tests** These are the sections containing all answers to activities, mini tests and revision tests found in the course.

English–Greek glossary This section of the book contains all words found in Units 1 to 15.

Taking it further This section has many useful Internet addresses for everyone interested in visiting websites about Greece. It includes many bilingual websites so you can easily access any area of particular interest about Greece and Greek.

Study guide

How to be successful at learning Greek

1 **Do a little bit every day**, between 20 and 30 minutes if possible, rather than two to three hours in one session.

2 **Try to work towards short-term goals.** For example, work out how long you'll spend in a particular unit and work within this time limit.

3 **Revise and test yourself regularly** using the **Learning tips** and **Mini tests** found in each unit.

4 **Listen to the recordings** as many times and as frequently as possible. If you don't have the recordings, grasp any opportunity to hear the language (by native speakers in Greece, on the radio, in films, in Greek restaurants or social clubs, etc.).

5 **Hear yourself speak!** If at all possible find yourself a quiet place to study where you can speak out loud. It will build up your listening and speaking skills as well as your confidence!

6 **Try every opportunity to speak the language.** You don't have to go to Greece to do this. Find a native Greek speaker to help you and find out about Greek social clubs, etc.

Symbols and abbreviations

▶ This indicates that the recording is needed for the following section.

ℹ This section contains information about Greek, Greece and the Greeks.

As in French, German, Spanish and other languages, Greek nouns have gender. In Greek, there are three genders: masculine, feminine and neuter. They are marked (m), (f) and (n). You will also find the following abbreviations:

(sing) singular	(fml) formal
(pl) plural	(infml) informal
(lit.) literally	

Punctuation

Greek punctuation is very similar to that of English. The only obvious difference is the semicolon [;] which is used as a question mark in Greek! The Greek semicolon looks like an English full stop, slightly raised [˙].

Pronunciation guide

▶ The Greek alphabet

The Greek alphabet has 24 capital letters and 25 small letters. This is because the letter Σ [sígma] becomes a small σ in any position of a word except at the end, where it is ς. If you have the recordings, listen to how the alphabet sounds when recited in Greek. Alternatively, check the names below:

Α α	[álfa]	Ν ν	[ni]
Β β	[víta]	Ξ ξ	[ksi]
Γ γ	[gáma]	Ο ο	[ómikron]
Δ δ	[THélta]	Π π	[pi]
Ε ε	[épsilon]	Ρ ρ	[ro]
Ζ ζ	[zíta]	Σ σ/ς	[sígma]
Η η	[íta]	Τ τ	[taf]
Θ θ	[thíta]	Υ υ	[ípsilon]
Ι ι	[yióta]	Φ φ	[fi]
Κ κ	[kápa]	Χ χ	[hi]
Λ λ	[lámTHa]	Ψ ψ	[psi]
Μ μ	[mi]	Ω ω	[oméga]

Greek, unlike English, is a phonetic language. This means that you can read or pronounce any word once you know the alphabet, something similar to German, Italian or Spanish.

Distinguish the different sound of [TH] and [th]. The first is used to produce the sound of Δ δ as in *this*, *though* or *thus*. The second is used to produce the sound of Θ θ as in *thin*, *thought*, or *thug*.

Be careful with two letters that have almost the same name: Ε ε [épsilon] and Υ υ [ípsilon].

Vowels and consonants

There are seven vowels and seventeen consonants in Greek.

Vowels	Consonants
α, ε, η, ι, ο, υ, ω	β, γ, δ, ζ, θ, κ, λ, μ, ν, ξ, π, ρ, σ/ς, τ, φ, χ, ψ

Two-letter vowels	Two-letter consonants
αι, ει, οι, ου	γγ, γκ, γχ, μπ, ντ, τσ, τζ

Vowel combinations	Two same-letter consonants
αυ, ευ	ββ, κκ, λλ, μμ, ππ, ρρ, σσ, ττ

The sounds of vowels and consonants in each sub-group above are explained in the following section.

Letters and sounds

In general, remember that all letters have one sound, except for **Γ γ** [gáma] and **Σ σ/ς** [sígma]. The vowel or consonant sounds are always pronounced in the same way in Greek, in contrast with English where one letter usually has more than one sound, e.g. *a* as in *mat, mate, mayor*, etc.

▶ Vowel sounds

A α	[álfa]	**a** as in *raft*
E ε	[épsilon]	**e** as in *met*
H η	[íta]	**i** as in *sit*
I ι	[yióta]	**i** as in *sit*
O o	[ómikron]	**o** as in *lot*
Y υ	[ípsilon]	**i** as in *sit*
Ω ω	[oméga]	**o** as in *lot*

Greek vowels can be short or long. The transliteration system used in this course does not show this since in Greek, unlike English, you will rarely find word pairs such as *fit-feet* or *sit-seat*. Consequently, the Greek word σπίτι house is transliterated as [spíti] although the first [i] is longer than the second.

Remember that **Hη, Iι,** and **Yυ** have the same sound (**i** as in *sit*). Also, **Oo** and **Ωω** have the same sound (**o** as in *lot*).

▶ Consonant sounds

B β	[víta]	**v** as in *vet*
Γ γ	[gáma]	1 **y** as in *yield*
		2 **g** as in *sugar*
Δ δ	[THélta]	**TH** as in *this*
Z ζ	[zíta]	**z** as in *zip*
Θ θ	[thíta]	**th** as in *thin*
K κ	[kápa]	**k** as in *kit*
Λ λ	[lámTHa]	**l** as in *let*
M μ	[mi]	**m** as in *met*
N ν	[ni]	**n** as in *net*
Ξ ξ	[ksi]	**ks** as in *banks*
Π π	[pi]	**p** as in *pet*
P ρ	[ro]	**r** as in *rest*
Σ σ/ς	[sígma]	1 **s** as in *set*
		2 **z** as in *zip*
T τ	[taf]	**t** as in *tea*
Φ φ	[fi]	**f** as in *fit*
X χ	[hi]	**h** as in *hit*
Ψ ψ	[psi]	**ps** as in *laps*

Remember that these are approximate sounds and only real words in context spoken by native speakers can present precise sounds.

The letter **Ξ ξ** [ksi] sounds also like the **x** in *six* or *box*.

▶ Two-letter vowels

αι	[álfa-yióta]	**e** as in *met*
ει	[épsilon-yióta]	**i** as in *sit*
οι	[ómikron-yióta]	**i** as in *sit*
ου	[ómikron-ípsilon]	**oo** as in *cool*

You are probably wondering about the sound **[i]** in Greek. Yes, it has five different spellings producing the same sound! Not an easy task for a spell-checker, is it?

▶ Two-letter consonants

The following two-letter consonants have only one sound:

γγ	[gáma-gáma]	**ng** as in *England*
		(Not as in *engine*)
γχ	[gáma-hi]	**nh** as in *inherent*
τσ	[taf-sígma]	**ts** as in *sets*
τζ	[taf-zíta]	**dz** as in *adze*

The remaining two-letter consonants have two different sounds each:

γκ	[gáma-kápa]	1 **g** as in *go*
		2 **ng** as in *England*
μπ	[mi-pi]	1 **b** as in *boy*
		2 **mb** as in *timber*
ντ	[ni-taf]	1 **d** as in *day*
		2 **nd** as in *end*

The **g**, **b** and **d** sounds occur at the beginning of Greek words, whereas the **ng**, **mb** and **nd** sounds occur within a Greek word.

▶ Vowel combinations

αυ	[álfa-ípsilon]	1 **af** as in *after*
		2 **av** as in *avenue*
ευ	[épsilon-ípsilon]	1 **ef** as in *left*
		2 **ev** as in *ever*

(The difference between the two depends on what letter follows.)

Two same-letter consonants

All two same-letter consonants have the same sound as the corresponding one-letter consonant, e.g. **β** [víta] or **ββ** [víta-víta] have the same sound **v** as in *vet*.

The transliteration system used in this book employs all the different sounds presented above. Once again, these sounds are a close approximation and cannot replace real native speakers.

The stress mark in Greek

A written accent is used in all words of more than one syllable to show where the stress falls, both in the Greek script and in the transliteration. Try to observe this as carefully as possible. Changing the stress can alter the meaning entirely, so pay close attention. Capital letters have no stress marks.

Final remarks

It is not absolutely vital to acquire a perfect accent. The aim is to be understood; here are a number of techniques for working on your pronunciation:

1 Listen carefully to the recordings, native speakers or your teacher. Whenever possible repeat aloud.
2 Record yourself and compare your pronunciation with that of a native speaker.
3 Ask native speakers to listen to your pronunciation and tell you how to improve it.
4 Ask native speakers how a specific sound is formed. Watch them and practise at home in front of a mirror.
5 Make a list of words that give you pronunciation trouble and practise them.

▶ Now practise your pronunciation by saying some names of geographical regions in Greece. If you have the recordings, listen to each one first and look them up on the map on page xx to see where each place is. One of the regions is not on the recording, see if you can find which one is missing.

a [atikí] – [nisiá saronikoó] ΑΤΤΙΚΗ – ΝΗΣΙΑ ΣΑΡΩΝΙΚΟΥ
b [kikláTHes] ΚΥΚΛΑΔΕΣ
c [THoTHekánisos] – ΔΩΔΕΚΑΝΗΣΟΣ
d [vorioanatoliká nisiá eyéoo] – ΒΟΡΕΙΟΑΝΑΤΟΛΙΚΑ ΝΗΣΙΑ ΑΙΓΑΙΟΥ
e [thráki] – [samothráki] – ΘΡΑΚΗ – ΣΑΜΟΘΡΑΚΗ
f [makeTHonía] – ΜΑΚΕΔΟΝΙΑ
g [thesalía] – ΘΕΣΣΑΛΙΑ
h [ípiros] – ΗΠΕΙΡΟΣ
i [évia] – [sporáTHes] – ΕΥΒΟΙΑ – ΣΠΟΡΑΔΕΣ
j [kendrikí eláTHa] – ΚΕΝΤΡΙΚΗ ΕΛΛΑΔΑ
k [nisiá oníoo] – ΝΗΣΙΑ ΙΟΝΙΟΥ
l [pelopónisos] – ΠΕΛΟΠΟΝΝΗΣΟΣ
m [kríti] – ΚΡΗΤΗ

Did you pick up the word for *Greece* **[eláTHa] Ελλάδα** and the word for *islands* **[nisiá] νησιά**? They will come in handy later on.

[kalí epitihía]! καλή επιτυχία means *good luck!* Now move on to the first unit.

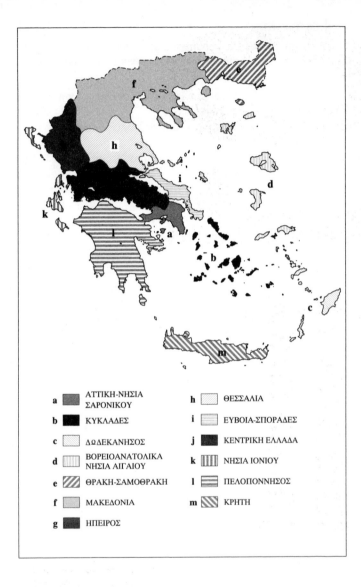

a		ΑΤΤΙΚΗ-ΝΗΣΙΑ ΣΑΡΟΝΙΚΟΥ	**h**	ΘΕΣΣΑΛΙΑ
b		ΚΥΚΛΑΔΕΣ	**i**	ΕΥΒΟΙΑ-ΣΠΟΡΑΔΕΣ
c		ΔΩΔΕΚΑΝΗΣΟΣ	**j**	ΚΕΝΤΡΙΚΗ ΕΛΛΑΔΑ
d		ΒΟΡΕΙΟΑΝΑΤΟΛΙΚΑ ΝΗΣΙΑ ΑΙΓΑΙΟΥ	**k**	ΝΗΣΙΑ ΙΟΝΙΟΥ
e		ΘΡΑΚΗ-ΣΑΜΟΘΡΑΚΗ	**l**	ΠΕΛΟΠΟΝΝΗΣΟΣ
f		ΜΑΚΕΔΟΝΙΑ	**m**	ΚΡΗΤΗ
g		ΗΠΕΙΡΟΣ		

1

γεια σου!
τι κάνεις;
hi! how are you?

In this unit you will learn

- how to say 'hello' and 'goodbye'
- how to exchange greetings
- how to ask and say how people are
- how to introduce yourself and your family
- how to address people when you meet them

Before you start

Read about the course in the introduction. This gives useful advice on how to make the best of this course. Everybody has a different learning style. You need to find the way that works best for you.

- Study regularly and in small amounts. It is much more effective to study 20 minutes each day rather than spending four hours in one go, once a week.
- Revise frequently. This will help you remember some things better and understand others more easily. Learning is based on regular revision.
- Use your recordings often. This will not only help you develop a better pronunciation but also will enable you to become increasingly more familiar with the rhythm of the language.

Speak to native speakers if it is at all possible. Practise with them what you learn in this book. This will help build your confidence in using Greek.

If you don't have the recordings and if you don't know any native speakers to help you with certain sounds and the pronunciation of new words and phrases, use the **Pronunciation guide** on p. xv.

Now before you start, read the **Final remarks** on p. xix once again. Remember that you should adapt this guide to your needs and learning style as you go along.

▶ Key words and phrases

Do you know any Greek already? People often know the word for both *hello* and *goodbye* in Greek which is **[yiásoo]** γεια σου or simply **[yia]** γεια. Read out loud the key words and phrases below. If you have the recordings, listen to one word or phrase at a time and (by using the pause button) repeat it once or twice. If you don't have the recordings, there are some pronunciation tips after this section. You can always check the **Pronunciation guide** at the beginning of the book and the **Greek alphabet** section at the back.

Greetings		
[kaliméra]	καλημέρα	*good morning*
[hérete]	χαίρετε	*hello / goodbye* (fml)
[yiásoo]	γεια σου	*hi / see you* (infml/sing)
[yiásas]	γεια σας	*hello / goodbye* (fml/pl)

| [kalispéra] | καλησπέρα | *good evening* |
| [kaliníhta] | καληνύχτα | *goodnight* |

Introductions

[na sas sistíso]	Να σας συστήσω ...	*Let me introduce ...*
		to you (fml/pl)
[na soo sistíso]	Να σου συστήσω ...	*Let me introduce ...*
		to you (infml/sing)
[apo'THó]	από' δω ...	*this is ...*
[héro polí]	χαίρω πολύ	*How do you do?*
		Pleased to meet you.
		(lit. *I'm very pleased*)
[hárika]	χάρηκα	*I am pleased to have*
		met you. (said when
		you take your leave
		of someone)

Polite phrases

[kalós orísate]!	Καλώς ορίσατε!	*Welcome!* (fml/pl)
[kalós órises]!	Καλώς όρισες!	*Welcome!* (infml/sing)
[kalós se/sas vríka]!	Καλώς σε/σας βρήκα!	*Nice to see you again!*
		[**se**] (infml), [**sas**] (fml)
[efharistó]	ευχαριστώ	*(I) thank you*
[efharistoóme]	ευχαριστούμε	*(We) thank you*
[parakaló]	παρακαλώ	*You're welcome*
		(lit. *please*)

Pronunciation tips

The word **[kaliméra]** *good morning* has three letters which have very similar sounds in both English and Greek. The letter κ **[k]** as in <u>k</u>arate, the letter λ **[l]** as in <u>l</u>ip, and the letter μ **[m]** as in <u>m</u>en. So, as you see, the Greek alphabet is not so difficult and you will be introduced to many more similar sounds in subsequent units. Remember that this section makes use of authentic visuals such as signs, adverts, cards, etc. associated with the sounds of each unit. You can take a moment and become familiar with them or copy them down as a spelling quiz!

▶ **[THiálogos 1] Διάλογος 1** *Dialogue 1*:
[sto aeroTHrómio] Στο αεροδρόμιο *At the airport*

[ángelos] Άγγελος (lit. Angel) is at Athens airport waiting for two friends from London when he meets his friend **[ána] Άννα** by chance.

[ána]	[kaliméra ángele]!	*Good morning, Angelos!*
[ángelos]	[yiásoo ána] [ti kánis]?	*Hello, Anna. How are you?*
[ána]	[íme kalá] [esí]?	*I'm fine (lit. well). You?*
[ángelos]	[kalá], [polí kalá].	*Fine, just fine.*
		(lit. Well, very well.)
[ána]	[yiatí íse eTHó]?	*Why are you here?*
[ángelos]	[periméno] [THío fíloos] [apó to lonTHíno].	*I'm waiting for two friends from London.*

Άννα	Καλημέρα, Άγγελε!
Άγγελος	Γεια σου, Άννα. Τι κάνεις;
Άννα	Είμαι καλά. Εσύ;
Άγγελος	Καλά, πολύ καλά.
Άννα	Γιατί είσαι εδώ;
Άγγελος	Περιμένω δύο φίλους από το Λονδίνο.

Notice that [ángelos] Ἄγγελος has a different form [ángele] Ἄγγελε when he is addressed directly. This is true for all Greek male names, whereas the Greek female names remain unchanged. Further comments on this will follow in subsequent units.

[sto]	στο	at the
[aeroTHrómio]	αεροδρόμιο	airport (n)
[kaliméra]	καλημέρα	good morning
[yiásoo]	γεια σου	hi / hello
[ti]	τι	what/how
[ti kánis]?	τι κάνεις;	how are you?
[íme]	είμαι	I am
[kalá]	καλά	OK, all right, well
[esí]?	Εσύ;	You?
[eTHó]	εδώ	here
[polí]	πολύ	much / very
[polí kalá]	πολύ καλά	just fine (lit. very well)
[yiatí]?	γιατί;	why?
[íse]?	είσαι;	are you?
[periméno]	περιμένω	I wait / I am waiting
[THío]	δύο	two
[fíloos]	φίλους	friends (m/pl)
[apó]	από	from
[to]	το	the
[lonTHíno]	Λονδίνο	London (n)

▶ [THiálogos 2] Διάλογος 2 Dialogue 2: [sistásis] Συστάσεις Introductions

[ángelos]	[na sas sistíso].	Let me introduce you.
	[apo'THó] [o John]	This is John
	[ke i Mary].	and Mary.
[ána]	[yiásas]. [héro polí].	Hello. Pleased to meet you.
	[kalós orísate]	Welcome
	[stin eláTHa].	to Greece!
John	[efharistó].	Thanks.
Mary	[efharistoóme]. [pos se léne]?	(We) thank you. What's your name?
[ána]	[ána]. [me léne ána].	Anna. My name is Anna.

| Ἄγγελος | Να σας συστήσω! Από'δω ο John και η Mary. |
| Ἄννα | Γεια σας. Χαίρω πολύ. Καλώς ορίσατε στην Ελλάδα! |

John	Ευχαριστώ.
Mary	Ευχαριστούμε! Πώς σε λένει;
Άννα	Άννα. Με λένε Άννα.

[sistásis]	Συστάσεις	*Introductions* (f/pl)
[na]	να	*to* (used with verbs)
[sas]	σας	*you* (pl/fml)
[sistíso]	συστήσω	*I introduce*
[apo'THó]	από'δω	*this is ...* (lit. from here…)
[ke]	και	*and*
[yiásas]	γεια σας	*hello*
[héro]	χαίρω	*I'm pleased / I'm happy*
[polí]	πολύ	*much, very*
[kalós orísate]	καλώς ορίσατε	*welcome*
[stin]	στην	*to / in / at* (used with nouns)
[eláTHa]	Ελλάδα	*Greece* (f)
[efharistó]	ευχαριστώ	*thanks* (lit. I thank you)
[efharistoóme]	ευχαριστούμε	*thanks* (lit. we thank you)
[pos]?	πως;	*how/what?*
[pos se léne]?	πώς σε λένε;	*what's your name?* (infml)
		(lit. what do they call you?)
[me léne]	με λένε	*my name is* (lit. they call me)

Note

Why contracted forms? Why [apo'THó] από'δω instead of [apó eTHó] από εδώ? Contracted forms are part of everyday, informal language. This course will make use of several contracted forms, which are used extensively in conversational Greek, explaining also the full forms of these words. Many other languages including English make use of contracted forms in everyday speech. Some examples include: '*What's* your name?', 'I *don't* understand.', '*I'm* not Greek.'

Language rules

As stated in the introductory section of this book, the aim is not to make you an expert in Greek grammar but 'to break the ice' as a beginner in simple, everyday language situations as well as interest and encourage you in advancing your learning of Greek. Keeping this in mind, you know that in this section you will be introduced and exposed to certain grammatical rules of Greek simply to make the language more understandable and your efforts more rewarding.

First things first. Greek is an inflected language. That simply means that many words have several different forms to express singular or plural, formal or informal language, male, female or neuter gender. English does have some ways of doing this, it simply uses fewer forms of words. Also, verbs in Greek change their endings depending on the subject (sing/pl) and the tense expressed. Without this becoming intimidating or confusing, it is important for you to focus for the time being only on the forms found in the dialogues or other explanations and activities.

1 [apó to lonTHíno] από το Λονδίνο from [the] London

Greek has several different forms for the word *the* (the definite article in English) because it changes with the gender, number, and function in the sentence of the noun it accompanies. There are further notes in the **Grammar summary**. In the two dialogues of this unit the Greek word for *the* appeared in the following instances:

[sto aeroTHrómio]	<u>στο</u> αεροδρόμιο	at <u>the</u> airport (n)
[to lonTHíno]	<u>το</u> Λονδίνο	(<u>the</u>) London (n)
[o John]	<u>o</u> John	(<u>the</u>) John (m)
[i méri]	<u>η</u> Mary	(<u>the</u>) Mary (f)
[stin eláTHa]	<u>στην</u> Ελλάδα	in (<u>the</u>) Greece (f)

The two words above [sto] στο and [stin] στην are a combination of the preposition [se] σε *to/in/at* plus the word for *the*. In Greek contracted words as above can be with or without an apostrophe ('), i.e. [apo'THó] or [sto] according to whether the second word begins with a vowel or not.

Notice also that the Greek word for *the* is used before names, i.e. [i méri] η Mary and not simply [méri] *Mary*.

2 [sto aeroTHrómio] Στο αεροδρόμιο At the airport

Words (nouns) that follow the word *the,* like airport, friend, language, have more than two forms in Greek. English has only two forms, i.e. the singular and the plural, for example, airport – airports, whereas Greek usually has three or four forms for the singular and three or four forms for the plural. Greek has three genders: masculine: [o fílos] ο φίλος *the friend*, feminine: [i eláTHa] η Ελλάδα *Greece*, and neuter: [to aeroTHrómio] το αεροδρόμιο *the airport*. More explanations will appear in the next few units about this, and in the **Grammar summary**.

3 [periméno] … περιμένω … I'm waiting

The words [íme] είμαι *I am*, and [periméno] περιμένω *I wait*, express an action or state of being and are called verbs. In English, verbs are often preceded by words such as *I, you, they*, etc.; these are called subject or personal pronouns. These words are generally omitted in Greek because the ending of the verb shows the subject, unless special emphasis is required: [egó íme kalá] Εγώ είμαι καλά *I am fine* (meaning *I and nobody else*) compared to [íme kalá] είμαι καλά *I am fine* (simply meaning that).

There is no difference in Greek between *I wait* and *I am waiting*. For both you say [periméno] περιμένω or [egó periméno] εγώ περιμένω.

The subject pronouns [egó] εγώ *I* and [esí] εσύ *you* are introduced in the second unit.

4 [íme kalá] Είμαι καλά *I am fine*

The verb [íme] είμαι *to be* is the most commonly used verb in both languages. Learn the different forms of this verb below and come back often to this section for the next few weeks of your studies until you become completely familiar with it. Greek has no root form (infinitive) for verbs, i.e. to be, to go, to eat, etc., so we use the 'I-form' when talking about a verb, i.e. I am, I go, I eat, etc.

[íme]	είμαι	I am
[íse]	είσαι	you are (sing/infml)
[íne]	είναι	he/she/it is
[ímaste]	είμαστε	we are
[ísaste] – [íste]	είσαστε – είστε	you are (either form is OK) (pl/fml)
[íne]	είναι	they are

Notes

- [pos íse]? Πώς είσαι; or [pos íste]? Πώς είστε; can be used for *How are you?*
- There is no different form for *he/she/it is* and *they are*. Both are [íne] είναι in Greek!
- The 'I-form' of Greek verbs is also the form found when you look up a verb in a dictionary. That is to say that the verb *to be* and its 'I-form' which is *I am*, are both [íme] είμαι in Greek.

ℹ️ [yiásoo] Γεια σου! *Hello! Hi!*

Even if you don't speak the language, knowing a few words of greetings, thanks or apologies will make you feel so much better in Greece and the Greeks will be delighted. And knowing some basic similarities or differences in social courtesies – when to shake hands, how to introduce people – can actually make all the difference.

[yia], **[yiásoo]** or **[yiásas]** are the most commonly heard greetings in Greece. They are used throughout the day. The first two are informal and used for children and young adults together, whereas the last one is used when addressing adults or older people. All three can also be used as a farewell, meaning *goodbye, so long,* or *see you.*

Otherwise, the normal greetings are **[kaliméra]** *good morning,* **[kalispéra]** *good evening,* and **[kaliníhta]** *good night.* Try to learn all these greetings and farewells by heart. You can also review the **Key words and phrases** section at the beginning of this unit if you want to check the Greek spelling of these words.

[héro polí] Χαίρω πολύ! *How do you do? Pleased to meet you!*

Greeks shake hands only in formal situations. Informally, good friends and relatives – men and women – kiss each other when they meet or depart.

Proximity, or use of space, is different in both cultures. Greeks usually allow less of a distance between themselves and the other person when talking or queuing up. Stepping back in a face-to-face conversation might only invite the other person to move forward and try to get closer to you! In general, Greeks are much more physical than north Europeans.

[na sas sistíso] Να σας συστήσω! *Let me introduce you!*

What do you say when introducing people to each other in Greek? **[na sas sistíso]** *let me introduce you* is the most common expression, followed by the names of the people being introduced. We can use just the first name when the introduction is informal, or both the first and last names if the introduction is more formal. **[yia]** and **[yiásoo]** can be used as informal answers to an introduction. **[yiásas]** and **[héro polí]** are more formal replies. **[héro polí]** means *very pleased to meet you* (lit. I am very pleased). From the same word root you have already met **[hárika]** *pleased to have met you* (lit. I was pleased) when you take your leave of someone you have met for the first time, and **[hérete]** *hello* used in formal situations. You can review the section **Key words and phrases** if you want to check the Greek spelling.

The phrase **[apó eTHó] από εδώ** or most commonly **[apo'THó] από'δω** in its contracted form, means *this is/these are* or *here is/here are* and also introduces people. It literally means *from here*. Practise some formal and informal introductions below while learning some Greek names:

> **[apo'THó o yiánis]. Από'δω ο Γιάννης.** *This is John.*
> (lit. the John)

> **[apo'THó] [o yiórgos ke i maría]. Από'δω ο Γιώργος και η Μαρία.** *Here are George and Mary.*

> **[apo'THó] [o dimítris ke i ioána]. Από'δω ο Δημήτρης και η Ιωάννα.** *Here are James and Joanna.*

> **[apo'THó] [o kírios yiánis mávros] [ke i kiría maría papá]. Από'δω ο κύριος Γιάννης Μαύρος και η κυρία Μαρία Παππά.** *This is Mr John Mavros* (lit. John Black) *and Mrs Mary Papa* (lit. Mary Priest).

Remember that the word for *the* comes before names in Greek, i.e. **[o yiánis] ο Γιάννης** (lit. *the John*) and not simply **[yiánis]**. From the very last example you realize that even in Greek as in many other languages, you have last names meaning colours, professions, etc. Some more names for you:

[ángelos ráftis]	Άγγελος Ράφτης	*Angelos Raftis* (lit. Angel Tailor)
[vasílis skoóros]	Βασίλης Σκούρος	*Vassilis Skouros* (lit. Bill Dark)
[angelikí mavromáti]	Αγγελική Μαυρομάτη	*Angeliki Mavromati* (lit. Angelica Black Eye)

Many names exist in both languages. For example, *John* is **[yiánis] Γιάννης**, *Mary* is **[méri] Μαίρη**, *Helen* is **[eléni] Ελένη**, and *Thomas* is **[thomás] Θωμάς**. Of course, there are names that are unique in either language, e.g. **[ángelos]** Άγγελος has no equivalent in English, neither has *Norman* an equivalent in Greek. More notes about names will follow in subsequent units.

4 [ne] Ναι *Yes*

The Greek word for *yes* is **[ne] ναι** and sounds a little like *no*. Be careful, because its sound is misleading! The Greek word for *no* is **[óhi] όχι**. Observe carefully the head movement that accompanies **[ne]** – the head is lowered – or **[óhi]** – the head is moved back and the eyebrows are raised.

NB It is always useful and practical to learn pairs of words that you associate together. Some examples from this unit are: **[kaliméra – kaliníhta]** καλημέρα – καληνύχτα, **[efharistó – parakaló]** ευχαριστώ – παρακαλώ – **[ne – óhi]** ναι – όχι.

Practice makes perfect

1 What greeting would you use at these times?

a 10:00 **b** 18:00 **c** 23:00

2 Match the words on the left with the words on the right to form word pairs.

a [yiásoo]	**i** [hárika]
b [kalispéra]	**ii** [parakaló]
c [héro políʃ]	**iii** [yia]
d [efharistó]	**iv** [kalós sas vríka]
e [kalós orísate]	**v** [kaliníhta]

3 Match each question with its corresponding answer.

a [yiatí íse eTHó]?	**i** [periméno fíloos]
b [ti kánis]?	**ii** [eléni]
c [pos se léne]?	**iii** [kalá]
d [pos íste]?	**iv** [ímaste polí kalá]

4 Rearrange these lines to make up a dialogue.

a [apo'THó] [o yiánis]
b [kalá, kalá] [yiatí íse eTHó]?
c [yiásoo yiáni]! [ti kánis]?
d [eTHó stin eláTHa]?
e [kalá efharistó]. [esí ti kánis]?

5 The English word *the* or *in the* has many forms in Greek because it changes with the gender, number, and function of the nouns it accompanies. Choose the correct one from the three choices given in each of the following examples.

a [méno] _____ [lonTHíno]   **i** [sto] **ii** [stin] **iii** [to]
b [íme apó] _____ [lonTHíno]   **i** [sto] **ii** [stin] **iii** [to]
c [íme apó] _____ [eláTHa]   **i** [tin] **ii** [stin] **iii** [i]
d [méno] _____ [athína]   **i** [tin] **ii** [stin] **iii** [i]

6 Someone introduces some Greek friends to you. Choose the correct form *[o]* before male names and *[i]* before female names.

a [apo'THó] _____ [ioána]   **d** [apo'THó] _____ [ángelos]
b [apo'THó] _____ [vasílis]   **e** [apo'THó] _____ [ána]
c [apo'THó] _____ [yiánis]   **f** [apo'THó] _____ [eléni]

▶**7** Listen again to Dialogue 2 of this unit and fill in the blanks. If you don't have the recordings, choose the missing words from the box below.

> [o]   [i]   [sas]   [stin]   [polí]   [se]   [me]

Angelos [na] **a** _____ [sistíso]. [apóTHo] **b** _____ [John] [ke] **c** _____ [Mary].
Anna [yiásas]. [héro] **d** _____. [kalós orísate] **e** _____ [eláTHa].
John [efharistó].
Mary [efharistoóme]. [pos] **f** _____ [léne]?
Anna [ána]. **g** _____ [léne ána].

8 How many Greek words can you find in this word search? As a hint, there are more than 10 words! The words read across, down, up, backwards, and diagonally.

k	a	l	i	m	e	r	a
a	p	o	p	s	t	i	n
l	o	o	o	t	h	i	o
a	y	i	a	s	o	o	t
p	e	r	i	m	e	n	o

Mini test

1 **Now you have arrived at the end of Unit 1. What would you say in the following situations?**

a You meet your friend [**ánna**] Άννα. Say 'hello'.
b Ask her how she is.
c Ask her why she is at the airport.
d You want to thank a friend.
e You want to say 'goodbye' to your teacher.
f What are the words for 'good morning' and 'good night'?
g 'I am pleased to meet you' is what you want to say when meeting Mr. X.

2 **What are the people in the pictures below saying?**

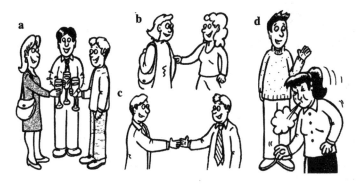

How many words can you translate from the word search in Exercise 8? If you have found more than ten, bravo! If you have fewer than ten, please revise the vocabulary of this unit once again!

You'll find the answers to **Practice makes perfect** and the **Mini test** in the **Key to the exercises** at the end of the book. If most of your answers are correct, you are ready to move on to Unit 2. If most of your answers were incorrect or you found the exercises and the **Mini test** difficult, spend more time revising this unit.

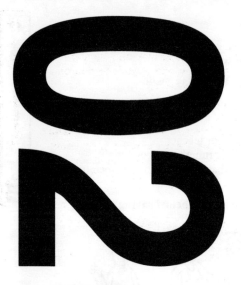

02

Μιλάτε Ελληνικά;
do you speak Greek?

In this unit you will learn
- how to ask about what languages people speak
- how to say what languages you speak
- how to ask and say where people come from
- the names of some cities and countries

Before you start

- Revise Unit 1. Hopefully by now you are familiar with most of the vocabulary of the previous unit. Remember that many words will be repeated in subsequent units, so you will be able to reinforce your learning and refresh your memory easier.
- How are you getting on with the transliteration of Greek used in this book? It helps you read words, expressions or even dialogues faster compared to reading them in original Greek. Keep in mind though that this transliteration does not exist in real life situations such as books, signs, or any other written material. Be also aware that the transliteration cannot be compared to listening to native speakers in Greece or the recordings. Use the **Pronunciation guide** frequently as a reference throughout your studies but ask native speakers whenever you get the chance for the 'real sound', which you should imitate as closely as possible.

Key words and phrases

It's still rather early for you to have a conversation in Greek so it is important in case of emergency to be able to ask people if they speak English. The question is **[milás angliká]? Μιλάς αγγλικά;** or **[miláte angliká]? Μιλάτε αγγλικά; [milás] Μιλάς** is informal and usually addresses younger people and **[miláte] Μιλάτε** is usually used either with strangers or older people.

Study the chart below of people from different cities and countries and the languages they speak.

Cities	Countries	Languages
[i athína] η Αθήνα *Athens*	[i eláTHa] η Ελλάδα *Greece*	[ta eliniká] τα Ελληνικά *Greek*
[to lonTHíno] το Λονδίνο *London*	[i anglía] η Αγγλία *England*	[ta angliká] τα Αγγλικα *English*
[to parísi] το Παρίσι *Paris*	[i galía] η Γαλλία *France*	[ta galiká] τα Γαλλικά *French*
[i rómi] η Ρώμη *Rome*	[i italía] η Ιταλία *Italy*	[ta italiká] τα Ιταλικά *Italian*

[to verolíno]	[i yermanía]	[ta yermaniká]
το Βερολίνο	η Γερμανία	τα Γερμανικά
Berlin	*Germany*	*German*
[i maTHríti]	[i ispanía]	[ta ispaniká]
η Μαδρίτη	η Ισπανία	τα Ισπανικά
Madrid	*Spain*	*Spanish*
[i néa iórki]	[i amerikí]	[ta angliká]
η Νέα Υόρκη	η Αμερική	τα Αγγλικά
New York	*America*	*English*
[to síTHnei]	[i afstralía]	[ta angliká]
το Σίδνεν	η Αυστραλία	τα Αγγλικά
Sydney	*Australia*	*English*

You are reminded that the word for *the* is used in Greek even with proper names. [o] **o** comes before masculine, [i] **η** before feminine and [to] **το** before neuter nouns. The words for languages have a plural form in Greek, which is why [ta] **τα**, the word for *the* before neuter nouns in the plural, is used here. Most words for countries take the article [i] **η**, whereas cities and towns take mostly [to] **το** or [i] **η**.

Some typical questions are:

[apó poo íse]?	Από πού είσαι;	*Where are you from?*
[apó pia póli]?	Από ποια πόλη;	*From which city?*
[apó pia hóra]?	Από ποια χώρα;	*From which country?*
[miláte angliká]?	Μιλάτε αγγλικά;	*Do you speak English?*
[katalavénis]?	Καταλαβαίνεις;	*Do you understand?* (sing/infml)
[katalavénete]?	Καταλαβαίνετε;	*Do you understand?* (pl/fml)

The sound of the word [**pia**] above is very similar to the first syllable of the word *piano*.

Some typical answers are:

[íme apó tin néa iórki].	Είμαι από την Νέα Υόρκη.	*I'm from New York.*
[apó to parísi].	Από το Παρίσι.	*From Paris.*
[íme apó tin anglía].	Είμαι από την Αγγλία.	*I'm from England.*
[ne], [miláo angliká].	Ναι, μιλάω αγγλικά.	*Yes, I speak English.*
[THen katalavéno].	Δεν καταλαβαίνω.	*I don't understand.*

If you are from Scotland [**i skotía**] you can say [**íme apó tin skotía**] **Είμαι από την Σκωτία.** *I'm from Scotland.* [**íme apó tin oo-alía**] **Είμαι από την Ουαλία** means *I'm from Wales,* and [**íme apó tin irlanTHía**] **Είμαι από την Ιρλανδία** means *I'm from Ireland.*

Pronunciation tips

The word [**parísi**] **Παρίσι** *Paris* has three letters, which have very similar sounds in both languages. The letter **π [p]** as in **p**apa, the letter **ρ [r]** as in **r**im, and the letter **σ [s]** as in **s**in. These Greek letters can be a little confusing at first as they are different from English script, but simply focus on word *sounds* rather than word *spelling* for the moment.

Listen to how native speakers roll the letter [**r**] **ρ**. Scots will have no problem with that!

▶ [THiálogos 1] Διάλογος 1 *Dialogue 1:* [miláte eliniká]? Μιλάτε Ελληνικά; *Do you speak Greek?*

Anna is surprised at their command of Greek.

| [**ána**] | [efharistó], [efharistoóme], *Thanks, we thank you! Wow!* |
| | [po-po]! [miláte eliniká]? *Do you speak Greek?* |

John	[ne], [angliká] [ke líga] [eliniká]. [esí]?	Yes, English and some Greek. You?
[ána]	[egó miláo eliniká], [angliká] [ke líga] [yermaniká].	I speak Greek, English and some German.
Mary	[brávo]!	Bravo!

Άννα	Ευχαριστώ, ευχαριστούμε! Πω, πω! Μιλάτε ελληνικα;
John	Ναι. Αγγλικά και λίγα ελληνικά. Εσύ;
Άννα	Εγώ μιλάω ελληνικά, αγγλικά και λίγα γερμανικά.
Mary	Μπράβο!

[po-po]!	πω, πω!	wow!
[miláte]	μιλάτε	you speak
[eliniká]	ελληνικά	Greek
[ne]	ναι	yes
[angliká]	αγγλικά	English
[líga]	λίγα	a little
[esí]	εσύ	you
[egó]	εγώ	I
[miláo]	μιλάω	I speak
[yermaniká]	γερμανικά	German
[brávo]	μπράβο	bravo

Note

[po-po] *Wow!* is a very common phrase that can express surprise, admiration, annoyance or even fear, depending on the context.

▶ **[THiálogos 2] Διάλογος 2** *Dialogue 2:*
[íste apó to lonTHíno]? Είστε από το Λονδίνο;
Are you from London?

Anna tries to find out where John and Mary come from.

[ána]	[íste] [apó to lonTHíno]?	Are you from London?
John	[óhi], [íme] [apó tin afstralía].	No, I'm from Australia.
Mary	[ki egó] [apó tin amerikí]. [esí]? [íse] [apó tin athína]?	And I (am) from America. You? Are you from Athens?
[ána]	[óhi], [íme] [apó ton póro], [alá tóra] [méno stin athína].	No, I'm from (the island of) Poros but I live in Athens now.

Άννα	Είστε από το Λονδίνο;
John	Όχι, είμαι από την Αυστραλία.
Mary	Κι'εγώ, από την Αμερική. Εσύ; Είσαι από την Αθήνα;
Άννα	Όχι. Είμαι από τον Πόρο, αλλά τώρα μένω στην Αθήνα.

[íste]?	είστε;	you are; are you? (pl/fml)
[tin]	την	the (with f nouns)
[afstralía]	Αυστραλία	Australia (f)
[óhi]	όχι	no
[ki]	κι'	and (contracted form of [ke] και)
[amerikí]	Αμερική	America (USA) (f)
[íse]?	είσαι;	you are; are you? (sing/infml)
[athína]	Αθήνα	Athens (f)
[ton]	τον	the (with m nouns)
[póro]	Πόρο	Poros (m)
[alá]	αλλά	but
[tóra]	τώρα	now
[méno]	μένω	I live

Language rules

1 [esí]? Εσύ; You? How about you?

It is important to know the subject pronouns* in Greek. Two of them [egó] *I* and [esí] *you* were mentioned in the first unit. Try to memorize these important words below:

[egó]	εγώ	I
[esí]	εσύ	you (sing)
[aftós]	αυτός	he
[aftí]	αυτή	she
[aftó]	αυτό	it
[emís]	εμείς	we
[esís]	εσείς	you (pl or sing. fml)
[aftí]	αυτοί	they (only males, or males and females)
[aftés]	αυτές	they (only females)
[aftá]	αυτά	they (only things and n nouns)

There is no difference in sound between the words for *she* and *they*. They are both [aftí], only the Greek spelling is different.

*Pronouns are also called 'personal pronouns' in grammar books.

2 [apó tin afstalía] Από την Αυστραλία *From Australia*

As mentioned in the **Key words and phrases** section at the beginning of this unit, Greek uses the word *the* much more than English. For instance, 'from Australia' is 'from *the* Australia' in Greek, [apó *tin* afstralía] από *την* Αυστραλία, or 'from London' is 'from *the* London', [apó *to* lonTHíno] από *το* Λονδίνο. Of course, as explained in Unit 1, the Greek word for *the* or *in the* has several different forms. Just learn them in context without trying to analyse them grammatically for the moment. Notice the different form used in the examples below depending on the gender (m, f, n) of the city or country:

[íme apó tin afstralía]. Είμαι από *την* Αυστραλία.
I'm from Australia. BUT
[méno stin afstralía]. Μένω *στην* Αυστραλία.
I live in Australia.

[íme apó tin athína]. Είμαι από *την* Αθήνα.
I'm from Athens. BUT
[méno stin athína]. Μένω *στην* Αθήνα.
I live in Athens.

[íme apó to lonTHíno]. Είμαι από *το* Λονδίνο.
I'm from London. BUT
[méno sto lonTHíno]. Μένω *στο* Λονδίνο.
I live in London.

Remember that **[stin]** or **[sto]** as explained in Unit 1 are words formed from the combination of the preposition **[se]** σε *at/in/to* and the word **[tin]** την *the* (f) or **[to]** το *the* (n). Interestingly, the two words cannot stand alone. We cannot say **[méno se tin afstralía]** or **[méno *se to* lonTHíno].** You can read some further notes about this in the **Grammar summary**.

Here are some other examples of different forms for the word *the*.

Different forms

[íme apó] [ton póro].   [ton] τον (m/sing)
Είμαι από τον Πόρο.
I'm from Poros (island).

[íme apó] [tin pátra].   [tin] την (f/sing)
Είμαι από την Πάτρα.
I'm from Patras (city).

[íme apó] [to náfplio].   [to] το (n/sing)
Είμαι από το Ναύπλιο.
I'm from Nafplio (town).

If you add the [s] from [se] at the beginning of these words you can use them with the word [méno] *I live*. Some examples:

[méno] [ston póro]. Μένω στον Πόρο. *I live in Poros.*
[méno] [stin pátra]. Μένω στην Πάτρα. *I live in Patras.*
[méno] [sto náfplio]. Μένω στο Ναύπλιο. *I live in Nafplio.*

3 [miláo eliniká] Μιλάω Ελληνικά *I speak Greek*

[miláo] *I speak*, like [íme] *I am* and [periméno] *I wait*, is another Greek verb. As you remember from Unit 1 you do not need to use words like *I*, *you* and *they* before the verb because the change in the ending of the verb tells you who is doing the action. You have already met three forms of this verb so far, that is [miláo], [milái], [miláte]. Let's see all the different forms below:

[miláo]	μιλάω	*I speak*
[milás]	μιλάς	*you speak*
[milái]	μιλάει	*he/she/it speaks*
[miláme]	μιλάμε	*we speak*
[miláte]	μιλάτε	*you speak*
[miloón(e)]	μιλούν(ε)	*they speak*

Remember that there is no difference in Greek between *I speak* and *I am speaking*. They are both [miláo].

ℹ️ [ta eliniká] Τα Ελληνικά *The Greek language*

Greek is one of the Indo-European languages, with more than 4,000 years of development and history. It is spoken by about 10 million people in Greece and 3.5 million elsewhere, including 1 million in Melbourne, 1 million in New York City, and 500,000 in Chicago. Fortunately for non-Greek speakers, many signs are in English, for instance advertisements for accommodation or airport signs. Some signs are bilingual, with good or bad English translations (as you will notice)! However, many other signs are only in Greek, including street signs, shop signs, etc.

Although it is not the aim of this book to teach the Greek alphabet fully, it will still provide you with some practical assistance on how to read public signs through authentic visuals, e.g. photos, adverts, cards and menus. For those of you who are interested in the Greek alphabet, the dialogues in Greek script in every unit are a good source of practice.

Remember that although many learners and visitors talk about a totally new alphabet, they forget to mention that most letters are identical in both alphabets and most sounds are already familiar to you. In the part of **Key words and phrases** you will encounter several suggestions about Greek sounds and spelling. The most important advice here is just to leave some initial concerns behind you and persevere.

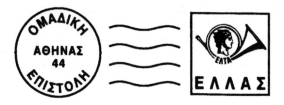

[i eláTHa] Η Ελλάδα *Greece*

Most visitors who decide to come to Greece enjoy their summer vacation on one of the many Greek islands. More and more people, however, have started visiting unspoiled and unexplored places, trekking through lesser-known mountain areas, or reaching remote villages on the mainland. Many also visit Greece during the autumn and winter months. There are several books covering Greece exhaustively. Below you will find some brief information about some distances, sizes and population figures of the different regions of Greece.

Some important geographical data about Greece

Greece occupies an area of 132,000 square km, which is about 4% of the EU. The distance from North to South is about 800 km and from East to West 1,000 km. 81% of the country is on the mainland whereas the remaining 19% are islands. Mount Olympus is the tallest mountain (2,920 m). Crete is the largest island with an area of 8,380 square km and Euboea (or Evvoia) comes in second (3,800 square km). Lesbos (or Lesvos) and Rhodes cover an area of 1,630 square km and 1,400 square km respectively. Greece is divided into nine large geographical areas: Sterea (pop. 4.5 million), Macedonia (pop. 2.3 million), Peloponnese (pop. 1 million), Thessaly (pop. 750,000), Crete (pop. 550,000), the Aegean Islands (pop. 500,000), Epirus (pop. 350,000), Thrace (pop. 350,000), and the Ionian Islands (pop. 200,000). Look back at the map on page xx and see if you can identify these regions.

3 [kiríes ke kíri-i]! Κυρίες και Κύριοι! *Ladies and Gentlemen!*

When addressing people you can use [kírie] **κύριε** *Sir* or [kiría] **κυρία** *Madam*. Notice where the stress comes in the two words. The plural form of those two words serves as the expression 'Ladies and Gentlemen'. The root words are [kírios] **κύριος** for *Mr/Sir*, [kiría] **κυρία** for *Mrs/Madam*, and [THespiníTHa] **δεσποινίδα** for *Miss*. These words are sometimes used with the first name only, for example [kiría ána] *Mrs Anna*, which is a semi-formal way of addressing a person you don't know very well. This form does not exist in English. *Ms* does not exist in Greek either.

Practice makes perfect

1 Patras is a bustling harbour in the Western Peloponnese, where many visitors arrive by boat from the Italian ports of Bari, Brindisi, Ancona and Venice. You see some cars with the following stickers. Please say and write in transliteration or Greek script the countries they come from with the corresponding languages.

Symbol	Country	Language
GR	a	i
E	b	ii
I	c	iii
F	d	iv
GB	e	v

2 Match each question with the most appropriate answer.

a [apó poo íse]?

b [apó pia póli]?

c [miláte italiká]?

d [poo ménete]?

i [stin athína].

ii [lonTHino].

iii [óhi].

iv [apó tin anglía].

3 Monsterwords! The author has forgotten to separate the words in the following sentences. Can you do it for him? Can you also translate them into English?

a [íneapótinthesaloníki].

b [alátoraménostinpátra].

c [miláoitalikákelígaispaniká].

d [iathínaínestineláTHa].

e [ketoparísistingalía].

4 Are you interested in geography? The six largest cities and towns in Greece with their population numbers are listed on the next page. Can you find them on the map below?

[i athína] η Αθήνα	4,000,000
[i thesaloniki] η Θεσσαλονίκη	1,000,000
[i pátra] η Πάτρα	170,000
[to iráklio] το Ηράκλειο	125,000
[i lárisa] η Λάρισα	120,000
[o vólos] ο Βόλος	80,000

5 The different forms of the Greek word *the* need more practice. Remember [sto] and [stin] mean *at/in/to + the* in Greek.

a [íme apó] _____ [lonTHíno].   **i** [o]   **ii** [to]   **iii** [sto]
b [méno] _____ [lonTHíno].   **i** [o]   **ii** [to]   **iii** [sto]
c [íme apó] _____ [amerikí].   **i** [i]   **ii** [tin]   **iii** [stin]
d [apó] _____ [néa iórki].   **i** [i]   **ii** [tin]   **iii** [stin]
e _____ [néa iórki íne stin amerikí].   **i** [i]   **ii** [tin]   **iii** [stin]
f _____ [lonTHíno íne stin anglía].   **i** [o]   **ii** [to]   **iii** [sto]

6 Place the names of the following European capitals on the map. Can you also say and write in transliteration or Greek script the names of the corresponding countries?

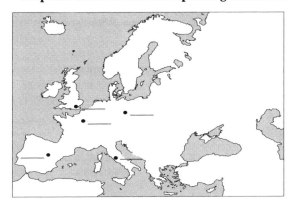

a [i rómi] η Ρώμη
b [to lonTHíno] το Λονδίνο
c [i maTHríti] η Μαδρίτη
d [to parísi] το Παρίσι
e [to verolíno] το Βερολίνο

7 Listen again to Dialogue 2 of this unit and fill in the blanks. If you don't have the recording, choose the missing words from the box below.

Anna   [íste] **a** ____ [to lonTHíno]?
John   **b** ____. [íme] [apó tin afstralía].
Mary   [ki] **c** ____ [apó tin amerikí]. **d** ____? [íse] [apó tin athína]?
Anna   **b** ____. [íme] [apó ton póro]. **e** ____ [tóra] [méno stin athína].

[alá]   [apó]   [esí]   [egó]   [óhi]

Mini test

[bravo]!Μπράβο! Congratulations, you have just completed the second unit. Keep up the good work! If you find the following **Mini test** a little bit difficult, do not be discouraged. Simply revise Unit 2 once again and then proceed to Unit 3. A lot of things will fall into place in the subsequent units.

a How would you ask for someone's country of origin?
b 'Where do you live now?' is what you want to know.
c 'I'm from Cardiff but I live in Manchester now.' I know this is a long sentence but try it...
d Name three European languages.
e Name three European cities.
f Have you started writing down word pairs? Are the following easy for you? 'yes-no', 'city-country', 'Greek-English', 'Madrid-Paris', 'I-you', and 'we-they'.

03

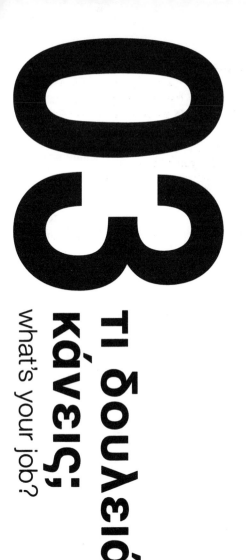

Τι δουλειά κάνεις;
what's your job?

In this unit you will learn
- how to ask about different jobs and professions
- how to answer a question about your job
- how to describe the place where you live
- the names of different professions

Before you start

- Revise Unit 2 once again. Going back to familiar materials makes you feel more confident.

- Remember, this is *your* book! Feel free to underline, circle and note down anything you like. Don't be afraid to use markers and highlighters and put some colour in this book. It will make your life easier when you retrace your steps for revision or quick reference. Always remember that your individual learning style suits you best and no one else.

- One last suggestion: it is you who decides what is important in every unit and how you would want to use the information with native speakers. The materials here will introduce you to certain topics, but it is up to you to personalize them. So, if your own job is not mentioned in this unit, please look it up in a dictionary.

▶ Key words and phrases

Discussions about jobs and professions emerge quite early on when you meet Greek people. So be prepared to understand or use the question [ti THooliá kánis]? Τι δουλειά κάνεις; in informal situations and [ti THooliá kánete]? Τι δουλειά κάνετε; in formal situations. Both questions mean 'What's your job?', 'What's your profession?', 'What do you do for a living?'. You should know the words [kánis] and [kánete] by now. The literal translation of the questions above is 'What work do you do?'. Typical answers could be [íme ...] είμαι *I am* ..., or [THoolévo sto/stin ...] δουλεύω στο/στην *I work at...*, or [THoolévo yia ...] δουλεύω για *I work for...*. Notice that the chart below showing different professions contains two columns for masculine and feminine words, something like *waiter-waitress* in English. Some professions are the same for both sexes, with just the article changing.

Masculine	Feminine
[o arhitéktonas] ο αρχιτέκτονας *architect*	[i arhitéktonas] η αρχιτέκτονας *architect*
[o moosikós] ο μουσικός *musician*	[i moosikós] η μουσικός *musician*
[o pianístas] ο πιανίστας *pianist*	[i pianístria] η πιανίστρια *pianist*
[o servitóros] ο σερβιτόρος *waiter*	[i servitóra] η σερβιτόρα *waitress*

[o yiatrós] ο γιατρός	**[i yiatrós]** η γιατρός
doctor	*doctor*
[o THáskalos] ο δάσκαλος	**[i THaskála]** η δασκάλα
teacher	*teacher*
[o sigraféas] ο συγγραφέας	**[i sigraféas]** η συγγραφέας
writer	*writer*

Interestingly enough, you do not need the word *a* when you state your profession in Greek. **[íme yiatrós]** Είμαι γιατρός *I am (a) doctor* literally translates to 'I am doctor'.

Pronunciation tips

The word **[servitóra]** σερβιτόρα *waitress* has four letters which have very similar sounds in English and Greek. The letter ε **[e]** as in *sell*, the letter ι **[i]** as in *sit*, the letter ο **[o]** as in *Tom*, and the letter α **[a]** as in *cat*.

Let's revise our pronunciation a little. So far you have been introduced to six consonant sounds and four vowel sounds. They are:

Consonants	**Vowels**
κ [k]	α [a]
λ [l]	ε [e]
μ [m]	ι [i]
π [p]	ο [o]
ρ [r]	
σ [s]	

You can always go back to the **Pronunciation guide** or the **Greek alphabet** section to review letters and sounds. Frequent revision will soon build up your confidence and make you more familiar with the new alphabet in a short period of time.

More pronunciation tips will follow in the subsequent units. If you have the recording, pay attention to the individual sounds in words found in the dialogues or try to listen to some native speakers if that is at all possible.

Αγγελική Κουκουλά
ΕΠΙΜΕΛΕΙΑ ΥΛΗΣ

Εκδοτική ΑΛΦΑ ΕΠΕ

ΕΚΔΟΣΕΙΣ • ΒΙΒΛΙΟΠΩΛΕΙΟ

▶ [THiálogos 1] Διάλογος 1 *Dialogue 1:*
[ti]? Τι; *What?*

Anna was not expecting such replies and now she is trying to find out why they live in London.

[ána]	[ti]? [afstralía]? [amerikí]?	*What? Australia? America?*
	[ke tóra] [ménete sto	*And now you live in*
	lonTHíno]?	*London?*
John	[ne]. [THoolévo]	*Yes. I work*
	[sto lonTHíno].	*in London.*
	[íme arhitéktonas].	*I'm an architect.*
Mary	[ki' egó] [íme sigraféas].	*And myself, I'm a writer.*
	[gráfo pediká vivlía].	*I write children's books.*
	[esí]?	*How about you?*
	[ti THooliá kánis]?	*What do you do for a living?*
[ána]	[íme THaskála].	*I'm a teacher.*

Άννα	Τι; Αυστραλία; Αμερική; Και τώρα μένετε στο Λονδίνο;
John	Ναι. Δουλεύω στο Λονδίνο. Είμαι αρχιτέκτονας.
Mary	Κι' εγώ είμαι συγγραφέας. Γράφω παιδικά βιβλία. Εσύ;
	Τι δουλειά κάνεις;
Άννα	Είμαι δασκάλα.

[ménete]	μένετε	*you live* (pl/fml)
[sto]	στο	*in the*
[THoolévo]	δουλεύω	*I work*
[arhitéktonas]	αρχιτέκτονας	*architect* (m/f)
[sigraféas]	συγγραφέας	*writer* (m/f)
[gráfo]	γράφω	*I write*
[pediká]	παιδικά	*children's*
[vivlía]	βιβλία	*books* (n/pl)
[THooliá]	δουλειά	*work* (f)
[THaskála]	δασκάλα	*teacher* (f)

Note

Both words **[sigraféas]** and **[gráfo]** have the combination of the two letters **[gr]** which sounds softer compared to the same combination in English words like *graph*, *gram* or *greet*. Listen to the recordings or a native speaker pronouncing these words.

▶ [THiálogos 2] Διάλογος 2 *Dialogue 2*

John now asks Anna if she knows London and about her home.

John	[ána], [kséris to lonTHíno]?	*Anna, do you know London?*
[ána]	[óhi] [THen kséro to lonTHíno]. [kséro móno tin athína].	*No, I don't know London. I know only Athens.*
Mary	[poo ménis]? [ménis kondá ston ángelo]?	*Where do you live? Do you live near Angelos?*
[ána]	[ne]. [méno] [kondá ston ángelo].	*Yes. I live near Angelos.*

John	Άννα, ξέρεις το Λονδίνο;
Άννα	Όχι, δεν ξέρω το Λονδίνο. Ξέρω μόνο την Αθήνα.
Mary	Πού μένεις; Μένεις κοντά στον Άγγελο;
Άννα	Ναι. Μένω κοντά στον Άγγελο.

[kséris]	ξέρεις	*you know* (sing./infml)
[THen]	δεν	*not*
[kséro]	ξέρω	*I know*
[poo]	πού	*where*
[kondá]	κοντά	*near, close to*
[ston]	στον	*at the*

Language rules

1 [THoolévo] [sto lonTHíno] Δουλεύω στο Λονδίνο *I work in London*

Verbs and nouns are very important words in most languages. Sentences are constructed around them, so you need to focus on them as you go along and become familiar with their different forms. Unit 1 introduced you to the verb **[íme]** είμαι *I am*, Unit 2 to the verb **[miláo]** μιλάω *I speak*, and now in this unit you will meet the verb **[THoolévo]** δουλεύω *I work*. These verbs belong to three different verb groups. The verb **[THoolévo]** is part of the largest verb group in the Greek language. That simply means that most Greek verbs have the same endings in their different forms. Look at the verb **[THoolévo]** below:

[THoolévo]	**δουλεύω**	*I work*
[THoolévis]	**δουλεύεις**	*you work* (sing/infml)
[THoolévi]	**δουλεύει**	*he/she/it works*
[THoolévoome]	**δουλεύουμε**	*we work*
[THoolévete]	**δουλεύετε**	*you work* (pl/fml sing)
[THoolévoon(e)]	**δουλεύουν(ε)**	*they work*

Remember that **[THoolévete]** *you work* can be used for only one person usually older than us to show respect (sing/fml), but it can also be used for several people (pl). **[THoolévis]** *you work* is always used with only one person (sing/infml). This is true for all Greek verbs.

Similarly, the following verbs use the endings **[-o]**, **[-is]**, **[-i]**, **[-oome]**, **[-ete]**, and **[-oon]**:

[periméno] περιμένω *I wait*, **[káno]** κάνω *I do/I make*, **[méno]** μένω *I live/I stay*, **[kséro]** ξέρω *I know*, **[gráfo]** γράφω *I write*.

Remember that the same form can be used to express 'I am working', 'I am waiting', 'I am doing', 'I am living', or 'I am writing'. Note the examples:

[THoolévo] [san servitóros].	*I work as a waiter.*
[THoolévo] [tóra].	*I am working now.*

2 [poo ménis]? Πού μένεις; Where do you live?

You already know four question words in Greek: **[poo]?** πού; *where?*, **[ti]?** τι; *what?*, **[pos]?** πώς; *how?*, and **[pia]?** ποια; *who?/which?/what?* **[pia]** is the feminine singular form here – this word changes with the gender, number and function of the noun it precedes. You can use these words with the verbs that you learn in order to form questions in Greek. For instance:

[poo ménis]?	**Πού μένεις;**	*Where do you live?*
[ti grafis]?	**Τι γράφεις;**	*What do you write?*
[pos kséris]?	**Πώς ξέρεις;**	*How do you know?*
[pia kséris]?	**Ποια ξέρεις;**	*Who [a female person] do you know?*

In English the auxiliary verb *do* is needed to form questions. In Greek you don't change the order of words as you do in English, you simply make your voice go up: **[ménis]** with a falling tone means 'you live' or 'you are living' and **[ménis]**? with a rising tone means 'do you live?' or 'are you living?'. Remember this important fact when you want to ask questions in Greek by making your voice go up without adding new words or changing the sequence of the words. One more example: (falling tone) **[íste apó tin anglía]**. *You are from England*; (rising tone) **[íste apó tin anglía]**? *Are you from England?*

3 [ki'egó] Κι'εγώ *And myself* (lit. *and I*)

In Unit 2, you were introduced to the subject pronouns, those words that express the meaning of *I*, *you*, *he/she/it*, *we*, *you*, *they* preceding verbs. It was also mentioned that these words are not necessarily used in Greek (because the verb ending shows the subject) unless you want to emphasize who is carrying out an action. Revise these important words again and compare their corresponding verb endings with **[méno]** μένω *I live* below:

[egó] εγώ	**[mén-o]** μένω	*I live*
[esí] εσύ	**[mén-is]** μένεις	*you live*
[aftós]/[aftí]/[aftó] αυτός/αυτή/αυτό	**[mén-i]** μένει	*he/she/it lives*
[emís] εμείς	**[mén-oome]** μένουμε	*we live*
[esís] εσείς	**[mén-ete]** μένετε	*you live*
[aftí]/[aftés]/[aftá] αυτοί/αυτές/αυτά	**[mén-oon(e)]** μένουν(ε)	*they live*

4 [THen kséro] Δεν ξέρω *I don't know*

[THen] δεν (sometimes **[THe]** δε, dropping the final letter **[-n]** ν) is the word used to make negative sentences. It simply precedes the verb. Note the examples below:

[ménoome stin athína]. Μένουμε στην Αθήνα. *We live in Athens.*
[THen] [ménoome stin thesaloníki]. Δεν μένουμε στην Θεσσαλονίκη. *We don't live in Thessaloniki.*
[íme sigraféas]. Είμαι συγγραφέας. *I am a writer.*
[THen] [íme arhitéktonas]. Δεν είμαι αρχιτέκτονας. *I am not an architect.*
[kséri angliká] Ξέρει αγγλικά. *He knows English.*
[THen] [kséri italiká]. Δεν ξέρει ιταλικά. *He does not know Italian.*

ⓘ [ti THooliá kánis]? Τι δουλειά κάνεις; *What's your job?*

Many Greeks are self-employed. From small one-man businesses to large companies, they enjoy being self-employed despite the risks this might have. There is something in the Greek character that highly values independence. Others become public employees, a life's ambition for many since it provides security. New professions are bank executives or stock brokers. Shipping has a long tradition in Greece and it is a sector occupying a large number of Greek workers. Equally important for the Greek economy is the tourist industry which generates one-eighth of the gross national income and employs a large number of people, especially during the summer. Last but not least, Greece is also an agricultural country, producing olive oil, wine, milk products, fruit, vegetables and cereals.

Many foreigners come to work in Greece, as employees for large multinational companies, as spouses of Greeks returning from abroad or as economic migrants hoping for a better future. Greece is not yet prepared to assimilate the large influx of foreign workers who come to Greece from countries such as Albania, Poland, Pakistan or countries of the former Soviet Union.

Practice makes perfect

1 **Fill in the blanks using the words provided in the box below. You might have more than one option in some instances. The first one has been done for you.**

> [egó]   [esí]   [aftós]   [aftí]   [aftó]
> [emís]   [esís]   [aftí]/[aftés]/[aftá]

a [esís] [poo ménete]?
b _____ [kséris eliniká]?
c _____ [ménoon stin pátra].
d _____ [THen periméno].
e _____ [íne o thomás].
f _____ [íne i ána].
g _____ [ímaste apó tin eláTHa].
h _____ [periménoon THío fíloos].

2 Change the following into negative sentences.

Look at the example: [miláo galiká]. → [eliniká] [THen miláo eliniká].

Now do the same to the following:

a [miláme angliká]. → [yermaniká]
b [kséro ton yiáni]. → [ángelo]
c [ksérete tin ioána]. → [ána]
d [periméni THío fíloos]. → [tris fíloos]
e [ménoon stin athína]. → [sta yánena]
f [íme apó tin anglía]. → [amerikí]
g [íne apó tin eláTHa]. → [italía]

3 Change the following sentences into questions as in the example:

[kséro yermaniká]. → [esí] [kséris yermaniká]?

a [ménoome stin yermanía]. → [esís]
b [aftós íne apó tin afstralía]. → [aftí]
c [kséroon líga eliniká]. → [esí]
d [aftí periménoon THío fíloos]. → [aftés]
e [miláo angliká]. → [esí]
f [THen miláme ispaniká]. → [esís]
g [ímaste apó tin anglía] → [esís]

4 Look at the cartoons below and write down the appropriate jobs in transliteration or Greek script. Item c has been answered for you.

a _____   d _____

b _____   e _____

c [nosokóma] νοσοκόμα *nurse*   f _____

5 Match each question with the most appropriate answer.

a [íse arhitéktonas]?   **i** [óhi], [íne pianístas].

b [íste yiatrós]?   **ii** [óhi], [íne servitóra].

c [o yiánis íne servitóros]?   **iii** [ne, íne THáskalos].

d [i ána íne sigraféas]?   **iv** [óhi, íme moosikós].

e [o ángelos íne THáskalos]?   **v** [ne, íme yiatrós].

6 Let's practise again some different forms of the Greek word for *the* or *in/at/to the*.

a [kséro] ___ [lonTHíno kalá].   **i** [o] **ii** [to] **iii** [sto]

b ___ [thomás íne yiatrós].   **i** [o] **ii** [i] **iii** [to]

c ___ [ioána íne arhitéktonas].   **i** [o] **ii** [i] **iii** [to]

d [méno] ___ [pátra tóra].   **i** [i] **ii** [tin] **iii** [stin]

e [alá íme apó] ___ [yiánena].   **i** [to] **ii** [ta] **iii** [sta]

7 Monsterwords! The author has forgotten to separate the words in the following sentences again. Can you do it? Can you also translate them into English?

a [ímeservitóraTHenímepianístria].

b [THenímesigraféas].

c [ísteyiatrósóhiímemoosikós].

d [ménokondástinthesaloníki].

e [THenímasteapótinanglía].

▶ **8 Listen again to Dialogue 2 of this unit and fill in the blanks. If you don't have the recordings, choose the missing words from the box below.**

John   [ána], **a** ___ [to lonTHíno]?

Anna   **b** ___ [THen kséro to lonTHíno]. [kséro] **c** ___ [tin athína].

Mary   **d** ___ [ménis]? [ménis] **e** ___ [ston ángelo]?

Anna   **f** ___ [méno] **e** ___ [ston ángelo].

| [ne] | [óhi] | [poo] | [móno] | [kondá] | [kséris] |

Mini test

Bravo again! You are now at the end of Unit 3. See how quickly and easily you can answer the following questions.

a 'What's your job?' is what you want to ask.

b If they ask you the question above, do you have an answer?

c [íme sigraféas] somebody replied. What did he say?

d Someone said [méno sto Manchester] and [méno kondá sto Manchester]. What is the difference?

e Name three male names in Greek.

f Name three female names in Greek.

g Name three professions.

h Let's revise four important question words: [ti], [pos], [poo], [pia]. How would you translate them?

i What's the difference between [íse apó tin anglía]? and [íste apó tin anglía]?

j 'I don't understand' is what you want to say.

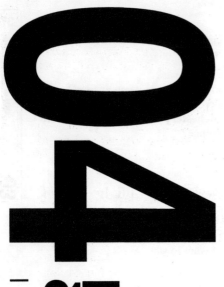

04

μένω σε
διαμέρισμα

I live in an apartment

In this unit you will learn
- how to talk about your home
- how to count from 1 to 10
- some Greek nouns in singular and plural forms

Before you start

- Revise Unit 3 once again, especially if you have used a highlighter or if you have underlined, or circled, or written down any remarks. Those are the points you should focus on whenever you go back to previous units.

- Language learning is based on two different stages. First there is the stage of passive learning which relies on you to absorb and digest as much new information and vocabulary as possible. At this stage grammatical rules and other explanations may not be quite clear. This is where you are at the moment and you may be a little frustrated. But not for too long! Remember that soon you will be approaching the second stage: active learning. Here you will be able to rely on the information you have acquired and actually use it to create your own thoughts and sentences in Greek. At this stage, your attitude changes, your motivation is raised and you become more confident. All this will contribute to your ability to make your own statements in Greek, that will not only surprise others but even yourself! So keep up the pace and efforts made so far and you will soon be happily surprised and rewarded.

▶ Key words and phrases

Everybody talks about home one way or another. You might be visiting different homes or even staying in some of them while in Greece. People will always ask you about your home, so you should be prepared perhaps to explain expressions such as 'detached' or 'semi-detached house' to your Greek friends. Read and try to memorize the vocabulary below:

Types of accommodation

[i katikía]	η κατοικία	residence (f)
[to spíti]	το σπίτι	house/home (n)
[to THiamérizma]	το διαμέρισμα	apartment/flat (n)
[i garsoniéra]	η γκαρσονιέρα	studio/bedsit (f)
[to retiré]	το ρετιρέ	penthouse (n)
[i monokatikía]	η μονοκατοικία	one-family house (f)
[i polikatikía]	η πολυκατοικία	apartment building (f)

Rooms

[to salóni]	το σαλόνι	living room (n)
[to kathistikó]	το καθιστικό	sitting room (n)
[i koozína]	η κουζίνα	kitchen (f)
[i trapezaría]	η τραπεζαρία	dining room (f)

[to ipnoTHomátio]	το υπνοδωμάτιο	*bedroom* (n)
[to bánio]	το μπάνιο	*bathroom* (n)
[i tzamaría]	η τζαμαρία	*conservatory* (f)

An important expression with this vocabulary can be: **[méno se…]** *I live in a...*

> **[méno se THiamérizma/retiré/monokatikía…]**
> *I live in a flat/penthouse/one-family house...*

[monokatikía] *one-family house* can be used as 'detached house'; 'semi-detached house' is more difficult to explain at this stage.

Pronunciation tips

Certain words have come up in the last three units where **[th]** and **[TH]** have been used in transliteration. Two examples from the vocabulary above are **[kathistikó]** and **[ipnoTHomátio]**. **[th]** θ is the sound in words like *thanks* or *theme* and **[TH]** δ is the sound in words like *than* or *them*. Would you be able to find some familiar sounds from the last three units? To help you start the list:

[th]	**[TH]**
[athína] *Athens* (Unit 2)	[eTHó] *here* (Unit 1)
_____	_____
_____	_____
_____	_____

ΔΕΗ is the Public Electricity Company in Greece

▶ [THiálogos 1] Διάλογος 1 Dialogue 1: [se spíti]? Σε σπίτι; In a house?

Anna describes her flat to John and Mary.

Mary	[ménis] [se spíti]?	Do you live in a house?
[ána]	[óhi], [méno] [se THiamérizma] [se mía polikatikía]. [éhi] [tésera THomátia], [mía koozína], [éna bánio] [kéna mikró hol].	No, I live in an apartment in a block of flats. It has four rooms, a kitchen, a bathroom and a small hallway.
Mary	[po-po], [íne megálo]!	Wow, it's big!

Mary	Μένεις σε σπίτι;
Άννα	Όχι, μένω σε διαμέρισμα σε μία πολυκατοικία. Έχει τέσσερα δωμάτια, μία κουζίνα, ένα μπάνιο, κι'ένα μικρό χωλ.
Mary	Πω, πω, είναι μεγάλο!

[se]	σε	in
[spíti]	σπίτι	house (n)
[THiamérizma]	διαμέρισμα	flat, apartment (n)
[mía]	μία	a, an; one (with f nouns)
[polikatikía]	πολυκατοικία	block of flats, apartment building (f)
[éhi]	έχει	it has
[tésera]	τέσσερα	four
[THomátia]	δωμάτια	rooms (n/pl)
[koozína]	κουζίνα	kitchen (f)
[éna]	ένα	a/an/one
[kéna]	κι'ένα	and + a/an/one (with m + n nouns)
[bánio]	μπάνιο	bathroom (n)
[mikró]	μικρό	small
[hol]	ωλ	hallway (n)
[megálo]	μεγάλο	big, large

▶ [THiálogos 2] Διάλογος 2 *Dialogue 2:*
[megálo spíti]! Μεγάλο σπίτι! *Big house!*

Angelos now describes his new house to his friends.

[ángelos]	[ksérete] [egó méno] [sálo spíti tóra]. [íne mía monokatikía].	*You know, I live in a different house now. It's a one-family house.*
Mary	[pósa THomátia éhi]?	*How many rooms does it have?*
[ángelos]	[éhi] [éna megálo salóni], [mazí me mía trapezaría], [éna bánio] [kéna vesé], [ke pénde ipnoTHomátia].	*It has one big living room, along with a dining room, a bathroom and a WC, and five bedrooms.*
Mary	[megálo spíti]!	*Big house!*
John	[polí megálo spíti]!	*Very big house!*

Άγγελος	Ξέρετε, εγώ μένω σ'άλλο σπίτι τώρα. Είναι μία μονοκατοικία.
Mary	Πόσα δωμάτια έχει;
Άγγελος	Έχει ένα μεγάλο σαλόνι, μαζί με μία τραπεζαρία, ένα μπάνιο κι'ένα WC, και πέντε υπνοδωμάτια.
Mary	Μεγάλο σπίτι!
Ξοην	Πολύ μεγάλο σπίτι!

[sálo]	σ'άλλο	*in a different* (lit. another)
[monokatikía]	μονοκατοικία	*one-family house* (f)
[pósa]	πόσα	*how many*
[salóni]	σαλόνι	*living room* (n)
[mazí me]	μαζί με	*along with*
[trapezaría]	τραπεζαρία	*dining room* (f)
[vesé]	WC (no Greek script)	*WC* (n)
[pénde]	πέντε	*five*
[ipnoTHomátia]	υπνοδωμάτια	*bedrooms* (n, pl)
[megálo]	μεγάλο	*big, large* (m, n nouns)

Language rules

1 [mía koozína] Μία κουζίνα *A kitchen*

In Dialogue 1 Anna says **[mía koozína]** *a kitchen* and **[éna bánio]** *a bathroom*. You will probably wonder why there are two Greek words **[mía]** and **[éna]** for one English word *a*. For now, just remember that **[mía]** goes with feminine nouns like **[i koozína]** → **[mía koozína]** μία κουζίνα *a/one kitchen* and [éna] goes with neuter nouns like [to bánio] → [éna bánio] ένα μπάνιο *a/one bathroom*. More information can be found in the **Grammar summary**, including the masculine form [énas] ένας – see also 1 below.

▶ 2 [arithmí] Αριθμοί *Numbers 1–10*

Look at the numbers 1–10 below and try to memorize them. You can come back to this list over and over again until you feel confident that you remember them all.

1	[énas] ένας (m), [mía] μία (f), [éna] ένα (n)	*one*
2	[THío] δύο	*two*
3	[tris] τρεις (m/f), [tría] τρία (n)	*three*
4	[téseris] τέσσερις (m/f), [tésera] τέσσερα (n)	*four*
5	[pénde] πέντε	*five*
6	[éksi] έξι	*six*
7	[eptá]/[eftá] επτά/εφτά	*seven*
8	[októ]/[ohtó] οκτώ/οχτώ	*eight*
9	[enéa]/[eniá] εννέα/εννιά	*nine*
10	[THéka] δέκα	*ten*

[miTHén] μηδέν means *zero*.

The numbers 1, 3 and 4 have more than one form because they have to agree with the gender (m, f, n) of the noun. The numbers 7, 8, and 9 have two different pronunciations. You can use either. Greeks also use them interchangeably.

3 [tésera THomátia] Τέσσερα δωμάτια *Four rooms*

As has been mentioned in the previous units, Greek nouns have more than two forms for singular and plural. At present, we will focus only on two of them, something similar to 'room/rooms' or 'house/houses' in English. Bear in mind that even in English not all plurals are the same. Notice the following examples: book/books, beach/beaches, ox/oxen, tooth/teeth. The Greek nouns below have been grouped according to masculine, feminine or neuter gender:

Masculine nouns

[o filos] – [i fili] ο φίλος – οι φίλοι *friend – friends*
[o THáskalos] – [i THáskali] ο δάσκαλος – οι δάσκαλοι
teacher – teachers
[o THiálogos] – [i THiálogi] ο διάλογος – οι διάλογοι
dialogue – dialogues

Feminine nouns

[i THaskála] – [i THaskáles] η δασκάλα – οι δασκάλες
  teacher – teachers
[i servitóra] – [i servitóres] η σερβιτόρα – οι σερβιτόρες waitress –
waitresses
[i THooliá] – [i THooliés] η δουλειά – οι δουλειές job – jobs

Neuter nouns

[to aeroTHrómio] – [ta aeroTHrómia] το αεροδρόμιο –
  τα αεροδρόμια airport – airports
[to vivlío] – [ta vivlía] το βιβλίο – τα βιβλία book – books
[to spíti] – [ta spítia] το σπίτι – τα σπίτια house – houses

Notice that the ending for masculine nouns changes from [-os] -ος to
[-i] -οι, the ending for feminine nouns from [-a] -α to [-es] -ες, and
the ending for neuter nouns from [-o] -o to [-a] -α. This explanation
is sufficient for the moment. We will get back to singular and plural
forms of Greek nouns in subsequent units.

4 [éhi tésera THomátia] Έχει τέσσερα δωμάτια
It has four rooms

The verb [ého] έχω *I have* is as important for you to learn as the verb
[íme] είμαι *I am* in Unit 1. The different endings of [ého] are exactly
the same as in [káno] κάνω *I do*, or [periméno] περιμένω *I wait*, or
[THoolévo] δουλεύω *I work*. Read them and try to memorize them.

Do not confuse the word [ého] έχω *I have* with the word [óhi] όχι
no because of how they sound.

[ého]	έχω	*I have*
[éhis]	έχεις	*you have*
[éhi]	έχει	*he/she/it has*
[éhoome]	έχουμε	*we have*
[éhete]	έχετε	*you have*
[éhoon]	έχουν	*they have*

5 [se spíti]? Σε σπίτι; *In a house?*

You probably remember [pos se léne]? Πώς σε λένε; *What's your
name?* in Unit 1. [se] Σε looks and sounds exactly the same but has
two different functions: the first is used with the meaning of
in/at/to/on and the second with the meaning of *you/your*. The literal
translation of [pos se léne]? is 'How do they call you?'

Similarly, it is also potentially confusing with the word [me] με which in Unit 1 again was used in [me léne ána] *my name is Anna* (lit. they call me Anna). A similar-looking word is used in this unit in Dialogue 2: [mazí me trapezaría]. Here it means *with*. Remember that some words sound the same, but have more than one distinct meaning and this is true for many languages. For example in English the word 'fair' means 1. *honest, right* in '*a fair fight*', 2. *mediocre, a little bit* in '*his Greek is fair*', 3. *clear* in '*fair weather*', or even 4. *blonde, light colour* in '*fair complexion*'!

6 [kéna mikró hol] Κι'ένα μικρό χωλ *And one small hallway*

[kéna] κι'ένα is a contraction of two words, i.e. [ke] και + [éna] ένα: *and* + *one*. So far you have encountered some other contracted forms, which are used more frequently than in uncontracted form. This is true even in English where contracted forms like *don't, can't* or *isn't* are used more frequently than *do not, cannot,* or *is not*. Let's list some other contracted forms in Greek:

[sto] στο → [se] + [to]	*at the*	(Unit 1)
[stin] στην → [se] + [tin]	*in the*	(Unit 1)
[kegó] or [ki'egó] κι'εγώ → [ke] + [egó]	*and I*	(Unit 2)
[ston] στον → [se] + [ton]	*at the*	(Unit 3)
[kéna] or [ki'éna] κι'ένα → [ke] + [éna]	*and one*	(Unit 4)
[sálo] σ'άλλο → [se] [álo]	*in another*	(Unit 4)

[sto], [stin] and [ston] cannot be heard or used as separate words whereas the other three examples can.

ⓘ [méno se THiamérizma] Μένω σε διαμέρισμα *I live in an apartment*

Most Greeks used to own their place of residence. However nowadays, more and more new families rent rather than buy a new home. Mortgages are abundant and have brought along a new culture as well. In the 1970s home owners used to make a down payment of at least 60 per cent to 80 per cent of the total value, whereas now a down payment can be as low as 10 per cent. Also, the time for paying off the loan has changed: people used to pay off the remaining amount in five to ten years. Today payment plans can reach 25 to 30 years.

Apartments are available everywhere around Greece. Rents can easily reach 400€ or more, which does not sound a lot in sterling when converted, but it represents about half an average monthly salary at the beginning of this millennium. Building one's own apartment or house is still a dream that many seek to fulfil, in spite of the increase in property taxes and the cost of land and building permits.

Greek homes follow several different architectural schools. Modern buildings coexist with neoclassical buildings. New apartments have fewer dividing walls, open kitchens, more bathrooms, larger balconies and more colours. Sometimes the method of building can be characterized as old fashioned and not very time- or money-effective. Different construction crews build and un-build several times before the completion of a property and create such an amount of rubble that it makes you wonder how anything gets finished!

Concrete is still the predominant material compared to wood, metal or other building materials. Flat roofs, slanted roofs, and more and more red tiled roofs can be seen with white, pink, blue and other colourful facades. Local styles prevail in the countryside and on the islands, such as the famous white-washed houses in the Cyclades or the stone houses built of grey slate in the Zagori villages in Epirus.

Practice makes perfect

1 **Word pairs have been greatly emphasized so far. See if you can match the words on the left with their pairs on the right.**

a [kondá]   i [THiamérizma]
b [póli]   ii [kathistikó]
c [spíti]   iii [megálo]
d [salóni]   iv [hóra]
e [koozína]   v [makriá] *far*
f [mikró]   vi [trapezaría]

[makriá] *far* is a new word for you here. Be careful because it sounds a little like [mikró] which means *small*.

2 **Now translate the word pairs in Exercise 1 into English. The answer key at the back includes the Greek script as well so you can try to challenge yourself one step further.**

3 **Match each question with its corresponding answer.**

a [poo ménete]?   i [óhi], [alá íne kondá].
b [íne megálo]?   ii [óhi], [íne mikró].
c [íne] [stin athína]? iii [rafína] [íne] [éna limáni]
d [poo íne]?   iv [méno] [se THiamérizma].
e [ti íne] [rafína]?   v [íne stin rafína]

[rafína] Ραφήνα is a port [limáni] λιμάνι one hour away from Athens. Boats leave from there to many islands in the Cyclades, e.g. Andros, Tinos and Mykonos.

4 Rearrange these lines to make up a dialogue.

a [éna salóni] [kéna ipnoTHomátio].
b [pósa THomátia éhi]?
c [éhis megálo spíti]?
d [móno THío THomátia].
e [óhi polí megálo].
f [ti THomátia]?

5 Below is a plan of an apartment. Can you write the name of each room?

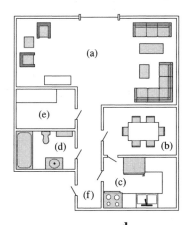

a _____   **d** _____
b _____   **e** _____
c _____   **f.** _____

6 Knowing numbers is essential if you want to give telephone numbers, room numbers, bus numbers, etc. Below is a list of emergency numbers in Greece. Can you read them out loud, number by number? The number 1 reads as [éna] ένα below.

a 100 – Police
b 134 – Telephone Operator
c 166 – Medical Assistance
d 169 – International Operator
e 171 – Tourist Police
f 199 – Fire Department

Can you also say the corresponding numbers in the UK or USA to a Greek friend?

7 The crossword puzzle below includes different kinds of residences and rooms in Greek. Can you work out the details? The vertical, shaded word means *living room*.

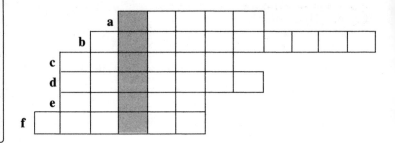

a residence   **d** room
b residence   **e** room
c room   **f** residence

▶8 Listen again to Dialogue 2 of this unit and fill in the blanks. If you don't have the recordings, choose the missing words from the box below.

[**ángelos**] [ksérete] [egó méno] **a** _____ [spíti tóra]. [íne mía monokatikía].

Mary   **b** _____ [THomátia éhi]?

[**ángelos**] [éhi] [éna] **c** _____ [salóni], **d** _____ [me trapezaría], [éna bánio]/[kéna vesé], [ke] **e** _____ [ipnoTHomátia].

Mary   [megálo spíti]!

John   **f** _____ [megálo spíti]!

[megálo]   [sálo]   [polí]   [mazí]   [pénde]   [pósa]

Mini test

You are now at the end of Unit 4. Let's see how easy the following questions are for you.

a What are the three Greek words for 'bathroom – toilet – WC'?
b Name four rooms in a house (exclude the three words above).
c Name four different residences in Greek.
d 'I live in a detached house in London' is what you want to say.
e What are the opposites: [**megálo**], [**kondá**], [**monokatikía**]?
f What are the synonyms for [**salóni**], [**bánio**], [**spíti**] in Greek?

g A Greek is giving out the telephone number of a hotel. Can you read the numbers out loud one by one? The telephone number is 7645138 and the area code is 0249.

It was an easy **Mini test**, wasn't it? Now, get prepared for Unit 5. See you there!

05

μία μεγάλη οικογένεια
a big family

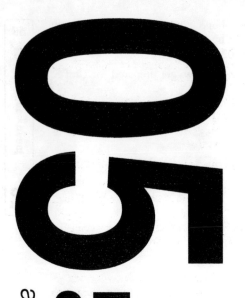

In this unit you will learn

- how to ask questions about family and children
- how to describe your family
- how to ask questions about people's age
- how to count from 11 to 20

Before you start

Hopefully, you are following the advice about frequent revision. If you go back to Unit 1 now, for instance, it shouldn't be that difficult or challenging for you any more. Is that right?

When you complete this unit you will have covered one third of this book successfully. How can you be sure, though, that most things are clear to you? Here are two simple suggestions: first, organize your learning materials, and second, test yourself!

• Here are some simple steps to help you follow the first suggestion:

Step 1: Organize your vocabulary from Units 1 to 5 in different groups. Make a list of all the important verbs you have found. Make some lists of nouns in groups, e.g. rooms, languages, countries, etc. Make a list of question words in Greek or even a list of important words like *yes, no, and, only, but,* etc. You decide how many lists you need to create.

Step 2: Write down a set of phrases and expressions you consider important for you to understand or use with Greeks. In Units 1 to 5, you are introduced to quite a few of them and some examples are provided for you below. What you have to keep in mind in this step is that certain phrases and expressions are 'formula' questions or answers. Note the following:

[pos se/sas léne]? Πώς σε/σας λένε; *What's your name?*
[me léne]... Με λένε... *My name is...*
[apó poo íse/íste]? Από πού είσαι/είστε; *Where are you from?*

Can you continue this list?

Step 3: Make a note of all points that you still find difficult to understand in the first five units. Keep those points handy. They might be explained further in subsequent units or you might get the chance to ask a native speaker.

• The second suggestion is to test yourself. This is not difficult since there is a comprehensive **Revision test** at the end of Units 5, 10 and 15.

Of course, some of you hate doing tests, especially language tests! If that's the case, don't worry! Omit the **Revision test** altogether and go directly to Unit 6 when you've finished this unit.

▶ Key words and phrases

Discussions about family and children are a central theme in Greek society. Many people will ask you

> [éhis ikoyénia]? Έχεις οικογένεια; or [éhete ikoyénia]?
> Έχετε **οικογένεια**; *Have you got a family?* and
> [éhete peTHiá]? Έχετε παιδιά; *Have you got any children?*

The easy answer to these questions of course is [ne] ναι *yes* or [óhi] όχι *no*. Look at Angelos' family tree below. Meet his family members and try to memorize most of the words.

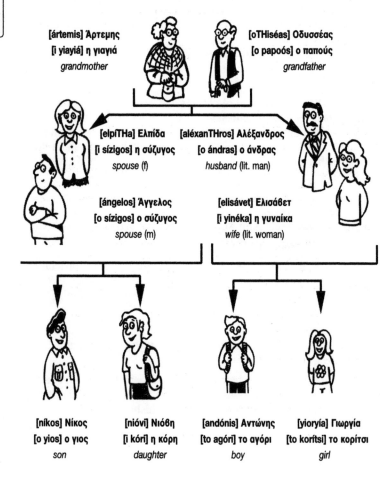

[ártemis] Άρτεμης
[i yiayiá] η γιαγιά
grandmother

[oTHiséas] Οδυσσέας
[o papoós] ο παπούς
grandfather

[elpíTHa] Ελπίδα
[i sízigos] η σύζυγος
spouse (f)

[aléxanTHros] Αλέξανδρος
[o ándras] ο άνδρας
husband (lit. man)

[ángelos] Άγγελος
[o sízigos] ο σύζυγος
spouse (m)

[elisávet] Ελισάβετ
[i yinéka] η γυναίκα
wife (lit. woman)

[níkos] Νίκος
[o yios] ο γιος
son

[nióvi] Νιόβη
[i kóri] η κόρη
daughter

[andónis] Αντώνης
[to agóri] το αγόρι
boy

[yioryía] Γιωργία
[to korítsi] το κορίτσι
girl

Study the box below of family relationships.

Masculine	Feminine	Neuter
[o patéras] ο πατέρας *father*	[i mitéra] η μήτερα *mother*	[to peTHí] το παιδί *child*
[o papoós] ο παπούς *grandfather*	[i yiayiá] η γιαγιά *grandmother*	[to moró] το μωρό *baby*
[o yios] ο γιος *son*	[i kóri] η κόρη *daughter*	
[o egonós] ο εγγονός *grandson*	[i egoní] η εγγονή *granddaughter*	[to egóni] το εγγόνι *grandchild*
[o aTHelfós] ο αδελφός *brother*	[i aTHelfí] η αδελφή *sister*	
[o (e)ksáTHelfos] ο (ε)ξάδελφος *cousin (m)*	[i (e)ksaTHélfi] η (ε)ξαδέλφη *cousin (f)*	

▶ [THiálogos 1] Διάλογος 1 *Dialogue 1*

Anna is trying to get some personal information about Mary and John.

[ángelos]	[páme spíti tóra]?	*Shall we go home now?*
[ána]	[misó leptó]. [áli mía erótisi]: [éhete peTHiá]?	*Just a minute.* (lit. half a minute) *One more question: Do you have any children?*
Mary	[ne]. [éhoome] [THío peTHiá]: [éna agóri], [pénde hronón], [kéna korítsi], [trión hronón].	*Yes. We have two children: one boy, five years old, and one girl, three years old.*
John	[esí]? [éhis ikoyénia]?	*How about you? Do you have a family?*
[ána]	[ne]. [ého] [mía megáli ikoyénia].	*Yes. I have a big family.*

Άγγελος	Πάμε σπίτι τώρα;
Άννα	Μισό λεπτό. Άλλη μία ερώτηση; έχετε παιδιά;
Mary	Ναι. Έχουμε δύο παιδιά: ένα αγόρι, πέντε χρονών, κι'ένα κορίτσι, τριών χρονών.
John	Εσύ; Έχεις οικογένεια;
Άννα	Ναι. Έχω μία μεγάλη οικογένεια.

[páme]	πάμε	we go (here: shall we go?)
[misó]	μισό	half
[leptó]	λεπτό	minute (n)
[misó leptó]	μισό λεπτό	just a minute
		(lit. half a minute)
[áli]	άλλη	another (f)
[erótisi]	ερώτηση	question (f)
[éhete]	έχετε	you have, do you have?
[peTHiá]	παιδιά	children (n/pl)
[éhoome]	έχουμε	we have
[THío]	δύο	two
[agóri]	αγόρι	boy (n)
[pénde hronón]	πέντε χρονών	five years old
		(lit. five of years)
[korítsi]	κορίτσι	girl (n)
[trión hronón]	τριών χρονών	three years old
		(lit. three of years)
[éhis]	έχεις	you have, do you have?
		(sing/infml)
[ikoyénia]	οικογένεια	family (f)
[ého]	έχω	I have
[megáli]	μεγάλη	large, big (with f noun)

▶ [THiálogos 2] Διάλογος 2 Dialogue 2

Anna describes her family to Mary and John and hopes to see them again soon.

[ána]	[o ándras moo] [íne servitóros].	*My husband is a waiter.*
	[ton léne] [yiórgo]. [éhoome]	*His name is George. We have*
	[tría peTHiá]: [THío agória]	*three children: two boys*
	[kéna korítsi].	*and one girl.*
	[ta onómata toos]	*Their names are*
	[íne] [yiánis], [THéspina]	*John, Despina*
	[ke níkos].	*and Nick.*
Mary	[póso hronón íne]?	*How old are they?*
[ána]	[o yiánis] [íne THóTHeka],	*John is twelve,*
	[i THéspina] [íne THéka] [ke	*Despina is ten and*
	o níkos] [íne eptá]. [ah]! [yiatí	*Nick is seven. Oh! Why are*
	févyete]? [thélo] [na sas	*you leaving? I want to see*
	ksanaTHó]!	*you again!*

Άννα   Ο άντρας μου είναι σερβιτόρος. Τον λένε Γιώργο. Έχουμε τρία παιδιά: δύο αγόρια κι'ένα κορίτσι. Τα ονόματά τους είναι Γιάννης, Δέσποινα και Νίκος.

Mary   Πόσο χρόνων είναι;

Άννα   Ο Γιάννης είναι δώδεκα, η Δέσποινα είναι δέκα κι ο Νίκος είναι επτά. Αχ! Γιατί φεύγετε; Θέλω να σας ξαναδώ!

Note

It was noted in Unit 1 that Greek male names have a different ending according to their function (case in grammar – see **Grammar summary**). This is also true here for the name *George* above as [**yiórgo**] **Γιώργο**, which has the form [**yiórgos**] **Γιώργος** in the nominative case, i.e. when it is the subject of the sentence.

[ándras]	άντρας	husband (m)
[moo]	μου	my
[servitóros]	σερβιτόρος	waiter (m)
[ton léne]	τον λένε	his name is
		(lit. they call him)
[tría]	τρία	three
[agória]	αγόρια	boys (n/pl)
[ta]	τα	the (n/pl)
[ta onómata toos]	τα ονόματα τους	their names
[póso hronón]	πόσο χρονών	how old
[THóTHeka]	δώδεκα	twelve
[THéka]	δέκα	ten
[eptá]	επτά	seven
[ah]!	αχ!	oh!
[yiatí]?	γιατί;	why?
[févyete]	φεύγετε	you leave, are you leaving? (pl/fml)
[thélo na]	θέλω να	I want to
[sas]	σας	you
[ksanaTHó]	ξαναδώ	see again
[na sas ksanaTHó]	να σας ξαναδώ	to see you (pl) again

Language rules

1 [páme spíti tóra]? Πάμε σπίτι τώρα; *Are we going home now?*

How are you getting on with Greek questions? Don't you think that it's getting easier now? The verb **[páme]** *we go* comes from **[páo]** πάω *I go* and it is often used in everyday conversations. Try to memorize its basic forms below:

[páo]	πάω	*I go*
[pas]	πας	*you go*
[pái]	πάει	*he/she/it goes*
[páme]	πάμε	*we go*
[páte]	πάτε	*you go*
[páne]	πάνε	*they go*

[páme]! can also be used for the phrase 'Let's go!'. The different pitch of the voice will distinguish the three uses:

[páme]. with a falling tone of voice → *We go/we are going.*
[páme]? with a rising tone of voice → *Do we go?/Are we going?*
[páme]! with a more emphatic tone of voice → *Let's go!*

2 [o ándras moo] Ο άντρας μου *My husband* (lit. *the husband of mine*)

You were introduced to subject or personal pronouns in Unit 2. These are words like *I, you, they*, etc. This unit introduces another group of extremely important and frequent words in everyday conversations. Words like *my, your, his, our*, etc. are called possessive pronouns in grammar. In Greek, these words come *after* the noun they modify whereas in English they come *before* the noun they modify. This difference will present you with a challenge in the beginning, but the examples below will make you more familiar with it.

Masculine	Feminine	Neuter
[o ándras moo]	**[i yinéka moo]**	**[to spíti moo]**
ο άντρας μου	η γυναίκα μου	το σπίτι μου
my husband	*my wife*	*my house*
[o papoós moo]	**[i yiayiá moo]**	**[to THomátio moo]**
ο παππούς μου	η γιαγιά μου	το δωμάτιο μου
my grandfather	*my grandmother*	*my room*
[o yios moo]	**[i kóri moo]**	**[to peTHí moo]**
ο γιος μου	η κόρη μου	το παιδί μου
my son	*my daughter*	*my child*

Study the possessive pronouns below and come back to this reference table as often as needed.

[moo]	μου	my
[soo]	σου	your (infml/sing)
[too]	του	his
[tis]	της	her
[too]	του	its
[mas]	μας	our
[sas]	σας	your (fml/pl)
[toos]	τους	their

These words are called possessive pronouns in Greek grammar and possessive adjectives in English grammar!

There is only one word for *his* and *its* in Greek: [**too**] του.

3 [ton léne yiórgo] Τον λένε Γιώργο *His name is George*

Early in this course, starting in Unit 1, you were introduced to the important question [**pos se léne**]? *What's your name?* (lit: What do they call you?) and its equally important answer [**me léne**]... *My name is...* (lit: They call me...). Of course, in the explanations above it was just mentioned that words like *my, your, our*, etc. come *after* the noun they modify. Here we have a new group of words *preceding* the verb [**léne**] *they call*, which is used as an idiomatic expression for *My (your, his, etc.) name is...* . Go over them below:

[me léne]	με λένε	my name is (lit. they call me)
[se léne]	σε λένε	your name is (lit. they call you) (infml)
[ton léne]	τον λένε	his name is (lit. they call him)
[tin léne]	την λένε	her name is (lit. they call her)
[to léne]	το λένε	its name is (lit. they call it)
[mas léne]	μας λένε	our name is (lit. they call us)
[sas léne]	σας λένε	your name is (lit. they call you) (fml)
[toos léne]	τους λένε	their name is (lit. they call them) (m)
[tis léne]	τις λένε	their name is (lit. they call them) (f)
[ta léne]	τα λένε	their name is (lit. they call them) (n)

You realize that the three forms [**mas**], [**sas**], and [**toos**] are identical to the possessive pronouns in the previous paragraph. All other forms are new. You can read more about pronouns in the **Grammar summary**.

4 [thélo na sas ksanaTHó] Θέλω να σας ξαναδώ *I want to see you again*

The same group of words as listed in section 3 on page 57 can be used here again. In the example [**thélo na sas ksanaTHó**], [**sas**] means *you* and precedes the verb. Look at the examples below:

[thélo na <u>sas</u> miláo eliniká].	*I want to speak Greek to <u>you</u>.*
[thélo na <u>ton</u> periméno].	*I want to wait for <u>him</u>.*
[thélo na <u>tin</u> páo stin anglía].	*I want to take* (lit. go) <u>*her*</u> *to England.*
[thélete na <u>me</u> periménete]?	*Do you want to wait for <u>me</u>?*
[théloome na <u>toos</u> ksanaTHóome].	*We want to see <u>them</u> again.*

In Unit 1 you were introduced to [**na sas sistíso**] which is a shorter version of [**thélo na sas sistíso**] *I want to introduce <u>you</u>*. You simply need to have patience. Things like this will become clearer in subsequent units.

5 [póso hronón íne]? Πόσο χρονών είναι; *How old are they?*

This is a typical and frequent question in Greek. Many people ask others directly and openly about their age. Addressing friends, you can ask [**póso hronón íse**]? Πόσο χρονών είσαι; *How old are you?* [**póso hronón íste**]? Πόσο χρονών είστε; is simply more formal. The usual reply is [**íme … hronón**] Είμαι … χρονών. *I am … years old.* As you can see, knowing the numbers here can be really handy. Of course, the previous unit introduced you to the numbers from 0 to 10. This unit will take you from 11 to 20, and Unit 6 will take you up to 100. You probably need all three units in order to express how old you 'feel' and how old you 'really' are! Study and memorize the numbers 11 to 20 below:

▶ 6 [arithmí] Αριθμοί *Numbers 11–20*

11	[éndeka] έντεκα	*eleven*
12	[THóTHeka] δώδεκα	*twelve*
13	[THekatrís] δεκατρείς (m/f)	*thirteen*
	[THekatría] δεκατρία (n)	

14	[THekatéseris] δεκατέσσερις (m/f)	fourteen
	[THekatésera] δεκατέσσερα (n)	
15	[THekapénde] δεκαπέντε	fifteen
16	[THekaéksi] δεκαέξι	sixteen
17	[THekaeftá] δεκαεφτά	seventeen
18	[THekaoktó] δεκαοκτώ	eighteen
19	[THekaeniá] δεκαεννιά	nineteen
20	[íkosi] είκοσι	twenty

The numbers 17, 18 and 19 have two interchangeable forms like 7, 8 and 9, i.e. [THekaeptá], [THekaohtó] and [THekaenéa].

🅘 [éhete peTHiá]? Έχετε παιδιά; Have you got any children?

The family is still a strong force in Greek society. Most parents have close ties with their children and monitor their education, development, progress and friends very closely. In fact, in comparison to other western countries, they can seem to be somewhat overprotective.

Be prepared to face very direct, personal questions about your family from people you have just met for the first time! For many Greeks it is a way of breaking the ice and they do not mean to invade your privacy. The most frequent questions are: [éhete peTHiá]? Έχετε παιδιά; Do you have children?, [póso hronón íne]? Πόσο χρονών είναι; How old is he/she? How old are they?, and [páne sholío]? Πάνε σχολείο; Do they go to school?. Some other questions are: [íste pandreménos]? Είστε παντρεμένος; or [íste pandreméni]? Είστε παντρεμένη; Are you married? (the first addresses a man and the latter a woman), or [éhis ikoyénia]? Έχεις οικογένεια; or [éhete ikoyénia]? Έχετε οικογένεια; Do you have a family?

Family ties keep family members at home much longer than in other cultures, where children start moving away at the age of 18 or 19. In Greece, other than for army service or studies away from home, unmarried children may easily stay with their parents until 25 or 30 years of age. Marriage unavoidably separates members of Greek families but that doesn't necessarily mean that many won't return home frequently to have a cup of mum's coffee or mum's homemade meal!

The previous units have introduced you to some Greek names such as [yiánis] Γιάννης John. More Greek names mentioned in this unit are [THéspina] Δέσποινα (Debbie would be the closest translation) and **[níkos] Νίκος** *Nick*. Other common Greek names are: **[pétros] Πέτρος** *Peter*, **[andónis] Αντώνης** *Anthony*, **[vasílis] Βασίλης** *Bill*, and **[kóstas] Κώστας** or **[konstandínos] Κωνσταντίνος** *Constantine* for men and **[yioryía] Γιωργία** *Georgia*, **[eléni] Ελένη** *Helen*, or **[katerína] Κατερίνα** *Catherine* for women. *Sir!* or *Madam!* are **[kírie] κύριε** and **[kiría] κυρία** when you call out to someone in the street. And the expression *Ladies and Gentlemen* is **[kiríes ke kíri-i] κυρίες και κύριοι.**

'Yiorgos Stavrou' is the name.

'George Manglaras' is the name of a famous pastry maker in Athens. Can you find it in this advert?

Name days (the days of the saints, whose names Greeks often give to their children) are observed and celebrated more in Greece than people's actual birthdays. Most people will remember your name day and pay you a visit at home, usually without any prior invitation or confirmation. Many people know the dates of several name days by heart, e.g. **[vasílis]** on January 1st, **[yiánis]** on January 7th, **[yioryía]** on April 23rd, and **[níkos]** on December 6th. Most birthdays will pass by unnoticed except perhaps for children's birthdays, which are often celebrated at fast food restaurants or special playgrounds.

It is still customary to name your child after its grandparents. Even the order of name-giving is set, starting with the grandparents on the paternal side. Of course, there are always exceptions, which can create a serious objection from the grandparent concerned! Most

Greek children are baptized, the majority in the Greek Orthodox faith. For these reasons, Greek saints' names are still dominant: first, to satisfy traditional name-giving, and second, to satisfy religious views. The words **[moró]** μωρό *baby* (n) or **[bébis]** μπέμπης *baby boy* (m), and **[béba]** μπέμπα *baby girl* (f) are used for unbaptized children. So, a two-year-old child who is not baptized will be addressed as 'baby' until the holy day of baptism!

Practice makes perfect

1 **Angelos has a family photo which shows some family members and explains who is who. Match the words below with their English translation.**

| i | ii | iii | iv | v | vi |

a [o patéras moo]
b [i mitéra moo]
c [i aTHelfí moo]
d [o yios moo]
e [i kóri moo]
f [o exáTHelfos moo]

i my sister
ii my mother
iii my cousin
iv my father
v my daughter
vi my son

2 **Now match the six words with the right people in the photo in Exercise 1.**

a [yios]
b [mitéra]
c [patéras]

d [exáTHelfos]
e [kóri]
f [aTHelfí]

3 Match each question with the most appropriate answer.

a [éhete peTHiá]?
b [éhis ikoyénia]?
c [pos léne ton ándra soo]?
d [pos léne tin sízigo soo]?
e [póso hronón íse]?

i [ton léne yiórgo].
ii [íme THóTHeka].
iii [óhi], [THeného].
iv [ne], [ého éna peTHí].
v [tin léne ioána].

▶ 4 Someone asks some schoolchildren about their age. Listen to the recording and write the age next to the name of each child.

a [yiórgos] Γιώργος *George* ☐
b [panayiótis] Παναγιώτης ☐
c [kóstas] Κώστας *Constantine* ☐
d [elpíTHa] Ελπίδα *Hope* ☐
e [ioána] Ιωάννα *Joanna* ☐
f [ariána] Αριάννα *Arianna* ☐

▶ 5 Some friends are giving out their telephone number at home [sto spíti] and at work [stin THooliá]. Listen to the recording and write down both numbers.

a [spíti] _____
b [THooliá] _____

6 Possessive pronouns like *my/your/his/her/its/our/your/their* are very important. Try to translate the following into Greek.

a his flat →
b our home →
c their grandfather →

d her mother →
e my room →
f your husband →

7 Let's have some fun now! How many Greek words can you find in this word search? Hint: there are more than 10 words. They read across, up and down.

p	a	p	o	o	s	y
a	n	p	l	h	e	i
m	y	i	n	e	k	a
e	o	a	e	n	a	y
k	o	r	i	t	s	i
k	m	i	t	e	r	a

▶8 **Listen again to Dialogue 2 of this unit and fill in the blanks. If you don't have the recordings, choose the missing words from the box below.**

[ána]   [o a _____ moo] [íne servitóros]. b _____ [léne] [yiórgo].
          [éhoome] [tría] c _____ : [THío agória] [kéna] d _____.
          [ta onómatá toos] [íne] [yiánis], [THéspina] [ke]
          e _____.
Mary   [póso] f _____ [íne]?
[ána]   [o yiánis [íne] g _____, [i THéspina] [íne] h _____ [ke-o]
          e _____ [íne] i _____. [ah]! j _____ [févyete]? [THélo] [na
          sas ksanaTHó]...

[níkos]   [ándras]   [korítsi]   [peTHiá]   [ton]   [hronón]
[yiatí]   [eptá]   [THéka]   [THóTHeka]

Mini test

Congratulations! You have already completed one third of this book! Let's see how well you remember this unit.

a Name six words that describe family relations.
b What are the numbers 11, 12, 14, 17, 19 and 20 in Greek?
c Can you describe your family in Greek?
d Someone wants to know your age: What is the question?
e Some people are called [**pétros**], [**elpíTHa**], [**andónis**], [**nióvi**], [**dimítris**], [**eléni**]. Is there a translation in English?
f 'What is it called in Greek?' is an important question. Do you know it?

Now try **Revision test 1** before moving on to Unit 6.

06

καλώς ορίσατε!
welcome!

In this unit you will learn
- how to welcome people
- how to reply to welcoming remarks
- how to ask for or offer refreshments
- how to count from 21 to 100

Before you start

- Did you score satisfactorily in the first **Revision test** of Units 1 to 5? If you didn't want to do the **Revision test**, how do you feel about the language covered so far? Are you on top of things? Studying alone sometimes can be a challenge. It also requires you to be disciplined and committed to regular study habits. Now you're at Unit 6, however, you've got what it takes to study successfully.

- Have you applied the [**simvoolés**] **συμβουλές** *tips* given to you in Unit 5? No matter what your learning style, these tips will help you in your efforts. They can be applied to every single unit. Make this a rewarding learning experience. Go ahead, sort out and apply all the learning tips you found helpful in the past five units.

▶ Key words and phrases

This unit will introduce you to very useful vocabulary about refreshments. No matter how short your visit to Greece might be, you will probably have a [**métrio**] **μέτριο** (*Greek coffee*, medium sweet: a teaspoonful each of coffee and sugar served in a small cup).

There is more on coffee and drinks later in this unit. Some frequent questions on this subject are:

[**THipsás**]? **Διψάς**; or [**THipsáte**]? **Διψάτε**; *Are you thirsty?*
[**thélis**] **Θέλεις** or [**thélete**] [**na pjíte káti**]? **Θέλετε να πιείτε κάτι;**
Would you like (lit. do you want) *to drink something?*
[**tha párete proinó**]? **Θα πάρετε πρωινό;** *Will you have*
(lit. take) *breakfast?*

Some important vocabulary about refreshments, snacks or breakfast can be found below. The nouns have been grouped by their gender, i.e. m/f/n.

Note that the common endings for masculine nouns are [**-es**] **-ες** and [**-os**] **-ος**, for feminine nouns [**-a**] **-α**, and for neuter nouns [**o**] **-ο** and [**-i**] **-ι**.

Masculine
[o kafés] ο καφές *coffee*
[o himós] ο χυμός *juice*
[o frapés] ο φραπές *iced coffee*

Feminine
[i portokaláTHa] η πορτοκαλάδα *orangeade*
[i lemonáTHa] η λεμονάδα *lemonade*
[i kóka kóla] η κόκα κόλα *Coca-Cola*
[i marmeláTHa] η μαρμελάδα *jam*

Neuter
[to tsái] το τσάι *tea*
[to noótiro] το βούτυρο *butter*
[to gála] το γάλα *milk*
[to psomí] το ψωμί *bread*

Pronunciation tips

The sound [ps] in the words [THipsás] *are you thirsty?* or [psomí] *bread* exists in English words like *tips* or *lips*. In Greek, the same sound can be used for words starting with [ps] like [psomí]. In English, the combination of those letters at the beginning of a word has a soundless [p] at the beginning of a word, e.g. *psychology* or *psalm*.

The sound [ts] in the word [tsái] *tea* is pretty much similar to the words like *sets*, *nets*, or *seats*. This sound can be found in the beginning or middle of Greek words and very seldom at the end, which is very common in English.

▶ [THiálogos 1] Διάλογος 1 *Dialogue 1:*
[kalós orísate]! Καλώς ορίσατε! *Welcome!*

Άγγελος drives them home now. Ελπίδα [elpíTHa] *Hope*, his wife, and Αντώνης [Andónis] *Anthony* and Γιωργία [yioryía] *Georgia*, his children, are there waiting for Mary and John.

[elpíTHa]	[kalós orísate]! [hérome] [poo sas ksanavlépo]!	*Welcome! Glad to see you again!*
John	[yiásoo elpíTHa]. [kalós se vríkame].	*Hi, Hope. Glad to be here again.*
Mary	[yiásoo elpíTHa], [yiásas peTHiá].	*Hi, Hope, hi kids.*
[andónis]	[yiásas] [kírie John]. [yiásas] [kiría Mary].	*Hello, Mr John. Hello, Mrs Mary.*
[yioryía]	[yiásas]	*Hello.*

Ελπίδα	Καλώς ορίσατε! Χαίρομαι που σας ξαναβλέπω!
John	Γεια σου, Ελπίδα. Καλώς σε βρήκαμε.
Mary	Γεια σου, Ελπίδα. Γεια σας, παιδιά.
Αντώνης	Γεια σας, κύριε John. Γεια σας, κυρία Mary.
Γιωργία	Γεια σας.

[elpíTHa] Ελπίδα *Hope* as a name is rather uncommon in the UK, although more common in the US. In Greece, it is not as common as Αντώνης *Anthony* or Γιωργία *Georgia*, but some people still like naming their daughters Hope, Love or Peace. [agápi] Αγάπη is *Love* and [iríni] Ειρήνη is *Peace*.

[hérome]	χαίρομαι	*I'm glad*
[poo]	που	*that*
[ksanavlépo]	ξαναβλέπω	*I see again*
[kalós se vríkame]	καλώς σε βρήκαμε	*Glad to be here again*
		(lit. glad to find you)
[kírie]	κύριε = κ.	*Mister* = *Mr* (m)
[kiría]	κυρία = κα.	(lit. *Mistress*) = *Mrs* (f)

▶ [THiálogos 2] Διάλογος 2 *Dialogue 2:*
[thélete énan kafé]? Θέλετε έναν καφέ; *Would you like a coffee?*

[elpíTHa] asks if they'd like any coffee or refreshments.

[ángelos]	[eláte], [kathíste ston kanapé]. [John], [páre mía karékla] [kondá moo].	*Come on in, have a seat on the sofa. John, take a chair close to me.*
John	[efharistó].	*Thanks.*
Mary	[oréo spíti], [polí oréo] [ke polí megálo].	*Nice house, very nice and very large.*
[elpíTHa]	[pináte]? [THipsáte]? [Thélete] [énan kafé], [mía kóka kóla]?	*Are you hungry? Are you thirsty? Would you like a coffee, a coke?*
Mary	[éhis portokaláTHa]?	*Do you have orangeade?*
John	[énan frapé] [yia ména].	*An iced coffee for me.*

Άγγελος	Ελάτε, καθίστε στον καναπέ. John, πάρε μία καρέκλα κοντά μου.
John	Ευχαριστώ.
Mary	Ωραίο σπίτι, πολύ ωραίο και πολύ μεγάλο.
Ελπίδα	Πεινάτε; Διψάτε; Θέλετε έναν καφέ, μία κόκα κόλα;
Mary	Έχεις πορτοκαλάδα;
John	Έναν φραπέ για μένα.

ΠΟΤΑ – ΑΝΑΨΥΚΤΙΚΑ

☆ *Πορἀδοση στο σπίτι ή στο γραφείο*

Αναψυκτικά διάφορα ποτήρι 300ml	0,91 €
Αναψυκτικά διάφορα ποτήρι 480ml	1,32 €
☆ *Αναψυκτικά διάφορα κουτί 380ml*	0,99 €
☆ *Νερό εμφιαλωμένο 1/2lt*	0,47 €
Καφές Φίλτρου 300ml	1,17 €
☆ *Κρασί Παψάνη (ροζέ) 187ml*	1,38 €
☆ *Κρασί Μακεδονικός (λευκό) 187ml*	1,32 €
☆ *Κρασί Μακεδονικός (λευκό) 750ml*	5,44 €
☆ *Κρασί Μακεδονικός (κόκκινο) 750ml*	5,44 €
☆ *Ούζο Τσάνταλη 40ml*	1,32 €
Μπύρα Amstel ποτήρι 250ml	1,23 €
Μπύρα Amstel ποτήρι 500ml	1,65 €
☆ *Μπύρα Amstel κουτί 500ml*	1,17 €
☆ *Μπύρα Heineken κουτί 330ml*	1,32 €
	0,12 €

A list of refreshments from a Greek menu.

[eláte]	ελάτε	*come* (pl/fml)
[kathíste]	καθίστε	*have a seat, sit down* (pl/fml)
[kanapé]	καναπέ	*sofa* (m)
[páre]	πάρε	*take* (sing/infml)
[karékla]	καρέκλα	*chair* (f)
[kondá]	κοντά	*close to*
[moo]	μου	*me* (after a preposition)
[efharistó]	ευχαριστώ	*thanks*
[oréo]	ωραίο	*nice, beautiful*
[pináte]?	πεινάτε;	*Are you hungry?* (pl/fml)
[THipsáte]?	διψάτε;	*Are you thirsty?* (pl/fml)
[thélete]?	θέλετε;	*Would you like?*
		(lit. *Do you want?*) (pl/fml)
[kafé]	καφέ	*coffee* (m)
[kóka kóla]	κόκα κόλα	*coke* (f)
[éhis]	έχεις	*you have, do you have?* (sing/infml)
[portokaláTHa]	πορτοκαλάδα	*orangeade* (f)
[frapé]	φραπέ	*iced coffee, frappé* (m)
[yia]	για	*for*
[ména]	μένα	*me*

Note

In this unit you have encountered [yia]: in [yiásas] γεια σας *hello* and [yia ména] για μένα *for me*. Although the sound is identical, the Greek spelling for these two words changes: The first is γεια and the second is για. Something similar in English would be *too*, *two* and *to*.

Language rules

1 [énan kafé] Έναν καφέ *A coffee*

The word [énan] έναν *a* is an article. Articles are words meaning *the*, *a*, *an*. You know by now some different words for *the* in Greek (the definite article). Similarly, the indefinite article *a* or *an* also varies according to the gender (m, f, n). [éna(s/n)] Ένα(ς/ν) is used before masculine nouns depending on their role in the sentence, [mía] μία before feminine nouns, and [éna] ένα before neuter nouns. This explains the different forms of the article used in the dialogues, e.g. [énan kafé] έναν καφέ *a coffee* (m noun), μία καρέκλα [mía karékla] *a chair* (f noun), [éna spíti] ένα σπίτι *a house* (n noun). You can check the **Grammar summary** and go over the numbers 1 to 10, particularly number 1 in Unit 4.

2 [yiásas] [kírie John] Γεια σας, κύριε John! Hello, Mr John!

This semi-formal way of usually younger people addressing older people does not exist in English. It was mentioned in Unit 3. Remember that it is very common and very frequent in Greek. [kiría] κυρία would be the corresponding word for women. You can always use these two words to express the meaning of 'Sir' or 'Madam' addressing people you do not know. Note the different position of the stress in these two words in the examples below:

[kírie] [poo íne to aeroTHrómio]? *Sir, where is the airport?*
[kírie] [to portofóli sas]! *Sir, your wallet!*
[kiría] [pos sas léne]? *Madam, what is your name?*

3 [thélete] [énan kafé]? Θέλετε έναν καφέ; Do you want/Would you like a coffee?

[thélete] Θέλετε comes from [thélo] θέλω *I want* and is a very common verb in Greek. Greek people use it to express 'I simply want', 'I want it here and now!', 'I want it if it is possible', 'I would like' or even 'I'd love to'! Note the different forms of this important verb below:

[thélo]	θέλω	I want
[thélis]	θέλεις	you want
[théli]	θέλει	he/she/it wants
[théloome]	θέλουμε	we want
[thélete]	θέλετε	you want
[théloon(e)]	θέλουν(ε)	they want

There are no new surprises in the verb endings. That's a relief, isn't it?

4 [hérome poo sas ksanavlépo]! Χαίρομαι που σας ξαναβλέπω! *Glad to see you again!*

The word **[poo]** in this sentence means *that* and not *where*, a meaning you already know. The sentence literally means 'I am glad that I see you again!' Keep in mind this dual function of **[poo]** which is *where?* in questions and *that* in statements. In Greek, the question word has a stress mark. **Πού**; *Where?* in contrast to **που** *that* which has no stress.

In Dialogue 2 of Unit 5 you were introduced to **[ksanaTHó]** ξαναδώ *I see again* and now you find **[ksanavlépo]** ξαναβλέπώ *see again*! These are two forms of a compound verb (compound words are made up from two different words together – see below) that belong to the same root word. In order not to make things difficult here with complicated explanations, a similar aspect can be seen in English with *go* and *went*. They do not look the same but they still belong to the same root word! We call these *irregular verbs*.

[ksanavlépo] is a compound word from **[ksaná]** *again* and **[vlépo]** *I see*. Some other compound words you have found in previous units include:

> **[periméno]** *I wait* → **[péri]** *around* + **[méno]** *I stay/I live*
> **[monokatikía]** *one-family house* → **[móno]** *single*
>   + **[katikía]** *residence*
> **[polikatikía]** *apartment complex* → **[polí]** *much/many*
>   + **[katikía]** *residence*
> **[eksáTHelfos]** *cousin* → **[eks]** *from* + **[aTHelfós]** *brother*
> **[eksaTHélfi]** *cousin* → **[eks]** *from* + **[aTHelfí]** *sister*
> **[THekapénde]** *fifteen* → **[THéka]** *ten* + **[pénde]** *five* and, of course, many more numbers…

This unit will introduce the numbers 21 to 100. The word above [arithmí] probably sounds to you like *arithmetic*. Are you good at it? Look at and study the numbers below:

21	[íkosiéna] είκοσι ένα	*twenty one*
22	[íkosiTHío] είκοσι δύο	*twenty two*
30	[triánda] τριάντα	*thirty*
31	[triandaéna] τριάντα ένα	*thirty one*
40	[saránda] σαράντα	*forty*
50	[penínda] πενήντα	*fifty*
60	[exínda] εξήντα	*sixty*
70	[evTHomínda] εβδομήντα	*seventy*
80	[ogTHónda] ογδόντα	*eighty*
90	[enenínda] ενενήντα	*ninety*
100	[ekató] εκατό	*one hundred*

The endings [-ánda], [-índa] or [-ónda] correspond to the English *-ty* as in *thirty, forty,* etc.

What you have learnt about 1, 3 and 4 applies to all numbers that include those numbers, e.g. 41 can be [saránda éna(n)] for masculine nouns, [saránda mía] for feminine nouns and [saránda éna] for neuter nouns.

ℹ [efharistó]! Ευχαριστώ! *Thanks!*

No matter how little you can converse in a foreign language, greetings, farewells and wishes will always be important. Unit 1 introduced you to some very useful and common words and expressions. Unit 6 introduces you to some other important words and expressions. Let's start with [efharistó] ευχαριστώ *thanks* or [efharistó polí] ευχαριστώ πολύ *thanks a lot.* [parakaló] παρακαλώ *you're welcome* (lit. please) or [típota] τίποτα *don't mention it* (lit. nothing) are two typical answers.

Greeks use plenty of expressions when welcoming someone. [kalós órises]! καλώς όρισες! or [kalosórises] καλωσόρισες as a compound word, means *welcome* and addresses one person informally in a friendly circle. The following expressions are used when addressing one person formally or more than one person: [kalós orísate]! καλώς ορίσατε! or [kalosorísate]! καλωσορίσατε!. The most typical answers to these expression are: [kalós se vríka]! καλώς σε βρήκα! one person replying informally to another person, or [kalós sas vríka]! καλώς σας βρήκα! one person replying formally to one person. The closest translation for all these phrases is perhaps 'nice seeing/meeting you again' or even 'nice/glad to be here'.

[énan frapé parakaló]! Έναν φραπέ, παρακαλώ!
An iced coffee, please!

[frapés] Φραπές *iced coffee* is the most popular drink consumed during the summer months. You can always order [nes] νες or [nes kafés] νες καφές which is a cup of hot instant coffee or [elinikós kafés] ελληνικός καφές *Greek coffee* which is a small cup of coffee, drunk without milk, that used to be called Turkish coffee, but don't call it that now! When ordering Greek coffee at a [kafenío] καφενείο *(traditional)* caf*é* or [kafetéria] καφετέρια *café*, you should specify how sweet you would like it to be: [skéto] σκέτο *no sugar*, [métrio] μέτριο *one spoon of sugar (medium)* or [glikó] γλυκό *two spoons of sugar (sweet)*. [frédo] freddo *iced cappuccino*, regular cappuccino or espresso are other coffee options.

The final [-s] is deleted in the words [frapés] and [kafés] when you order these coffees from a waiter, e.g. [énan frapé parakaló] or [énan elinikó kafé parakaló]. See the **Grammar summary** for further details.

Some popular refreshments are [lemonáTHa] λεμονάδα *lemonade,* [portokaláTHa] πορτοκαλάδα *orangeade* and, of course, all international soft drinks. You can always ask for [neró] νερό *water*, or [emfialoméno neró] εμφιαλωμένο νερό *bottled water*, or even [éna potíri neró] ένα ποτήρι νερό *a glass of water*. Some refreshments come in a [bookáli] μπουκάλι *bottle* or in a [kootí] κουτί *can*, so you can always ask for [éna bookáli kóka kóla]/[éna kootí kóka kóla] *a bottle/can of Coke*.

'Zagori' bottled water. One of the most popular brands in Greece.

Practice makes perfect

1 Mary has taken out a family photo and talks about the people in it. Match the words below with the right people in the photo.

a [o papoós moo]
b [i yiayiá moo]
c [o aTHelfós moo]
d [i eksaTHélfi moo]
e [o yios moo]
f [o ándras moo]

i   ii   iii   iv   v   vi

2 Can you match the above-mentioned six words with their English translation?

a [papoós]
b [yiayiá]
c [aTHelfós]
d [eksaTHélfi]
e [yios]
f [ándras]

i son
ii husband
iii grandfather
iv brother
v grandmother
vi cousin

3 Match each question with the most appropriate answer.

a [éhis oréo spíti]?
b [thélis énan kafé]?
c [thélis mía portokaláTHa]?
d [THipsáte]?
e [ti thélis]?

i [óhi], [mía lemonáTHa].
ii [éna tsái], [efharistó].
iii [óhi], [pináme]!
iv [polí oréo ke polí megálo].
v [ne], [éna frapé parakaló].

4 Rearrange these lines to make up a dialogue.

a [ti thélis] [na pjis]?
b [éna himó] [se parakaló].
c [ángele]! [THipsás]?
d [THen kséro]. [ti éhi]?
e [ne polí] [mitéra].
f [éhi himó lemonáTHa]
[ke fisiká kafé].

a Τι θέλεις να πιεις;
b Ένα χυμό σε παρακαλώ.
c Άγγελε, διψάς;
d Δεν ξέρω. Τι έχει;
e Ναι πολύ, μητέρα.
f Έχει χυμό λεμονάδα
και φυσικά καφέ.

5 Translate the English phrases into Greek to complete the following dialogue.

[fílos] [páre mía karékla] [kondá moo].
You   a *Close to you? Why?*
[fílos] [yiatí] [thélo na miláme] [angliká].
You   b *English? I want to speak Greek!*
[fílos] [eliniká]? [oréa]! [kafé stin arhí]?
You   c *Why not? Coffee to start with* (lit. *in the beginning*). *A frappé for me.*

6 Crossword puzzle. The shaded vertical word means *butter*.

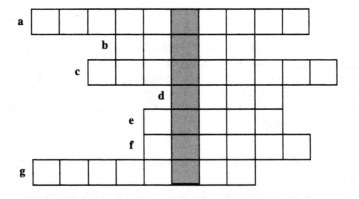

a I see again
b bread
c lemonade
d tea

e juice
f iced coffee
g coke

▶ **7** **Listen again to Dialogue 2 of this unit and fill in the blanks. If you don't have the recordings, choose the missing words from the box below.**

[ángelos]	**a** _____, [kathíste ston] **b** _____. [John], [páre mía] **c** _____ [kondá moo].
John	[efharistó].
Mary	[oréo spíti], [polí oréo] [ke polí megálo].
[elpíTHa]	**d** _____? [THipsáte]? [thélete] **e** _____ [kafé], **f** _____ [kóka kóla]?
Mary	**g** _____ [portokaláTHa]?
John	[éna frapé] **h** _____ **i** _____.

[pináte]	[kanapé]	[éna]	[ména]	[eláte]	[mía]
	[yia]	[karékla]	[éhis]		

Mini test

Unit 6 was not very long or very difficult, was it? Let's see how you are handling the new vocabulary. Remember that whenever you find the **Mini tests** difficult, you should revise the unit once again.

a Name five Greek refreshments. **[kóka kóla]** doesn't count!
b 'Come close to me' and 'Let's go close to him' is what you want to say.
c 'Do you have an orangeade or juice?' is what you want to ask.
d 'Have a seat!' or 'Take a chair!' How can you say that in Greek?
e Can you say your home and business telephone numbers? Instead of saying the numbers one by one, say them in twos.
f What number was the page where Unit 6 started and what page does it finish on?

[oréa]! [polí oréa]! [tha se ksanaTHó] [stin enótita] (unit) **[eptá]! [yiásoo]!**

Ωραία! Πολύ ωραία! Θα σε ξαναδώ στην ενότητα επτά! Γεια σου!

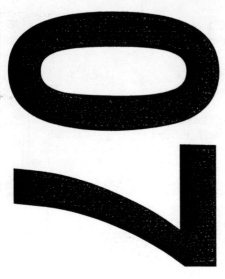

07

Τι ωραία πολυθρόνα!

what a nice armchair!

In this unit you will learn
- how to agree or disagree with someone
- how to say if you like or dislike something
- more Greek nouns in singular and plural form
- how to start using adjectives
- some colours

Before you start

You are now in Unit 7 – almost half way through this book. You're obviously making good progress and you're enjoying yourself. [sinharitíria]! Συγχαρητήρια! or [bravo]! Μπράβο! Sorry about the first word; it is rather long but it is the only one that means 'congratulations'!

Beginners sometimes get frustrated at this stage because of their limited vocabulary. They want to say things but don't have the right words at their fingertips. What can they do and more specifically, what can *you* do in a situation like this? Two suggestions here will help you get much further than you can imagine with native speakers whenever a situation like this arises:

* Use a small pocket dictionary! This is the best-known method to get you out of difficult situations quickly. Pocket dictionaries will always come in handy when travelling abroad even if you are quite proficient in the language in question.

* Use substitutions to build your confidence in Greek. What do we mean by substitutions? Here is an example: You have already learnt [íme kalá] είμαι καλά *I'm fine*, but how would you say 'I'm not so good' or 'I'm fairly OK' if you don't know the words 'so' or 'fairly'? You can substitute the unknown words by using words you are already familiar with and which can provide a possible alternative to what you're trying to say. [THen íme kalá] Δεν είμαι καλά lit. *I'm not fine* or [íme lígo kalá] Είμαι λίγο καλά (lit. *I'm a little fine*) use the words [THen] and [lígo] already known to you. You will find more explanations about substitutions in Unit 8.

Pronunciation tips

In the **Pronunciation guide** at the beginning of the book you were introduced to five vowel sounds in Greek. If you want to practise them again, you can always go back to Unit 3 as well where four out of these five vowel sounds were presented.

The word [arésoon] *like* has three vowel sounds: [a] and [e] and [oo] which have very similar sounds in both languages. The word [protimó] *I prefer* has the other two vowel sounds: [o] and [i] which also have very similar sounds in both languages. Let's see the five vowels in Greek once again: [a] as in '*fan*', [e] as in '*ten*', [i] as in '*sit*', [o] as in '*not*', and [oo] as in '*boot*'. Remember that they can be both short and long in Greek. As a rule of thumb, stressed vowels are always long.

ο κόσμος της επικοινωνίας

'OTE' is the main telephone company in Greece.

▶ Key words and phrases

All of us agree and disagree with people. All of us like and dislike things. All of us prefer some things to others. Unit 7 is a good start for you to become familiar with these important concepts and the words behind them. Look at and study the two lists below. They will often come in handy.

Likes		Dislikes	
[moo arési] μου αρέσει or [marési] μ'αρέσει	I like (one person or thing; lit. it pleases me)	[antipathó] αντιπαθω	I dislike
[moo arésoon] μου αρέσουν or [marésoon] μ'αρέσουν	I like (more than one person or thing; lit. they please me)	[THen m'arési] δεν μ'αρέσει or [THen m'arésoon] δεν μ'αρέσουν	I don't like
[simfonó] συμφωνώ	I agree	[THiafonó] διαφωνώ	I disagree
[protimó] προτιμώ	I prefer	[THen protimó] δεν προτιμώ	I don't prefer
[ého THíkio] έχω δίκιο	I'm right (lit. I have right)	[ého áTHiko] έχω άδικο	I'm wrong (lit. I have wrong)

Look at the examples below:

[ého THíkio i áTHiko]? Έχω δίκιο ή άδικο; *Am I right or wrong?*
[simfonó mazí soo]. Συμφωνώ μαζί σου. *I agree with you.*
[moo arési i maría]. Μου αρέσει η Μαρία. *I like Maria.*

[THen moo arésoon o THimítris ke i María]. Δεν μου αρέσουν ο Δημήτρης και η Μαρία. *I don't like Jim and Mary.* [protimó kafé ke óhi tsái]. Προτιμώ καφέ και όχι τσάι. *I prefer coffee and not tea.*

In the examples above [i] is used with two different meanings. [i] ή with a stress mark means *or* and [i] η without a stress mark means *the* (f definite article).

▶ [THiálogos 1] Διάλογος 1 *Dialogue 1*

Ελπίδα (*Hope*) is proud of their new house and shows Mary around.

[elpíTHa]	Mary [éla na soo THíxo] [to spíti].	*Mary, let me show you the house.*
Mary	[ne] [to thélo polí]. [páme].	*Yes, I'd like that a lot. Let's go.*
[elpíTHa]	[eTHó íne to ipnoTHomátio mas].	*Here's our bedroom.*
Mary	[ti oréa polithróna] [ke ti megálo kreváti]!	*What a nice armchair and what a big bed!*
[elpíTHa]	[eTHó íne i koozína]. [éhi megálo pángo] [ke hóro yia megálo trapézi] [ke polés karékles].	*Here's the kitchen. It has a long counter and space for a big table and a lot of chairs.*
Mary	[vlépo], [vlépo]. [brávo, elpíTHa].	*I see, I see. Bravo, Hope.*

Ελπίδα	Mary, έλα να σου δείξω το σπίτι.
Mary	Ναι, το θέλω πολύ. Πάμε.
Ελπίδα	Εδώ είναι το υπνοδωμάτιο μας.
Mary	Τι ωραία πολυθρόνα και τι μεγάλο κρεβάτι!
Ελπίδα	Εδώ είναι η κουζίνα. Έχει μεγάλο πάγκο και χώρο για μεγάλο τραπέζι και πολλές καρέκλες.
Mary	Βλέπω, βλέπω. Μπράβο, Ελπίδα.

[éla]	έλα	*come* (sing/infml)
[éla na soo THíkso]	έλα να σου δείξω	*let me show you* (lit. come to show you)
[páme]	πάμε	*we go, let's go*
[oréa]	ωραία	*beautiful, nice* (with f noun)
[ipnoTHomátio]	υπνοδωμάτιο	*bedroom* (n)

[polithróna]	πολυθρόνα	*armchair* (f)
[kreváti]	κρεβάτι	*bed* (n)
[koozína]	κουζίνα	*kitchen* (f)
[pángo]	πάγκο	*counter* (m)
[hóro]	χώρο	*space, area* (m)
[trapézi]	τραπέζι	*table* (n)
[karékles]	καρέκλες	*chairs* (f/pl)
[vlépo]	βλέπω	*I see, I understand, I realize*

Notes

* [ipnoTHomátio] υπνοδωμάτιο *bedroom* is a compound word from [ípnos] ύπνος *sleep* (m) and [THomátio] δωμάτιο *room* (n). [krevatokámara] κρεβατοκάμαρα also means *bedroom*. It is also a compound word from [kreváti] κρεβάτι *bed* (n) and [kámara] κάμαρα *room* (f).

* The main form of the word for 'space' is χώρος [hóros]. The two different forms: with the final [-s] and without, apply to all masculine nouns. This relates to the different 'cases' in Greek grammar. The main form is the one usually listed in dictionaries, and is in the nominative case (used for nouns before the verb, the subject of the sentence) and the form without the final [-s] is the accusative case (usually used for nouns after the verb, the object of the sentence). Other examples from past units include [kafés] – [kafé], [frapés] – [frapé] as well as proper names such as [níkos] – [níko] and [kóstas] – [kósta]. See also the notes on cases in the **Grammar summary**.

▶ **[THiálogos 2] Διάλογος 2** *Dialogue 2:* **[soo arési]? Σου αρέσει;** *Do you like it?*

Hope takes Mary further around the house.

[elpíTHa]	[eTHó] [íne to vesé]. [íne lígo mikró] [alá polí praktikó] [ótan íne anángi].	*Here's the WC. It's a little bit small but very practical when necessary.*
Mary	[ne], [vévea].	*Yes, of course.*
[elpíTHa]	[apo'THó to lootró]. [soo arési]?	*This is the bathroom. Do you like it?*
Mary	[moo arési polí]. [moo arésoon] [ta hrómata polí] [ke o strongilós kathréftis].	*I like it a lot. I like the colours and the round mirror.*
[elpíTHa]	[ne] [to mávro ke áspro] [kánoon] [megáli antíthesi] [alá moo arésoon].	*Yes, black and white create a great contrast and* (lit. but) *I like them.*

Mary	[simfonó]. [éhis THíkio].	*I agree. You're right.*

Ελπίδα	Εδώ είναι το WC. Είναι λίγο μικρό αλλά πολύ πρακτικό όταν είναι ανάγκη.
Mary	Ναι, βέβαια.
Ελπίδα	Από'δω το λουτρό. Σου αρέσει;
Mary	Μου αρέσει πολύ. Μου αρέσουν τα χρώματα πολύ και ο στρογγυλός καθρέφτης.
Ελπίδα	Ναι, το μαύρο και άσπρο κάνουν μεγάλη αντίθεση αλλά μου αρέσουν.
Mary	Συμφωνώ. Έχεις δίκιο.

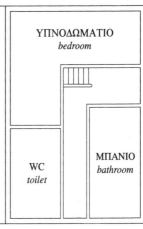

[praktikó]	πρακτικό	*practical* (with n noun)
[ótan]	όταν	*when* (within a sentence, not as a question)
[anángi]	ανάγκη	*necessity* (f), *necessary*
[vévea]	βέβαια	*of course, naturally*
[lootró]	λουτρό	*bath, bathroom* (n)
[soo arési]?	σου αρέσει;	*Do you like?* (sing/infml)
[hrómata]	χρώματα	*colours* (n/pl)
[strongilós]	στρογγυλός	*round* (with m noun)
[kathréftis]	καθρέφτης	*mirror* (m)
[mávro]	μαύρο	*black*
[áspro]	άσπρο	*white*
[antíthesi]	αντίθεση	*contrast* (f)
[simfonó]	συμφωνώ	*I agree*
[THíkio]	δίκιο	*right* (n)

Notes

- **[ótan íne anángi]** Όταν είναι ανάγκη *When it is necessary* is a useful phrase. Learn it by heart.

- You can also use **[bánio] μπάνιο** (n) in place of **[lootró] λουτρό** (n) for bathroom. **[vesé]** *WC* is also used and always written in English. The public bathrooms or toilets in hotels or airports are **[tooaléta] τουαλέτα** *toilet* (f).

Language rules

1 [ke polés karékles]... και πολλές καρέκλες... *and many chairs...*

In Unit 6 you were introduced to the word **[karékla] καρέκλα** *chair* and in this unit to its plural form **[karékles] καρέκλες** *chairs*. Study the list below without trying to memorize everything at once. Simply notice that certain nouns are consistent in their plural formation, e.g. feminine nouns change endings from **[-a]** to **[-es]** as in **[i karékla]** – **[i karékles]**, or neuter nouns from **[-i]** to **[-ia]** as in **[to trapézi]** – **[ta trapézia]**. Refer back to the similar list in Unit 4.

Masculine
[o kanapés] – [i kanapéTHes] ο καναπές – οι καναπέδες *sofa – sofas*
[o pángos] – [i pángi] ο πάγκος – οι πάγκοι *counter – counters*
[o kathréftis] – [i kathréftes] ο καθρέφτης – οι καθρέφτες
  mirror – mirrors

Feminine
[i karékla] – [i karékles] η καρέκλα – οι καρέκλες *chair – chairs*
[i polithróna] – [i polithrónes] η πολυθρόνα – οι πολυθρόνες
  armchair – armchairs
[i koozína] – [i koozínes] η κουζίνα – οι κουζίνες *kitchen – kitchens*

Neuter
[to THomátio] – [ta THomátia] το δωμάτιο – τα δωμάτια
  room – rooms
[to kreváti] – [ta krevátia] το κρεβάτι – τα κρεβάτια *bed – beds*
[to trapézi] – [ta trapézia] το τραπέζι – τα τραπέζια *table – tables*

Notes

- It might be useful to compare notes with the section on nouns in the **Grammar summary**.
- The above-mentioned masculine nouns for 'sofa', 'counter', and 'mirror' drop the final **-s** from the nominative when they are used in the accusative in their singular form, as already mentioned earlier in this Unit. In the **Glossary** at the back of the book or in any dictionary these nouns appear in their nominative form (including the final **-s**).
- The word **[políthróna]** is a compound word from **[polí]** *very/much/many* and **[thrónos]** *throne* which comes to 'very much a throne'. Interesting, isn't it?
- Be prepared to hear the word **[koozína]** κουζίνα *kitchen* with different meanings in other contexts. It can also mean 'cooker/stove' or even 'cuisine'.

2 [ta hrómata] Τα χρώματα *Colours*

Looking at the nouns above and how their forms change from singular to plural, you probably noticed the different forms for the word *the* in the plural. Let's summarize these forms below:

	masculine	feminine	neuter
singular	[o] ο	[i] η	[to] το
plural	[i] οι	[i] οι	[ta] τα

3 [moo arési polí]! Μου αρέσει πολύ! *I like (it/that) a lot!*

[moo arési] μου αρέσει *I like* (only one person or thing) and **[moo arésoon]** *I like* (more than one person or thing) are two very popular verbs, but not similar to what you have been introduced to so far. Possibly **[me léne]** *my name is/they call me* is the only verb that comes close to them. Note their different forms below:

[moo arési]	μου αρέσει	*I like* (only one person or thing)
[soo arési]	σου αρέσει	*you like*
[too arési]	του αρέσει	*he/it likes*
[tis arési]	της αρέσει	*she likes*
[mas arési]	μας αρέσει	*we like*
[sas arési]	σας αρέσει	*you like*
[toos arési]	τους αρέσει	*they like* (m/f/n)

[moo arésoon]	μου αρέσουν	*I like* (more than one person or thing)
[soo arésoon]	σου αρέσουν	*you like*
[too arésoon]	του αρέσουν	*he/it likes*
[tis arésoon]	της αρέσουν	*she likes*
[mas arésoon]	μας αρέσουν	*we like*
[sas arésoon]	σας αρέσουν	*you like*
[toos arésoon]	τους αρέσουν	*they like* (m/f/n)

The first two forms have an alternative contracted form: [marési], and [sarési]. Equally: [marésoon] and [sarésoon].

Some examples:

[moo arési o kanapés]. Μου αρέσει ο καναπές. *I like the sofa.*
[moo arésoon i karékles]. Μου αρέσουν οι καρέκλες.
I like the chairs.
[THen too arési o kathréftis]. Δεν του αρέσει ο καθρέφτης.
He doesn't like the mirror.
[THen mas arésoon ta hrómata]. Δεν μας αρέσουν τα χρώματα.
We don't like the colours.

4 [moo arésoon ta hrómata polí]! Μου αρέσουν τα χρώματα πολύ! *I like the colours a lot!*

This unit introduces you to two colours: [mávro] μαύρο *black* and [áspro] άσπρο *white*. Subsequent units will refer to more colours but if you are anxious to know them now, they are listed for you below:

[mov] μωβ *purple*   [ble] μπλε *blue*
[prásino] πράσινο *green*   [kítrino] κίτρινο *yellow*
[portokalí] πορτοκαλί *orange*   [kókino] κόκκινο *red*

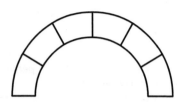

Put some colour in this book! If you have crayons or if you can borrow some from your children, you can colour the arch above. [mávro ke áspro] Μαύρο και άσπρο is not very exciting, is it?

5 [oréa polithróna]! Ωραία πολυθρόνα! *A nice armchair!*

All the units have had some words describing nouns. Here are some more examples:

[oréa polithróna]	ωραία πολυθρόνα	*nice* armchair (f)
[megálo kreváti]	μεγάλο κρεβάτι	*big* bed (n)
[megálo trapézi]	μεγάλο τραπέζι	*big* table (n)
[mikró vesé]	μικρό WC	*small* WC (n)
[praktikó vesé]	πρακτικό WC	*practical* WC (n)
[strongilós kathréftis]	στρογγυλός καθρέφτης	*round* mirror (m)
[megáli antíthesi]	μεγάλη αντίθεση	*big* contrast (lit. antithesis] (f)

These underlined words are called *adjectives* and are very useful in everyday conversations. These words, as with nouns in Greek, have different forms for singular and plural and also have different endings for masculine, feminine or neuter nouns. Note the change in the endings for the adjective for 'big':

Masculine
[megálos kathréftis] μεγάλος καθρέφτης *big mirror*

Feminine
[megáli karékla] μεγάλη καρέκλα *big chair*

Neuter
[megálo trapézi] μεγάλο τραπέζι *big table*

If you go back to the examples now, you will soon realize that these are the most common endings for the three genders with [oréa] being the only exception:

masculine: [strongilós] στρογγυλός
feminine: [megáli] μεγάλη, [oréa] ωραία
neuter: [megálo] μεγάλο, [mikró] μικρό, [praktikó] πρακτικό

Subsequent units will refer further to this new group of words. Don't worry too much about them at the moment.

6 [to lootró] Το λουτρό *The bathroom*

A lot of information about Greek houses was provided in Unit 4. It is often useful to know the names of different items found there.

Certain associations can be used as follows: [koozína] κουζίνα
kitchen with [pángos] πάγκος *counter*, [trapézi] τραπέζι *table* and
[karékla] καρέκλα *chair*; [ipnoTHomátio] υπνοδωμάτιο *bedroom*
with [kathréftis] καθρέφτης *mirror*, [kreváti] κρεβάτι *bed* and
[doolápa] ντουλάπα *closet/wardrobe*; and [salóni] σαλόνι *living
room* with [polithróna] πολυθρόνα *armchair* and [kanapés]
καναπές *sofa*. Some more important words in the home are:
[balkóni] μπαλκόνι *balcony/porch*, [paráthiro] παράθυρο *window*,
[pórta] πόρτα *door*, and [avlí] αυλή *yard*.

Now look at the picture below and see how many items of furniture
you can label in Greek. Use a dictionary if necessary.

ℹ️ [elinikí filoksenía] Ελληνική φιλοξενία *Greek
hospitality*

People often talk about Greek hospitality. Generally speaking,
Greeks are hospitable people; they open their homes to friends and
acquaintances and entertain generously. Of course, hospitality in its
broad sense can be interpreted differently among people in different
situations. You need to experience it in order to realize what it is like
and what lies between the reality and the myth. Many tourists and
visitors in Greece have experienced a combination of hospitality and
kindness as well as impoliteness and rudeness. Two typical
examples can be mentioned here: staying overnight in a rented room
on a small island and taking a taxi in Athens. Of course, we should
not over-generalize and put them in stereotypes like 'All rented
rooms in Greece are very nice!' and 'All Athenian taxi drivers are
rude!' Be prepared for both, though, and have a pleasant stay...

Practice makes perfect

1 Some people like repeating themselves. By mistake the author has put in the colour arch again. Without looking back can you fill in the colours with 'words' or real colours?

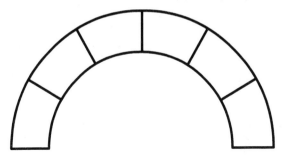

2 Are you good with flag colours? Six flags are listed for you below but unfortunately they are in black and white. What are their real colours?

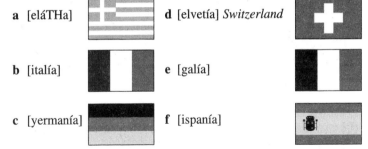

a [eláTHa]

d [elvetía] *Switzerland*

b [italía]

e [galía]

c [yermanía]

f [ispanía]

3 We live in a consumer society. The person below wants everything in big quantities. Can you change the sentences from singular to plural? The first sentence has been done for you.

[moo arési to trapézi] → [moo arésoon ta trapézia]

a [moo arési o kathréftis] → _____
b [moo arési o kanapés] → _____
c [moo arési i karékla] → _____
d [moo arési i polithróna] → _____
e [moo arési to bánio*] → _____
f [moo arési to kreváti] → _____

*The word [bánio] means 'bathroom' but also 'bathtub' and 'swimming'.

4 It is useful to learn some words in pairs (sometimes similar, sometimes opposite). The new group of words introduced in this unit (adjectives) are important when describing or comparing things. Find the pairs below. Some new words have been added for you.

a [strongilós] στρογγυλός
b [mikrós] μικρός
c [oréos] ωραίος
d [THíkeos] δίκαιος
e [lígos] λίγος

i [áshimos] άσχημος *ugly*
ii [polís] πολύς
iii [áTHikos] άδικος
iv [megálos] μεγάλος
v [tetrágonos] τετράγωνος *square*

5 In Exercise 4 above all words were given in the masculine gender. Can you change the endings to neuter? The first one has been done for you.

[strongilós] → [strongiló]

a [mikrós] → _____
b [oréos] → _____
c [THíkeos] → _____
d [lígos] → _____
e [áshimos] → _____

f [polís] → _____
g [áTHikos] → _____
h [megálos] → _____
i [tetrágonos] → _____

6 Rearrange these lines to make up a dialogue.

a [egó protimó ta mikrá spítia].

b [ne], [alá íne polí megálo].

c [THen éhis THíkio].

d [moo arésoon ta megála spítia].

e [soo arési to spíti mas]?

f [óhi]! [óhi]! [antipathó ta mikrá spítia]!

a Εγώ προτιμώ τα μικρά σπίτια.

b Ναι, αλλά είναι πολύ μεγάλο.

c Δεν έχεις δίκιο.

d Μου αρέσουν τα μεγάλα σπίτια.

e Σου αρέσει το σπίτι μας;

f Όχι, όχι! Αντιπαθώ τα μικρά σπίτια!

▶ **7** Listen again to Dialogue 2 of this unit and fill in the blanks. If you don't have the recording, choose the missing words from the box below.

[elpíTHa]   [eTHó] [íne to vesé]. [íne lígo mikró] [alá polí] a _____ .

Mary   [ne], b _____ .

[elpíTHa]   [apó'THo to] c _____ . [soo arési]?

Mary   [moo arési polí]. [moo] d _____ [ta hrómata polí] [ke o strongilós] e _____ .

[elpíTHa]   [ne] [to mávro ke] **f** _____ [kánoon] [megáli antíthesi]. **g** _____ [moo arésoon].

Mary   [simfonó]. [éhis] **h** _____ .

> [vévea]   [alá]   [THíkio]   [kathréftis]   [áspro]
> [arésoon]   [praktikó]   [lootró]

▶ **8 Read the conversation between Mary and Hope about Greece. Then say whether the sentences (a)–(e) are true or false.**

Mary   [moo arési i eláTHa] [yiatí íne mikrí].

[elpíTHa]   [THen simfonó]. [THen íne polí mikrí].

Mary   [THiafonó] [alá]… [moo arési] [o kerós*] [stin eláTHa].

[elpíTHa]   [eTHó] [simfonó mazí soo]. [éhis THíkio].

Mary   [vévea], [yiatí THen protimó] [tin vrohí*] [sto lonTHíno].

[elpíTHa]   [THen éhis áTHiko]

*[kerós] **καιρός** _weather_ (m) and [vrohí] **βροχή** _rain_ (f).

	True	False
a They both believe Greece is a small country.	☐	☐
b They both agree that Greece has nice weather.	☐	☐
c Mary dislikes rainy days in London.	☐	☐
d Mary dislikes the weather in Greece.	☐	☐
e Hope likes the weather in Greece.	☐	☐

9 Can you translate the dialogue in Exercise 8?

Mini test

How did you find Unit 7? It had some important new vocabulary for you to remember. Let's see how much you know:

a What are your favourite colours? Can you name four?

b What is the opposite of 'I like', 'I agree' and 'I'm right'?

c How would you translate 'I like', 'I agree', and 'I'm right' into Greek?

d There are two words for 'dislike' in Greek. What are they?

e Can you name at least five pieces of furniture?

f What is the opposite of 'square', 'big' and 'black' in Greek?

g How would you translate the three words in question **f** into Greek?

Now you're ready to go to Unit 8. **Θα σε δω εκεί!** Can you guess what this means?

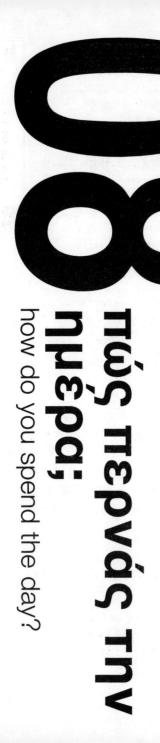

08

πώς περνάς την ημέρα;

how do you spend the day?

In this unit you will learn
- how to talk about daily routines
- how to tell the time
- how to count from 101 to 1,000
- about Greek adverbs

Before you start

Revise Unit 1 once again! Yes, Unit 1! This is not a mistake! You are now slowly moving towards the second stage of your learning where you actively participate and start to create Greek phrases all by yourself. Here are some suggestions for revising Unit 1:

1 Cover the transliteration column. Looking at the English column, can you translate it into Greek?

2 Cover the English column. Do you understand everything, looking at the transliteration column?

3 Check the Greek spelling. You can start creating a new list of words written in Greek. One word to include in this new list could be for example: **[aeroTHrómio]** αεροδρόμιο *airport*, which is important for you when travelling in Greece.

4 Use substitutions. By now you will have created a small vocabulary list that you can start using with alternative options or possible substitutions. Take for example the sentence: **[egó miláo angl18á]** Εγώ μιλάω αγγλικά *I speak English*. Using substitutions, you can: **a** talk about different people: *You speak, he speaks, we speak*, etc.; **b** make negative sentences: *I don't, you don't, he doesn't speak English*, etc.; **c** talk about other languages: *I speak German, Spanish, Italian*, etc; or express other options and possibilities.

Pronunciation tips

The word **[telióno]** *I finish* has three letters which have very similar sounds in both languages. The letters τ **[t]** as in '*tell*', λ **[l]** as in '*let*', and ν **[n]** as in '*not*'. These are three letters that you have found in many words throughout the previous units. Can you make a list, including at least five words for each sound? See if you can find an example of the sounds in the pictures on page 93.

ΞΕΝΟΔΟΧΕΙΟ
Ταξιάρχες

ΑΡΙΣΤΗ
ΖΑΓΟΡΙΟΥ
ΤΗΛ. 0653 - 41888

▶ Key words and phrases

In order to express yourself successfully when describing daily routines, you should study the pictures opposite with the corresponding action verbs. Most of us 'wake up, get up, wash, have breakfast, get ready, go to work' etc. So you should find this new vocabulary very useful. Come back to it whenever needed.

Match the phrases to the cartoons a–n. The first has been done for you:

[ftáno sti THooliá]. **Φτάνω στη δουλειά.**	I arrive at work. →	e
[sikónome argá]. **Σηκώνομαι αργά.**	I get up late. →	___
[epistréfo sto spíti argá]. **Επιστρέφω στο σπίτι αργά.**	I get home late. → _	___
[mathéno eliniká]. **Μαθαίνω ελληνικά.**	I study Greek. →	___
[páo sto kreváti argá]. **Πάω στο κρεβάτι αργά.**	I go to bed late. →	___
[páo sti THooliá]. **Πάω στη δουλειά.**	I go to work. →	___
[tró-o vraTHinó]. **Τρώω βραδινό.**	I eat dinner. →	___
[THen tró-o proinó]. **Δεν τρώω πρωινό.**	I don't eat breakfast. →	___
[tró-o mesimerianó norís]. **Τρώω μεσημεριανό νωρίς.**	I eat lunch early. →	___
[káno dooz]. **Κάνω ντους.**	I take a shower. →	___
[píno polí kafé]. **Πίνω πολύ καφέ.**	I drink a lot of coffee. →	___
[telióno ti THooliá]. **Τελειώνω τη δουλειά.**	I finish work. →	___
[pérno to asansér]. **Παίρνω το ασανσέρ.**	I use the lift. →	___
[vlépo lígo tileórasi]. **Βλέπω λίγο τηλεόραση.**	I watch some TV. →	___

▶ **[THiálogos 1] Διάλογος 1** *Dialogue 1:*
[ti óra íne]? Τι ώρα είναι; *What time is it?*

Hope tells Mary about her daily routine.

Mary	[ti óra íne tóra]?	*What time is it now?*
[elpíTHa]	[íne mía akrivós].	*It's one o'clock exactly.*
	[yiatí ti thélis]?	*Why, what do you want?*
Mary	[pes moo], [pos pernás tin iméra soo]? [ti kánis] [norís to proí]?	*Tell me, how do you spend your day? What do you do early in the morning?*
[elpíTHa]	[siníthos] [sikónome stis eptá], [etimázo proinó] [ke pérno ta peTHiá] [sto sholío]. [épita páo yia psónia]. [teliká mayirévo] ... [THistihós].	*I usually get up at seven, I prepare breakfast and I take the children to school. Then I go shopping. Finally, I cook ... unfortunately.*

Mary	Τι ώρα είναι τώρα;
Ελπίδα	Είναι μία ακριβώς. Γιατί, τι θέλεις;
Mary	Πες μου, πώς περνάς την ημέρα σου; Τι κάνεις νωρίς το πρωί;
Ελπίδα	Συνήθως σηκώνομαι στις επτά. Ετοιμάζω πρωινό και παίρνω τα παιδιά στο σχολείο. Έπειτα πάω για ψώνια. Τελικά, μαγειρεύω ... δυστυχώς.

[óra]	ώρα	*time* (f)
[ti óra íne tóra]?	τι ώρα είναι τώρα;	*what time is it now?*
[akrivós]	ακριβώς	*exactly*
[pes moo]	πες μου	*tell me* (sing/infml)
[pernás]	περνάς	*you spend* (sing/infml)
[norís]	νωρίς	*early*
[siníthos]	συνήθως	*usually*
[sikónome]	σηκώνομαι	*I get up*
[etimázo]	ετοιμάζω	*I prepare*
[proinó]	πρωινό	*breakfast* (n)

[pérno]	παίρνω	*I take*
[sholío]	σχολείο	*school* (n)
[épita]	έπειτα	*then, after that*
[páo]	πάω	*I go, I am going*
[psónia]	ψώνια	*shopping* (n/pl)
[teliká]	τελικά	*finally*
[mayirévo]	μαγειρεύω	*I cook*
[THistihós]	δυστυχώς	*unfortunately*

▶ **[THiálogos 2] Διάλογος 2** *Dialogue 2:*
[páo sti THooliá] Πάω στη δουλειά *I go to work*

Now Mary tells Hope about her daily routine.

[elpíTHa]	[esí ti kánis] [óli tin im.éra]?	*What do you do all day?*
Mary	[ksipnáo stis eptámisi] [káno éna dooz] [ke tró-o proinó]. [metá pérno to tréno] [ke páo sti THooliá].	*I wake up at 7:30, I take a shower and have breakfast. Then I take the train and go to work.*
[elpíTHa]	[ti óra epistréfis spíti]?	*What time do you get back home?*
Mary	[THoolévo siníthos] [apó tis THéka] [méhri tis téseris] [epistréfo spíti] [stis pendémisi].	*I usually work from 10:00 to 4:00. I get back home at 5:30.*
[elpíTHa]	[ti óra] [tróte vraTHinó]?	*What time do you have* (lit. eat) *dinner?*
Mary	[yíro stis eptá] [sto spíti] [i stis októ ékso].	*Around 7:00 at home or at 8:00 when eating out* (lit. at 8:00 out).

Ελπίδα	Εσύ, τι κάνεις όλη την ημέρα;
Mary	Ξυπνάω στις επτάμιση, κάνω ένα ντους και τρώω προινό. Μετά παίρνω το τρένο και πάω στη δουλειά.
Ελπίδα	Τι ώρα επιστρέφεις σπίτι;
Mary	Δουλεύω συνήθως από τις δέκα μέχρι τις τέσσερις. Επιστρέφω σπίτι στις πεντέμιση.
Ελπίδα	Τι ώρα τρώτε βραδινοί;
Mary	Γύρω στις επτά στο σπίτι ή στις οκτώ έξω.

[iméra]	ημέρα	day (f)
[óli tin iméra]	όλη την ημέρα	all day
[ksipnáo]	ξυπνάω	I wake up
[dooz]	ντους	shower (n)
[tró-o]	τρώω	I eat
[metá]	μετά	then, afterwards
[pérno]	παίρνω	I take
[tréno]	τρένο	train (n)
[epistréfis]	επιστρέφεις	you return (sing/infml)
[méhri]	μέχρι	to, until
[tróte]	τρώτε	you eat (pl/fml)
[vraTHinó]	βραδινό	dinner (n)
[yíro]	γύρω	around, about
[stis]	στις	at
[ékso]	έξω	out, outside

Language rules

1 [siníthos] Συνήθως *Usually*

The two dialogues in this unit introduce you to a new group of words that express frequency. They are called *adverbs of frequency* in grammar. Note the following:

[pánda]	πάντα	always
[sheTHón pánda]	σχεδόν πάντα	almost always
[sihná]	συχνά	often
[merikés forés]	μερικές φορές	sometimes
[spánia]	σπάνια	rarely
[sheTHón poté]	σχεδόν ποτέ	hardly ever
[poté]	ποτέ	never

Do not confuse the word [spánia] σπάνια *rarely* with the word [ispanía] Ισπανία *Spain* which you already know.

Also do not confuse the word [poté] ποτέ *never*, with the stress on the last syllable, with the word [póte] πότε *when?* which is a new word for you and has the stress on the first syllable.

2 [épita vlépo]... Έπειτα βλέπω...*Then I watch...*

Unit 8 also introduces you to another group of words that all belong to the same family of adverbs, this time expressing time, place and manner (how you do something), instead of frequency. These words are from this group:

[épita]	έπειτα	*then, later*
[teliká]	τελικά	*finally*
[THistihós]	δυστυχώς	*unfortunately*
[méhri]	μέχρι	*until*
[yíro]	γύρω	*around, about*
[metá]	μετά	*afterwards, later*
[norís]	νωρίς	*early*
[argá]	αργά	*late*

Don't confuse the word [**yíro**] **γύρω** *around, about, approximately*, with [**strongilós**] **στρογγυλός** *round (in shape)* from Unit 7.

▶ 3 [ti óra íne tóra]? Τι ώρα είναι τώρα; *What time is it now?*

Telling the time in Greek is not very difficult. Of course the most important thing is to remember the numbers from 1 to 60. Do you remember all of them? There are two different ways of telling the time: the easy way and the more challenging way! Let's start with the easy way. Simply say the numbers you see:

1:35   [**mía ke triánda pénde**] **μία και τριάντα πέντε**
       one thirty-five

2:20   [**THío ke íkosi**] **δύο και είκοσι**
       two twenty

3:30   [**tris ke triánda**] **τρεις και τριάντα**
       three thirty

4:15   [**téseris ke THekapénde**] **τέσσερις και δεκαπέντε**
       four fifteen

5:45   [**pénde ke saránda pénde**] **πέντε και σαράντα πέντε**
       five forty-five

After the hours, add the word [**ke**] **και** before the minutes.

The more challenging way requires you to remember some important words: [**ke**] **και** *past* (you already know it as 'and'), [**pará**] **παρά** *to, before*, [**tétarto**] **τέταρτο** *quarter* and [**misí**] **μισή** *half, half past*. Another thing you need to remember is that the *hour* [**óra**] **ώρα** comes before the *minutes* [**leptá**] **λεπτά**. Examples:

1:35   [**THío pará íkosi pénde**] **δύο παρά είκοσι πέντε**
       twenty-five (minutes) to two

2:20   [**THío ke íkosi**] **δύο και είκοσι**
       twenty past two

3:30   **[tris ke misí]** τρεις και μισή
half past three

4:15   **[téseris ke tétarto]** τέσσερις και τέταρτο
quarter past four

5:45   **[éksi pará tétarto]** έξι παρά τέταρτο
quarter to six

By the way, **π.μ.** [pi-mi] means *a.m.* and **μ.μ.** [mi-mi] means *p.m.*

Note that as **[óra]** ώρα *hour* is feminine so we use the feminine form of **[énas]** ένας → **[mía]** μία, [tría] τρία → **[tris]** τρεις and **[tésera]** τέσσερα → **[téseris]** τέσσερις.

[stis] Στις means *at* when telling the time, as the number is plural, except 'at 1:00 o'clock' which is in the singular: **[sti]** στη, e.g. **[sti mía i óra]** στη μία η ώρα *at one o'clock*. Look at your watch now. **[ti óra íne]?** How fast can you answer the question?

▶ 4 [i arithmí] Οι αριθμοί *Numbers 101–1,000*

Talking of numbers, let's continue from where we left off in Unit 6. Note and study the new numbers from 101 to 1,000:

101	**[ekatón éna]** εκατόν ένα	*one hundred and one*
105	**[ekatón pénde]** εκατόν πέντε	*one hundred and five*
170	**[ekatón evTHomínda]** εκατόν εβδομήντα	*one hundred and seventy*
200	**[THiakósia]** διακόσια	*two hundred*
300	**[trakósia]** τριακόσια	*three hundred*
400	**[tetrakósia]** τετρακόσια	*four hundred*
500	**[pendakósia]** πεντακόσια	*five hundred*
600	**[eksakósia]** εξακόσια	*six hundred*
700	**[eptakósia]** επτακόσια or **[eftakósia]** εφτακόσια	*seven hundred*
800	**[oktakósia]** οκτακόσια or **[ohtakósia]** οχτακόσια	*eight hundred*
900	**[eniakósia]** εννιακόσια	*nine hundred*
1,000	**[hílji]** χίλιοι (m), **[hílies]** χίλιες (f), **[hília]** χίλια (n)	*one thousand*

As you see, the important ending in the hundreds is **[-kósia]** before neuter nouns. It doesn't have an English equivalent. Learn the numbers above because many Greeks will tell you their telephone number as follows: 76-26-291 **[evTHomínda éksi]**, **[íkosi éksi]**, **[THiakósia enenínda éna]**. The ending **[-kósia] -κόσια** becomes **[-kósies] -κόσιες** before feminine nouns and **[-kósi] -κόσιοι** before masculine nouns.

ℹ [pos pernás tin iméra]? Πώς περνάς την ημέρα; *How do you spend the day?*

[méra] μέρα or **[iméra] ημέρα** means *day*. It is the main part of some compound words like **[kaliméra] καλημέρα** *good day* or **[mesiméri] μεσημέρι** *midday/afternoon*. One can always ask **[ti kánis to proí/mesiméri/ apóyevma/vráTHi]?** *What do you do in the morning/ afternoon/evening/at night?* There is probably no set answer to these questions. You might be doing some of the following: **[mayirévo] μαγειρεύω** / *cook*, **[THoolévo] δουλεύω** / *work*, **[kimáme] κοιμάμαι** / *sleep*, **[tró-o] τρώω** / *eat*, **[píno] πίνω** / *drink*, **[perpató] περπατώ** / *walk*.

Daily routines are pretty much universal one way or another. A typical day at home includes perhaps cooking, cleaning, reading or watching TV, whereas a day at school includes learning and playing, and a day at work hopefully includes working, if nothing else. Some typical Greek activities during the summer are having an afternoon siesta, eating out late at night in outdoor tavernas, staying for hours in local coffee houses discussing everything from politics to soccer, going to outdoor cinemas and open air concerts.

[tró-o proinó] Τρώω πρωινό / *have (I am having) breakfast*

[proinó] Πρωινό *breakfast* is almost non-existent in Greece. Very few people actually sit down at the breakfast table and have a full breakfast. Greek breakfast usually consists of **[kafé] καφέ** *coffee* or **[gála] γάλα** *milk* with perhaps a **[kooloóri] κουλούρι** *sesame breadstick*, **[krooasán] κρουασάν** *croissant* or **[dimitriaká] δημητριακά** *cereal*. Continental and English breakfasts are available in hotels and restaurants in summer resorts.

Επιλεγμένα Παραδοσιακά Προϊόντα

Σπιτικά Γλυκά του κουταλιού Μαρμελάδες Λικέρ Μελοδημιουργίες Λάδι και ξύδι με μυρωδικά Τουρσί Ζυμαρικά Ποτά Δώρα κά

Το γευστικόν μετά του ωφελίμου

In Greece **[mesimerianó] μεσημεριανό** *lunch* is often a full and at times heavy meal, which definitely requires an afternoon siesta! **[vraTHinó] βραδινό** *dinner* is usually a light snack or the leftovers from lunch. Eating is still an important event and can last 2 or 3 hours, especially on Sunday when people eat with family and friends. In later units certain local dishes will be mentioned but as eating has to do with taste it is better to be sampled rather than explained!

All three words for meals derive from the time of day they are taken: **[proinó] πρωινό** from **[proí] πρωί** *morning*, **[mesimerianó] μεσημεριανό** from **[mesiméri] μεσημέρι** *midday / afternoon* and **[vraTHinó] βραδινό** from **[vráTHi] βράδυ** *evening*.

Dinner at 'Epilekton' or 'Unique dishes'.

Practice makes perfect

1 **Below is Maria's daily routine in jumbled order. Can you put it in a more logical order? To make it more of a challenge, cover up the transliteration column and work only with the Greek script!**

[ftáno sti THooliá] [stis októ].　　a Φτάνω στη δουλειά στις οκτώ.
[sikónome norís].　　　　　　　　b Σηκώνομαι νωρίς.
[epistréfo sto spíti argá].　　　c Επιστρέφω στο σπίτι αργά.
[péfto sto kreváti argá].　　　　d Πέφτω στο κρεβάτι αργά.
[páo sti THooliá].　　　　　　　e Πάω στη δουλειά.
[pérno vraTHinó stis eniá].　　　f Παίρνω βραδινό στις εννιά.
[THen tró-o proinó móno kafé].　 g Δεν τρώω πρωινό, μόνο καφέ.

[tró-o mesimerianó sti THooliá]. **h** Τρώω μεσημεριανό στη δουλειά.
[káno dooz]. **i** Κάνω ντους.
[píno polí kafé sti THooliá]. **j** Πίνω πολύ καφέ στη δουλειά.
[telióno ti THooliá stis éksi]. **k** Τελειώνω τη δουλειά στις έξι.
[vlépo lígo tileórasi stis THéka]. **l** Βλέπω λίγο τηλεόραση στις δέκα.

2 Can you translate the above sentences into English?

3 How do you study Greek? This is a personal test and many answers are possible. Use the words in the box to express how frequently you do the following tasks:

a I listen to the recording. _____

b I speak to native speakers. _____

c I use a Greek dictionary. _____

d I revise past units. _____

e I make lists of important words. _____

f I listen to Greek music. _____

g I record myself speaking Greek. _____

```
100% = [pánda]   90% = [sheTHón pánda]
70% = [siníthos]   60% = [sihná]   40% = [merikés forés]
20% = [spánia]   10% = [sheTHón poté]   0% = [poté]
```

▶ 4 Now listen to the recording. People are telling you the times they do different activities. Match the times with the correct activities.

a 8:15   **i** [THen tró-o mesimerianó stis]
b 9:15   **ii** [pérno to tréno stis]
c 13:30   **iii** [tró-o proinó stis]
d 16:20   **iv** [ftáno sto spíti stis]
e 16:41   **v** [ftáno sti THooliá stis]
f 17:05   **vi** [telióno ti THooliá stis]

▶ 5 Some people are telling you the time. Listen to the recording and put the times in the right order.

a _____   **d** _____
b _____   **e** _____
c _____   **f** _____

```
8:30   7:05   10:30   11:45   1:45   8:05
```

6 Using substitutions is important. Below the author gives you four options but one is wrong in each case. Can you single out the wrong ones?

a [THoolévo]
    i [sto spíti]
    ii [sto kókino]
    iii [THistihós]
    iv [stis THéka]

b [epistréfo]
    i [sto THiamérizma]
    ii [sto vraTHinó]
    iii [sti THooliá]
    iv [sto aeroTHrómio]

c [telióno]
    i [ti THooliá]
    ii [ton kafé]
    iii [to mesimerianó]
    iv [to asansér]

d [pérno]
    i [to asansér]
    ii [to proinó moo]
    iii [kreváti argá]
    iv [THooliá sto spíti]

▶ 7 Listen again to Dialogue 2 of this unit and fill in the blanks. If you don't have the recording, choose the missing words from the box below.

[elpíTHa]   [esí ti kánis] **a** _____ [tin iméra]?

Mary   **b** _____ [stis eptámisi] [káno éna dooz] [ke] **c** _____ [proinó]. [metá] **d** _____ [to tréno] [ke páo sti THooliá].

[elpíTHa]   [ti óra] **e** _____ [spíti]?

Mary   [THoolévo siníthos] **f** _____ [tis THéka] **g** _____ [tis téseris] [epistréfo spíti] [stis pendémisi].

[elpíTHa]   [ti óra] **h** _____ [vraTHinó]?

Mary   **i** _____ [stis eptá] [sto spíti] [i stis októ] **j** _____.

[epistréfis]   [óli]   [tróte]   [méhri]   [apó]   [yíro]
[tró-o]   [ksipnáo]   [pérno]   [ékso]

Mini test

a Can you say the following numbers in Greek? 104 – 184 – 231 – 456 – 827 – 951 – 1,000

b Can you tell the following times? 7:20 – 8:30 – 9:00 – 11:15 – 1:30 – 4:10 – 5:45

c When talking about daily routines it's important to use set vocabulary. How do you say the following in Greek: get up, arrive, finish, come back, take.

d Can you translate the following sentences:

    i I always get up at 6:15.

    ii I never arrive at work early.

    iii I sometimes finish my work late.

    iv I seldom eat out.

    v I almost always take the train.

[páme kalá]! Πάμε καλά! This is an expression meaning that 'things are OK' (lit. *we are going well*), you are progressing satisfactorily! So keep up the good work, revise a lot, improvise sometimes and **[tha se THo stin enótita eniá], [okéi]? Θα σε δω στην Ενότητα εννιά, ΟΚ;**

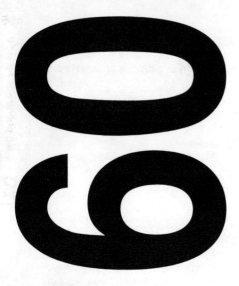

09

έχεις χόμπι;

do you have a hobby?

In this unit you will learn
- how to talk about your free time
- how to ask others if they have hobbies
- the names of different kinds of Greek music
- the names of different kinds of Greek films

Before you start

Revise Unit 2 now. Use the suggestions given to you in the previous unit. Although the Greek alphabet can be somewhat of a challenge at first, you should still aim to make and enlarge the list of new Greek words that you may come across when you are in Greece. Unfortunately, with public signs there is no way of knowing if they will be written in small or capital letters, so you should write both forms in your list. Remember the example in the previous unit αεροδρόμιο or ΑΕΡΟΔΡΟΜΙΟ for *airport*.

Key words and phrases

This unit can be used as a starting point for you to come up with different word lists in groups. For instance, if you like books, you should be able to say what kind of books you enjoy reading. If you like sports, you should be able to name a few and if you like music, you should be able to mention some local or international kinds of music. You can personalize the lists on the next page by highlighting all the important words for you. You can always add some words missing from the four lists below by using a dictionary.

[moosikí] Μουσική *Music*		
[rok]	ροκ	*rock*
[blooz]	μπλουζ	*blues*
[laiká]	λαϊκά	*pop*
[tzaz]	τζαζ	*jazz*
[rebétika]	ρεμπέτικα	*Greek blues*
[érga] Έργα *Films*		
[komoTHíes]	κωμωδίες	*comedies*
[THramatiká]	δραματικά	*dramas*
[thríler]	θρίλερ	*thriller/horror*
[astinomiká]	αστυνομικά	*crime stories*
[epistimonikís fantasías]	επιστημονικής φαντασίας	*science fiction*
[vivlía] Βιβλία *Books*		
[mithistorímata]	μυθιστορήματα	*novels*
[noovéles]	νουβέλες	*novels*
[astinomiká]	αστυνομικά	*crime stories*
[istoríes agápis]	ιστορίες αγάπης	*love stories*
[peripéties]	περιπέτειες	*adventure stories/ thrillers*

[spor] Σπορ Sports		
[poTHósfero]	ποδόσφαιρο	*football*
[ténis]	τένις	*tennis*
[vólei]	βόλεϋ	*volleyball*
[ping pong]	πίνκ πονκ	*table tennis*
[básket]	μπάσκετ	*basketball*

Many words in the list above are plural. The singular form is provided for you below:

[vivlío] βιβλίο *book* (n), [noovéla] νουβέλα *novel* (f), [mithistórima] μυθιστόρημα *novel* (f), [istoría] ιστορία *story/history* (f), [peripétia] περιπέτεια *adventure* (f), [komoTHía] κωμωδία *comedy* (f).

Two words are in the genitive case singular. The base form, in the nominative case, is [agápi] αγάπη *love* (f) and [fantasía] φαντασία *fiction* (lit. fantasy) (f).

Can you name the different types of films shown in the pictures below?

Here are some questions you can ask:

[soo arési i moosikí]? Σου αρέσει η μουσική;
Do you like music?
[sarési to sinemá]? Σ'αρέσει το σινεμά;
Do you like the cinema?
[soo arésoon ta spor]? Σου αρέσουν τα σπορ;
Do you like sports?
[ti hóbi éhis]? Τι χόμπυ έχεις; or [ti hóbi éhete]? Τι χόμπυ έχετε;
What hobby do you have?

[soo arési] Σου αρέσει and the contracted form [sarési] σ'αρέσει above are interchangeable. Similarly, you can construct the plural form [soo arésoon] σου αρέσουν or [sarésoon] σ'αρέσουν.

Pronunciation tips

The word **[blooz] μπλουζ** *blues* has two letters which have very similar sounds in Greek and English. The letters **μπ [b]** as in *blue* and the letter **ζ [z]** as in *zoo*. The sounds **[b]**, **[d]** and hard **[g]** exist in both languages. You need to be aware that these three sounds are represented in Greek words by a combination of <u>two</u> letters, which perhaps will make you stop and think for a second when you read a sign for example. The letters are:

μπ or **ΜΠ** for the sound **[b]** at the beginning of a word and **[mb]** within a word.

ντ or **ΝΤ** for the sound **[d]** at the beginning of a word and **[nd]** within a word.

γκ or **ΓΚ** for the sound **[g]** at the beginning of a word and **[ng]** within a word.

γγ for the sound **[ng]** appears only within a word, not at the beginning.

Some words with those sounds in the past units were:

[b] μπ	**[g] γκ** *or* **γγ**
[bébis] μπέμπης *baby boy*	**[ángelos] Άγγελος** *Angelos*
[béba] μπέμπα *baby girl*	**[garsoniéra] γκαρσονιέρα**
[brávo] μπράβο *bravo*	*studio apartment/bedsit*
[d] ντ	**[anglía] Αγγλία** *England*
[andónis] Αντώνης *Anthony*	
[éndeka] έντεκα *eleven*	
[kondá] κοντά *near*	

It is important for you to double check or cross reference from time to time the information provided in this section with the introductory notes found in the **Pronunciation guide** at the beginning of the book and the **Greek alphabet** section at the back of the book.

▶ [THiálogos 1] Διάλογος 1 *Dialogue 1:* [ti kánis ton eléfthero hróno soo]? Τι κάνεις τον ελεύθερο χρόνο σου; *What do you do in your free time?*

Angelos asks John about his free time.

[ángelos]	[John], [ti kánis] [ton eléfthero hróno soo]?	*John, what do you do in your free time?*
John	[marési nakoó-o moosikí].	*I like to listen to music.*

[ángelos]	[ti moosikí sarési]?	What kind of music do you like?
John	[kiríos laiká] [alá ke rok]. [esí pos pernás] [tis eléftheres óres soo]?	Mainly pop but rock too. How do you spend your free time (lit. free hours)?
[ángelos]	[vlépo tileórasi] [i akoó-o raTHiófono].	I watch TV or listen to the radio.
John	[polí oréa].	Very nice.

Άγγελος	John, τι κάνεις τον ελεύθερο χρόνο σου;
John	Μ'αρέσει ν'ακούω μουσική.
Άγγελος	Τι μουσική σ'αρέσει;
John	Κυρίως λαϊκά, αλλά και ροκ. Εσύ, πώς περνάς τις ελεύθερες ώρες σου;
Άγγελος	Βλέπω τηλεόραση ή ακούω ραδιόφωνο.
John	Πολύ ωραία.

[eléfthero]	ελεύθερο	free
[hróno]	χρόνο	time (m)
[marési]	μ'αρέσει	I like
[nakoó-o]	ν'ακούω	to listen
[moosikí]	μουσική	music (f)
[kiríos]	κυρίως	mainly
[laiká]	λαϊκά	popular music (n)
[rok]	ροκ	rock (n)
[óres]	ώρες	hours (f/pl)
[eléftheres óres]	ελεύθερες ώρες	free time (f) (lit. free hours)
[tileórasi]	τηλεόραση	television (f)
[raTHiófono]	ραδιόφωνο	radio (n)

▶ [THiálogos 2] Διάλογος 2 Dialogue 2: [éhis hóbi]? Έχεις χόμπυ; Do you have a hobby?

Now Mary asks Hope about her hobbies.

Mary	[elpíTHa], [éhis hóbi]?	Hope, do you have a hobby?
[elpíTHa]	[ne] [marésoon polí ta spor].	Yes, I like sports a lot.
Mary	[enTHiaféron]. [ti spor]?	Interesting. What sports?

[elpíTHa]	[marési to troháTHin] [to básket] [ke to ténis]. [polés forés páo théatro] [i sinemá]. [esí]? [ti hóbi éhis]?	I like running, basketball and tennis. Many times I go to the theatre or the movies. How about you? What are your hobbies?
Mary	[marési na piyéno vóltes] [i na káthome spíti] [ke na THiavázo].	I like to go for a stroll or stay at home and read.
[elpíTHa]	[ti vivlía siníthos THiavázis]?	What kind of books do you usually read?
Mary	[kiríos mithistorímata] [alá ke] [vivlía thríler].	Mainly novels but also thrillers.

Mary Ελπίδα, έχεις χόμπυ;
Ελπίδα Ναι, μ'αρέσουν πολύ τα σπορ.
Mary Ενδιαφέρον. Τι σπορ;
Ελπίδα Μ'αρέσει το τροχάδην, το μπάσκετ και το τένις. Πολλές φορές πάω στο θέατρο ή στο σινεμά. Εσύ; Τι χόμπυ έχεις;
Mary Μ'αρέσει να πηγαίνω βόλτες ή να κάθομαι σπίτι και να διαβάζω.
Ελπίδα Τι βιβλία συνήθως διαβάζεις;
Mary Κυρίως μυθιστορήματα αλλά και βιβλία θρίλερ.

[hóbi]	χόμπυ	hobby (n)
[spor]	σπορ	sports (n/pl)
[enTHiaféron]	ενδιαφέρον	interesting (n)
[troháTHin]	τροχάδην	running (n)
[básket]	μπάσκετ	basketball (n)
[ténis]	τένις	tennis (n)
[polés forés]	πολλές φορές	many times
[théatro]	θέατρο	theatre (n)
[sinemá]	σινεμά	cinema (n)
[vóltes]	βόλτες	walks, strolls, car rides (f/pl)
[káthome spíti]	κάθομαι σπίτι	I stay at home (lit. I sit home)
[THiavázo]	διαβάζω	I read, I study
[vivlía]	βιβλία	books (n)
[mithistorímata]	μυθιστορήματα	novels (n)

Note
The word *sport/s* is **[to spor]** το σπορ in the singular and **[ta spor]** τα σπορ in the plural.

Language rules

1 [marési nakoó-o moosikí] Μ'αρέσει ν'ακούω μουσική I like to listen to music

It has already been mentioned that Greek, like many other languages, uses a lot of contracted forms, i.e. two words joined together into one in everyday speech. This unit includes the following:

[marési] μ'αρέσει → [moo] + [arési] μου αρέσει I like
[nakoó-o] ν'ακούω → [na] + [akoó-o] να ακούω to listen
[sarési] σ'αρέσει → [soo] + [arési] σου αρέσει you like
[marésoon] μ'αρέσουν → [moo] + [arésoon] μου αρέσουν I like

You can use either form. Simply remember that in terms of frequency the contracted forms are more common. Look also at Note 5 in Unit 4.

2 [eléftheres óres] Ελεύθερες ώρες Free time (lit. hours)

[óres] ώρες is the plural form of [óra] ώρα hour. Do not confuse this word with the word [forés] φορές which you were introduced to in the last unit in [merikés forés] μερικές φορές sometimes and the phrase in Dialogue 2 of this unit [polés forés] πολλές φορές many times.

Let's look at some singular and plural nouns from this unit again:

[i vólta] – [i vóltes]	η βόλτα – οι βόλτες	walk – walks (f)
[to mithistórima] –	το μυθιστόρημα –	novel –
[ta mithistorímata]	τα μυθιστορήματα	novels (n)
[to vivlío] –	το βιβλίο –	book –
[ta vivlía]	τα βιβλία	books (n)
[to théatro] –	το θέατρο –	theatre –
[ta théatra]	τα θέατρα	theatres (n)

There are a lot of nouns in this unit that have only one form for singular and plural. These are foreign words that come from other languages including English. Some of them are below:

[to spor] – [ta spor]	το σπορ – τα σπορ	sport – sports (n)
[to sinemá] –	το σινεμά –	cinema –
[ta sinemá]	τα σινεμά	cinemas (n)
[to hóbi] – [ta hóbi]	το χόμπυ – τα χόμπυ	hobby – hobbies (n)

3 [káthome spíti] Κάθομαι σπίτι I stay at home (lit. I sit home)

[káthome] **κάθομαι** I sit is a verb that belongs to a new group of verbs with special endings not mentioned before. The verb [íme] **είμαι** I am which was presented in Unit 1 has certain similarities that you can draw upon. Study the verb below:

[káthome]	κάθομαι	I sit / I stay
[káthese]	κάθεσαι	you sit / you stay
[káthete]	κάθεται	he/she/it sits / he/she/it stays
[kathómaste]	καθόμαστε	we sit / we stay
[kathósaste]	καθόσαστε	you sit / you stay
[káthonde]	κάθονται	they sit / they stay

[káthome] **κάθομαι** is also the root verb for [kathíste]! **καθίστε!** Have a seat! Sit down! found in Unit 6.

The following verbs from past units belong to this new group: [hérome] **χαίρομαι** I am glad and [sikónome] **σηκώνομαι** I get up.

You might hear slightly different accents when native speakers pronounce these words. The difference in pronunciation is in the [o] which becomes [oo]. Note the examples:

[káthome] → [káthoome], [hérome] → [héroome], [sikónome] → [sikónoome]

🄹 [éhis hóbi]? Έχεις χόμπυ; Have you got a hobby?

Unit 9 introduces you to vocabulary about hobbies. Try to become familiar with this vocabulary and use it in your early attempts at conversation. Of course, a dictionary will help you expand this list, but keep it personal.

Many Greeks read a lot, from newspapers to novels and academic literature. They go to the cinema often and sometimes to the theatre. They also watch and participate in sports. New things have become fashionable in the last decade: television with its various private channels, going to the gym, acquiring computer skills and travelling outside Greece. There has also been a shift in popularity from soccer to basketball. Outdoor activities such as hunting, fishing, hiking, rafting, rock and mountain climbing and of course swimming are also popular.

[básket ke sinemá] Μπάσκετ και σινεμά
Basketball and cinema

You will have noticed the number of words borrowed between English and Greek. Remember, when countries come into contact with one another word borrowing between them is inevitable. Two lists are provided for you below. The first lists words of Greek origin, the second words of English origin. Test yourself by covering the translations given with a sheet of paper and guessing the meanings. Some are more obvious than others.

Words of Greek origin:

[moosikí] η μουσική	*music* (f)
[théatro] το θέατρο	*theatre* (n)
[ráTHio] το ράδιο	*radio* (n)
[mithistórima] το μυθιστόρημα	*novel* (lit. myth story) (n)
[istoría] η ιστορία	*history/story* (f)

Words of English origin:

rock (n)	[rok] το ροκ
hobby (n)	[hóbi] το χόμπυ
sports (n)	[spor] το σπορ
basketball (n)	[básket] το μπάσκετ
tennis (n)	[ténis] το τένις

Of course, some words are not so obvious at first glance. In **Dialogue 2** the word **[vivlía] βιβλία** is not so apparent but if you think of words like '*biblio*graphy' meaning 'reference books' and '*biblio*phile' meaning 'lover of books' then **[vivlía] βιβλία** and *books* are clearly related.

[laiká ke rok] Λαϊκά και ροκ *Popular and rock music*

Most people listen to music and Greeks are no exception. In Greece, international, or as Greeks say 'foreign' music, is not as popular as Greek music, which includes not only traditional Greek music but also modern songs with international melodies but Greek lyrics. In bars and nights clubs you will hear both 'foreign' and Greek songs.

The most important categories of Greek music are: **[laiká] λαϊκά** *Greek pop music*, **[elafrolaiká] ελαφρολαϊκά** *soft pop*, **[rebétika] ρεμπέτικα** *a kind of Greek blues*, **[rok] ροκ** *rock music, both Greek and international*, and **[nisiótika] νησιώτικα** *island music*. All Greek regions have their own traditional music including both local melodies and instruments. Some popular Greek instruments are the **[boozoóki] μπουζούκι** *bouzouki*, the **[baglamaTHáki] μπαγλαμαδάκι** *small bouzouki*, and the **[líra] λύρα** *lyre*.

Practice makes perfect

▶ 1 [THimítris], [níkos] and [maría] are asked the questions [ti kánis ton eléfthero hróno soo]? and [pos pernás tis eléftheres óres soo]? Listen to the recording and tick the boxes of the activities or hobbies they have.

Activity	[THimítris]	[níkos]	[maría]
1 smoke a			
2 stay at			
3 read a			
4 play			
5 drink			
6 listen to			
7 watch			

You will find the new vocabulary at the end of Exercise 2.

2 Match the cartoons in Exercise 1 with the phrases in either of the columns below. For more of a challenge, cover the transliteration column and work with the Greek script alone.

i [THiavázo efimeríTHa].   Διαβάζω εφημερίδα.
ii [pézo poTHósfero].   Παίζω ποδόσφαιρο.
iii [akoó-o raTHiófono].   Ακούω ραδιόφωνο.
iv [kapnízo tsigáro].   Καπνίζω τσιγάρο.
v [vlépo tileórasi].   Βλέπω τηλεόραση.
vi [káthome spíti].   Κάθομαι σπίτι.
vii [píno kafé].   Πίνω καφέ.

New words: **[kapnízo] καπνίζω** *I smoke*, **[tsigáro] τσιγάρο** *cigarette* (n), **[efimeríTHa] εφημερίδα** *newspaper* (f), **[pézo] παίζω** *I play*

3 Continue the sentences below to make full sentences. You can substitute more than one possibility. Whenever this is the case, make a note of your other options.

a [sheTHón poté THen vlépo   **i** … [káthome spíti].
   tileórasi ótan] …

b [pánda kapnízo tsigára ótan] …   **ii** … [éhi poTHósfero].

c [polés forés THiavázo vivlía ótan] …   **iii** … [íme megálos].

d [spánia pézo poTHósfero ótan] …   **iv** … [THen kséro ti álo
                                                           na káno].

e [merikés forés akoó-o   **v** … [píno kafé].
   raTHiófono ótan] …

4 The verbs are missing in the sentences below. Can you fill them in? The verbs in English in the box might help you a little, if you translate them first!

a [o níkos poté THen] _____ [tileórasi].

b [i maría ke o THimítris pánda] _____ [raTHiófono].

c _____ [ta laiká ke to rok].

d [emís stin eláTHa] _____ [polá vivlía].

e [egó] _____ [ta tsigára].

f _____ [to raTHiófono i tin tileórasi]?

| listen   watch   read   like   dislike   prefer |

5 Can you translate the sentences in Exercise 4 into English?

a _____
b _____
c _____
d _____
e _____
f _____

▶ **6** Listen to the recordings and tick the kinds of music [ángelos], [THéspina] and [ariána] like.

	[ángelos]	[THéspina]	[ariána]
1 [laiká]			
2 [elafrolaiká]			
3 [rebétika]			
4 [tzaz]			
5 [rok]			
6 [blooz]			

▶ 7 Listen again to Dialogue 2 of this unit and fill in the blanks. If you don't have the recordings, choose the missing words from the box below.

Mary	[elpíTHa], [éhis hóbi]?
[elpíTHa]	[ne] **a** ___ [polí ta spor].
Mary	**b** ___ [ti spor]?
[elpíTHa]	[marési to] **c** ___ [to básket] [ke to ténis]. [polés] **d** ___ [páo théatro] [i sinemá]. [esí]? [ti hóbi éhis]?
Mary	[marési na] **e** ___ [vóltes] [i na káthome spíti] [ke na] **f** ___.
[elpíTHa]	[ti vivlía] **g** ___ [THiavázis]?
Mary	[kiríos mithistorímata] [alá ke] [vivlía] **h** ___.

[forés] [piyéno] [siníthos] [marésoon] [THiavázo]
[enTHiaféron] [thríler] [troháTHin]

Mini test

a Name three different kinds of music (exclude jazz, rock and blues!)
b Name three different kinds of books.
c Name three different kinds of films.
d What are the two different questions in Greek when you want to find what someone does in his/her free time?
e How do you spend you free time? Give three possible answers.
f [troháTHin], [vóltes], [enTHiaféron], [siníthos] and [kiríos] were new words in Dialogue 2. Can you translate them into English?
g Can you find the opposites of the following words: [poté], [spánia], [marési], [komoTHíes]?

How did it go? Was it an easy test? Are you ready to move on to the next unit now?

10

στη λαϊκή αγορά

at the fruit and vegetable market

In this unit you will learn
- how to shop in a fruit and vegetable market
- the names of some fruits and vegetables
- how to ask other people to join you
- how to describe different moods
- how to count from 1,000 to 10,000

Before you start

Revise Unit 3 before you start this unit. Going back to past units
should be an interesting experience but also rewarding consolidation
for details and explanations which may not have made a lot of sense
a few weeks earlier. This is how you benefit from such revisions.

If you have 10 minutes, go over Unit 9 now. A quick look at the
previous unit will refresh at least five points made throughout that
unit. Some of them might be repeated or expanded in this unit, so you
need to keep them fresh in your mind.

Now, I think you are ready for this unit. Let's go! **[páme]! Πάμε!**

Key words and phrases

This unit introduces you to new vocabulary needed when you want
to buy fruit and vegetables. Of course, in large supermarkets there is
no conversation with anyone since you simply pick whatever you
want from the shelves and pay for it at the cash desk. In smaller
places, like a **[pandopolío]** παντοπωλείο *grocer's* or *mini market*,
[manáviko] μανάβικο *greengrocer*, **[oporopandopolío]**
οπωροπαντοπωλείο *fruit and vegetable store* or in open fruit and
vegetable markets **[laikí agorá]** λαϊκή αγορά, you need to converse.

[froóta] Φρούτα *Fruits*

[o ananás]	ο ανανάς	pineapple
[i banána]	η μπανάνα	banana
[i fráoola]	η φράουλα	strawberry
[to stafíli]	το σταφύλι	grape
[to pepóni]	το πεπόνι	melon

[lahaniká] Λαχανικά
[aromatiká fitá] αρωματικά φυτά
Vegetables and herbs

[o ánithos]	ο άνιθος	dill
[o maindanós]	ο μαϊντανός	parsley
[i patáta]	η πατάτα	potato
[i domáta]	η ντομάτα	tomato
[to karóto]	το καρότο	carrot
[to kolokitháki]	το κολοκυθάκι	courgette, zucchini

Important questions may include: **[pósa thélete]? Πόσα θέλετε;** *How many do you want?*, **[pósa kilá]? πόσα κιλά;** *How many kilos?*; **[póso káni]? Πόσο κάνει;** *How much is it?*, **[póso kánoon]? Πόσο κάνουν;** *How much are they?* Some possible answers include: **[éna kiló] ένα κιλό** *one kilo*, **[THío kilá] δύο κιλά** *two kilos*, **[káni] κάνει** or **[kánoon tría evró] κάνουν τρία ευρώ** *It is* or *they are three euros*.

Pronunciation tips

The word **[froóta] φρούτα** *fruits* has two letters which have a very similar sound in both languages. The letter **φ [f]** as in *fruit, frog, fry*, and the letter **τ [t]** as in *tar* or *tardy*. You can also read the notes about **[t]** in Unit 8. A third letter has a little more challenging sound for you to produce, that is **ρ [r]** which carries a stronger sound in Greek compared to English. If possible, listen to someone who can pronounce both words for you together to hear the difference. Some more explanations about **ρ [r]** can be found in the **Pronunciation guide** at the beginning of this book and in Unit 1.

'Flavour pastry shops'. Can you find the Greek flavour in this advert?

▶ **[THiálogos 1] Διάλογος 1** *Dialogue 1:* **[érhese mazí moo]? Έρχεσαι μαζί μου;** *Are you coming with me?*

Hope has to go to the local fruit and vegetable market. She asks Mary to join her.

[elpíTHa]	Mary, [íse koorazméni]?	*Mary, are you tired?*
Mary	[óhi], [yiatí rotás]?	*No, why are you asking?*

[elpíTHa]	[prépi na páo] [stin laikí agorá] [yia lígo]. [érhese mazí moo]?	*I have to go to the fruit and vegetable market for a little while. Are you coming with me?*
Mary	[oréa iTHéa]. [poo íne]?	*(That's a) good idea. Where is it?*
[elpíTHa]	[íne kondá]. [boroóme na páme] [me ta póTHia]. [thélo nagoráso] [meriká froóta] [ke lahaniká].	*It's close by. We can go on foot. I want to buy some fruit and vegetables.*
Mary	[éla]. [páme].	*Come on. Let's go.*

Ελπίδα	Mary, είσαι κουρασμένη;
Mary	Όχι, γιατί ρωτάς;
Ελπίδα	Πρέπει να πάω στην λαϊκή αγορά για λίγο. Έρχεσαι μαζί μου;
Mary	Ωραία ιδέα. Πού είναι;
Ελπίδα	Είναι κοντά. Μπορούμε να πάμε με τα πόδια. Θέλω ν' αγοράσω μερικά φρούτα και λαχανικά.
Mary	Έλα. Πάμε.

[koorazméni]	**κουρασμένη**	*tired* (f)
[yiatí rotás]?	**γιατί ρωτάς;**	*why are you asking?* (sing/infml)
[prépi na páo]	**πρέπει να πάω**	*I have to go*
[agorá]	**αγορά**	*market* (f)
[laikí agorá]	**λαϊκή αγορά**	*fruit and vegetable market* (f) (lit. people's market)
[yia lígo]	**για λίγο**	*for a little while*
[érhese]?	**έρχεσαι;**	*Are you coming?* (sing/infml)
[iTHéa]	**ιδέα**	*idea* (f)
[me ta póTHia]	**με τα πόδια**	*on foot* (lit. with the feet)
[meriká]	**μερικά**	*some* (n/pl)
[froóta]	**φρούτα**	*fruit* (n/pl)
[lahaniká]	**λαχανικά**	*vegetables* (n/pl)

Note

Do not confuse the word **[póTHia]** *feet* in this dialogue with the word **[peTHiá]** *children*, found in past units.

▶ [THiálogos 2] Διάλογος 2 Dialogue 2:
[sti laikí agorá] Στη λαϊκή αγορά At the fruit and vegetable market

Hope and Mary are walking in a noisy, crowded market among stalls with fresh fruit and vegetables.

Mary	[po-po kózmos]! [polís kózmos]!	Wow! Crowded! Very crowded!
[elpíTHa]	[ne], [pánda éhi poloós anthrópoos eTHó]. [na]! [eTHó ipárhoon] [oréa míla] [portokália ke banánes]. [ti sarési na pároome]?	Yes, it has always many people. Here! There are some nice apples, oranges and bananas. What would you like us to get?
Mary	[na pároome míla]. [ipárhoon karpoózia] [aftí tin epohí]?	Let's get some apples. Are there any watermelons at this time of the year?
[elpíTHa]	[ne, fisiká]. [lígo pio káto]. [eTHó éhi] [kalá ke fréska] [lahaniká]. [thélo nagoráso] [éna maroóli], [THío agoória] [kéna kiló domátes].	Yes, that's right (lit. naturally). A little bit further down. Here are some nice and fresh vegetables. I want to buy one lettuce, two cucumbers and one kilo of tomatoes.

Mary	Πω-πω κόσμος! Πολύς κόσμος!
Ελπίδα	Ναι, πάντα έχει πολλούς ανθρώπους εδώ. Να! Εδώ υπάρχουν ωραία μήλα, πορτοκάλια και μπανάνες. Τι σ'αρέσει να πάρουμε;
Mary	Να πάρουμε μήλα. Υπάρχουν καρπούζια αυτή την εποχή;
Ελπίδα	Ναι, φυσικά. Λίγο πιο κάτω. Εδώ έχει καλά και φρέσκα λαχανικά. Θέλω ν'αγοράσω ένα μαρούλι, δύο αγγούρια κι'ένα κιλό ντομάτες.

[kózmos]	κόσμος	people (m), (here: crowded place)
[poloós]	πολλούς	many (m, accusative case)
[anthrópoos]	ανθρώπους	people (m/pl, accusative case)
[pánda]	πάντα	always
[ipárhoon]	υπάρχουν	there are

[míla]	μήλα	apples (n/pl)
[portokália]	πορτοκάλια	oranges (n/pl)
[banánes]	μπανάνες	bananas (f/pl)
[na pároome]	να πάρουμε	to get/to buy (lit. to take)
[karpoózia]	καρπούζια	watermelons (n/pl)
[epohí]	εποχή	season (f)
[fisiká]	φυσικά	naturally
[pio]	πιο	more
[káto]	κάτω	down
[fréska]	φρέσκα	fresh (n/pl)
[maróoli]	μαρούλι	lettuce (n)
[agoória]	αγγούρια	cucumbers (n/pl)
[kiló]	κιλό	kilo (n)
[domátes]	ντομάτες	tomatoes (f/pl)

Notes

• Do not confuse the word [míla] μήλα *apples* found in this dialogue with the word [milá] μιλά *he/she/it speaks* found in past units. The stressed syllable, and also the spelling, are different.

• [kózmos] ο κόσμος (m) is an interesting word. In the dialogue above it means 'many people'. It also means 'world', which is where we get the word 'cosmopolitan' from. Remember that as a masculine noun it is possible to hear it as [kózmos] (nominative case – the noun before a verb) and [kózmo] (accusative case – the noun after a verb). Look at the comment before **Dialogue 2** in Unit 7.

Language rules

1 [íse koorazménos]? Είσαι κουρασμένος; *Are you tired?*

Be careful with the two alternative forms when addressing men or women. This is a very important point when asking questions in Greek. Note the difference below:

[íse koorazmé<u>nos</u>]? Είσαι κουρασμέν<u>ος;</u> *Are you tired?* (when addressing a man) (m gender)

[íse koorazmé<u>ni</u>]? Είσαι κουρασμέν<u>η;</u> *Are you tired?* (when addressing a woman) (f gender).

Remember, you use **είσαι** with someone you know, or a child, and **είστε/είσαστε** with an adult you don't know.

Look at the pictures showing different moods:

a [eftihizméni] ευτυχισμένη
b [thimoménos] θυμωμένος
c [lipiméni] λυπημένη
d [ékplikti] έκπληκτη
e [pinazménos] πεινασμένος
f [THipsazménos] διψασμένος
g [taragméni] ταραγμένη
h [koorazméni] κουρασμένη

The two words **[pinazménos] πεινασμένος** *hungry* and **[THipsazménos] διψασμένος** *thirsty* are not used very frequently. Usually, the questions are **[pinás]? πεινάς;** or **[pináte]? πεινάτε;** *Are you hungry?* and **[THipsás] διψάς;** or **[THipsáte]? διψάτε;** *Are you thirsty?* Actually those were the questions used in Unit 6.

2 [ipárhoon]... Υπάρχουν... *There are …*

The common phrases *there is* **[ipárhi] υπάρχει** and *there are* **[ipárhoon] υπάρχουν** come from the root word **[ipárho] υπάρχω** *I exist*. **[éhi] έχει** and **[éhoon] έχουν** are also used sometimes to express *there is* and *there are*. You remember the verb **[ého] έχω**, don't you? Here are some examples:

> **[ipárhi kafenío eTHó kondá]? Υπάρχει καφενείο εδώ κοντά;**
> *Is there a café near here?*

[ipárhoon polá kafenía eTHó kondá]. Υπάρχουν πολλά
καφενεία εδώ κοντά. *There are many cafés near here.*
[éhi éna kafenío stin gonía]. Έχει ένα καφενείο στην γωνία.
There is (lit. it has) *a café on the corner.*

3 [prépi na páo] Πρέπει να πάω / *must go*

[na] να *to* is a particle in Greek connecting two verbs. It is
sometimes omitted in English, for instance:

with *to:* I want to go. without *to:* I like buying fruits. I must go there.

In contrast, to translate all three examples above, [na] να is needed
in order to connect the two verbs in Greek. Note:

[thélo na páo]. Θέλω να πάω. *I want to go.*
[marési na agorázo froóta]. Μ'αρέσει να αγοράζω φρούτα.
I like buying fruit.
[prépi na páo ekí]. Πρέπει να πάω εκεί. *I must go there.*

There is no exception to this rule. Without getting into complex
grammar here, just bear in mind that after να, often a different form of
the verb is used. Some examples of this will appear in subsequent units.

Do not confuse the second meaning of [na] να found in Dialogue 2,
meaning 'Here it is!', 'Here you go!', 'Look!' when you show
something to someone.

Important verbal phrases for you to remember here are:

[prépi na] πρέπει να   *must / have to / is necessary to*
[boró na] μπορώ να   *can / be able to*
[borí na] μπορεί να   *may / is possible to*
[thélo na] θέλω να   *want to / would like to*
[marési na] μ'αρέσει να   *like to*

▶4 [arithmí] Αριθμοί *Numbers 1,000–10,000*

1,000	[hílji] χίλιοι (m), [hílies] χίλιες (f), [hília] χίλια (n)	*one thousand*
2,000	[THío hiliáTHes] δύο χιλιάδες (m/f/n)	*two thousand*
3,000	[tris hiliáTHes] τρεις χιλιάδες	*three thousand*
4,000	[téseris hiliáTHes] τέσσερις χιλιάδες	*four thousand*
5,000	[pénde hiliáTHes] πέντε χιλιάδες	*five thousand*
6,000	[éksi hiliáTHes] έξι χιλιάδες	*six thousand*
7,000	[eptá hiliáTHes] επτά χιλιάδες	*seven thousand*

8,000	[októ hiliáTHes] οκτώ χιλιάδες	*eight thousand*
9,000	[eniá hiliáTHes] εννιά χιλιάδες	*nine thousand*
10,000	[THéka hiliáTHes] δέκα χιλιάδες	*ten thousand*

ℹ️ Greek money

Greece's currency is the Euro. The Euro is spelt ευρώ and pronounced [evró] (note the stress on the second syllable), and, being a foreign word, has only this form, even in the plural. Its gender is neuter. So we say:

[éna evró] ένα ευρώ *one euro*
[THéka evró] δέκα ευρώ *ten euros*
[hília evró] χίλια ευρώ *one thousand euros*
[pénde hiliádes evró] πέντε χιλιάδες ευρώ *five thousand euros*

[laikí agorá] Λαϊκή αγορά *A fruit and vegetable market*

Visitors to Greece will probably come across a [laikí agorá] λαϊκή αγορά *fruit and vegetable market* one way or another. Many local farmers try to sell their produce in pre-selected neighbourhoods every day. If you miss the market close to where you are staying, you can always visit another market the next day a little farther away. You can also go directly to the [kendrikí laikí agorá] κεντρική λαϊκή αγορά *central* market, which is open 5 to 6 days a week in the same place. In many places, especially those close to the sea, there is also a [psaragorá] ψαραγορά *fish market*.

Greece produces several types of fruit. Some examples are: [stafília] σταφύλια *grapes*, [karpoózia] καρπούζια *watermelons*, [portokália] πορτοκάλια *oranges*, and [míla] μήλα *apples*. Some local fish in Greece are: [barboónia] μπαρμπούνια *red mullets*, [tsipoóres] τσιπούρες *dorados or giltheads*, [lavrákia] λαβράκια *bass* and [péstrofes] πέστροφες *trout*. Of course, different foods, regardless of size, colour or aroma, taste better when we actually experience them rather than try to explain them. And the hubbub of a Greek market is definitely something to be experienced...

NB The words for the fruit and fish above are in the plural. The singular forms are: [to stafíli] σταφύλι (n), [to karpoózi] καρπούζι (n), [to portokáli] πορτοκάλι (n), [to mílo] μήλο (n), and [to barboóni] μπαρμπούνι (n), [i tsipoóra] τσιπούρα (f), [to lavráki] λαβράκι (n), [i péstrofa] πέστροφα (f).

2 [ne] Ναι Yes

[ne] **ναι** *yes* and [óhi] **όχι** *no* are very important words in most languages. You might also hear some other options that carry a similar meaning like [fisiká] **φυσικά** *naturally*, [vévea] **βέβαια** *of course/sure*, [amé] **αμέ** *yeah!*, or even get just a nod of the head for 'yes'. Likewise, a 'no' can be expressed with a head shaking or a clicking of the tongue. Just remember that the non-verbal 'yes' and 'no' in Greek is not identical to what you are familiar with in your country. Once more, a Greek non-verbal 'yes' is expressed by tilting your head downwards and keeping it down. A Greek non-verbal 'no' is expressed by tilting your head backwards and looking up with your eyebrows raised. Sometimes just the eyebrows are raised as an answer.

Non-verbal communication is a vital part of everyday interaction and it delivers strong, positive or negative feelings to other people. Apart from non-verbal signs, Greeks have a tendency to speak very loudly, a fact that leads foreigners to assume that they are actually quarrelling instead of just having a nice, simple conversation! Keep an open mind and when in doubt just ask for extra explanations.

Practice makes perfect

1 **There are some fruits, herbs and vegetables mixed up in the box below. Can you separate them into two groups?**

> [banána]   [fráoola]   [kolokitháki]   [yiarmás]
> [agoóri]   [domáta]   [stafíli]   [mílo]   [karóto]
> [ánithos]   [maindanós]   [karpoózi]

ΦΡΟΥΤΑ   ΛΑΧΑΝΙΚΑ/ΑΡΩΜΑΤΙΚΑ ΦΥΤΑ

a _____   i _____

b _____   ii _____

c _____   iii _____

d _____   iv _____

e _____   v _____

f _____   vi _____

2 Remember that the various forms for the word *the* [definite article] are important and can be challenging in Greek. Add the necessary definite articles to the words in Exercise 1 both in the singular and plural. The first ones have been done for you.

a [i banána] –
[i banánes]

b _____

c _____

d _____

e _____

f _____

i [to kolokitháki] –
[ta kolokithákia]

ii _____

iii _____

iv _____

v _____

vi _____

3 Can you write the words in Exercise 2 in Greek script? Give it a try and see how familiar you have now become with the Greek alphabet. The first ones have been done for you.

a η μπανάνα –
οι μπανάνες

b _____

c _____

d _____

e _____

f _____

i το κολοκυθάκι –
τα κολοκυθάκια

ii _____

iii _____

iv _____

v _____

vi _____

4 Look at the picture below. Can you name the fruits and vegetables? Some new vocabulary is given in the box. Give the appropriate singular or plural form as needed. The first ones have been done for you.

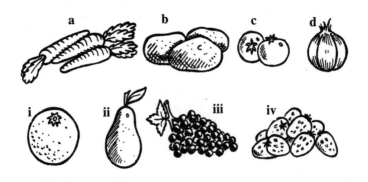

| [to skórTHo] | το σκόρδο | *garlic* |
| [to ahláTHi] | το αχλάδι | *pear* |

a	[ta karóta]	i	[to portokáli]
b	_____	ii	_____
c	_____	iii	_____
d	_____	iv	_____

5 Some shopkeepers have told you the amount you need to pay for the things you have just bought. Write the transliteration and/or Greek script for the amounts.

a	50€	c	100€	e	34€
b	17€	d	12€	f	70€

6 Match the numbers with the words.

a	16	1	ογδόντα τρία
b	25	2	πενήντα επτά
c	41	3	είκοσι πέντε
d	57	4	εξήντα εννέα
e	69	5	δέκα έξι
f	83	6	σαράντα ένα

7 Can you match your friends' moods in the cartoons with the words below? Work with the transliteration column or the Greek script for more of a challenge.

i	[lipiméni]	i	λυπημένη
ii	[thimoménos]	ii	θυμωμένος
iii	[eftihizméni]	iii	ευτυχισμένη
iv	[pinazménos]	iv	πινασμένος
v	[THipsazménos]	v	διψασμένος
vi	[koorazméni]	vi	κουρασμένη

8 **The box below will help you translate the following sentences.**

> [prépi na]   [thélo na]   [boró na]   [marési na]   [borí na]

a I like going for walks with you.
b I want to go to the fruit and vegetable market.
c I must see you.
d I can become angry.
e Perhaps her name is Helen.

▶ **9 Listen again to Dialogue 2 of this unit and fill in the blanks. If you don't have the recordings, choose the missing words from the box below. One answer is used twice.**

Mary   [po-po kózmos]! [polís kózmos]!
[elpíTHa]   [ne], [pánda éhi poloós anthrópoos eTHó]. [na]! [eTHó] **a** _____ [oréa míla] **b** _____ [ke banánes]. [ti sarési na pároome]?
Mary   [na pároome míla]. **a** _____ [karpoózia] [aftí tin] **c** _____?
[elpíTHa]   [ne] **d** _____. [lígo pio] **e** _____. [eTHó éhi] [kalá ke fréska] **f** _____. [thélo nagoráso] [éna maroóli], [THío] **g** _____ [kéna] **h** _____ [domátes].

> [kiló]   [fisiká]   [epohí]   [agoória]   [lahaniká]
> [káto]   [portokália]   [ipárhoon]

Mini test

a Name four different fruits that you like.
b Name four different vegetables and herbs that you like.
c Tell a friend about your moods. Name at least four.
d How do you say the following numbers in Greek? 450, 670, 1,200, 3,900, 5,000, 7,400, 9,500, 10,000.
e Words with the same sound as the word **[aftí]** *this* in the phrase **[aftí tin epohí]** *this time of year/season* in Dialogue 2 of this unit have been introduced before with two other meanings. What are they?
f Can you ask for the price of something? State both possible ways.

[**sinharitíria**]! **Συγχαρητήρια!** You have successfully completed two thirds of this book. Keep up the good work and soon you will have completed the whole book. [**brávo**]! **Μπράβο!** Now if you like tests, you can take the second **Revision test** at the back of the book. If not, move on to the next unit.

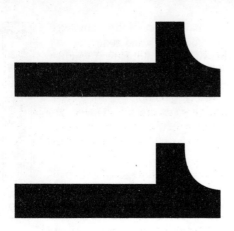

11

πού είναι η Τράπεζα;

where is the bank?

In this unit you will learn
- how to understand and ask for directions
- how to talk about distances
- how to describe the location of a landmark
- how to recognize the names of some places
- how to make a bank transaction

Before you start

- Did you do the second **Revision test**? Did you find it easy or difficult? If your score was less than 70%, it might be a good idea to look back at Units 6 to 10, revise some key points, and practise the vocabulary once again. Of course, if you don't like tests and you haven't done the **Revision test**, these comments do not affect you. Remember, however, that will help the learning process. For that reason, we suggest that you revise Unit 4 before you start this unit.

- In this unit the order of the transliteration and the Greek text will change. Now the Greek text will come before the transliteration. You should pay more attention to the Greek spelling of words that you might encounter while you are in Greece. This unit is helpful as it will introduce you to the names of some places and signs.

- Units 11 to 15 are also a little longer. This will require a little more effort and time on your part, but it will be worth it!

▶ Key words and phrases

Are you good at finding your way around? Some people can be in a place for the very first time and know their way around immediately, and some can't. Regardless of which group you belong to, the picture on the next page includes most places you will see during your visit. Come back to this section whenever you want to refresh your memory. The nouns in the list are grouped according to their gender. The number preceding the words can be found in the picture. Let's start now:

Masculine nouns

3	Ο ΣΤΑΘΜΟΣ ΛΕΩΦΟΡΕΙΩΝ	[o stathmós leoforíon]	*bus station*
6	Ο ΣΤΑΘΜΟΣ ΤΡΕΝΩΝ	[o stathmós trénon]	*train station*
18	Ο ΤΗΛΕΦΩΝΙΚΟΣ ΘΑΛΑΜΟΣ	[o tilefonikós thálamos]	*telephone booth*
24	Ο ΠΟΤΑΜΟΣ	[o potamós]	*river*

Feminine nouns

4	Η ΑΣΤΥΝΟΜΙΑ	[i astinomía]	*police*
11	Η ΔΙΣΚΟΘΗΚΗ	[i THiskothíki]	*discotheque*
12	Η ΑΓΟΡΑ	[i agorá]	*market*
15	Η ΣΤΑΣΗ ΛΕΩΦΟΡΕΙΩΝ	[i stási leoforíon]	*bus stop*
16	Η ΤΡΑΠΕΖΑ	[i trápeza]	*bank*
25	Η ΕΚΚΛΗΣΙΑ	[i eklisía]	*church*
26	Η ΓΕΦΥΡΑ	[i yéfira]	*bridge*

27	Η ΤΟΥΑΛΕΤΑ	[i tooaléta]	*toilet*
29	Η ΠΛΑΖ	[i plaz]	*beach*
30	Η ΘΑΛΑΣΣΑ	[i thálasa]	*sea*

Neuter nouns

1	ΤΟ ΑΕΡΟΔΡΟΜΙΟ	[to aeroTHrómio]	*airport*
2	ΤΟ ΣΙΝΕΜΑ	[to sinemá]	*cinema*
5	ΤΟ ΝΟΣΟΚΟΜΕΙΟ	[to nosokomío]	*hospital*
7	ΤΟ ΤΑΧΥΔΡΟΜΕΙΟ	[to tahiTHromío]	*post office*
8	ΤΟ ΕΣΤΙΑΤΟΡΙΟ	[to estiatório]	*restaurant*
9	ΤΟ ΣΧΟΛΕΙΟ	[to sholío]	*school*
10	ΤΟ ΞΕΝΟΔΟΧΕΙΟ	[to ksenoTHohío]	*hotel*
13	ΤΟ ΠΑΡΚΙΝ	[to párkin]	*car park*
14	ΤΟ ΘΕΑΤΡΟ	[to théatro]	*theatre*
17	ΤΟ ΒΙΒΛΙΟΠΩΛΕΙΟ	[to vivliopolío]	*book store*
19	ΤΟ ΦΑΡΜΑΚΕΙΟ	[to farmakío]	*pharmacy*
20	ΤΟ ΠΡΑΤΗΡΙΟ ΒΕΝΖΙΝΗΣ	[to pratírio venzínis]	*petrol / gas station*
21	ΤΟ ΓΚΑΡΑΖ	[to garáz]	*garage*
22	ΤΟ ΜΟΥΣΕΙΟ	[to moosío]	*museum*
23	ΤΟ ΣΟΥΠΕΡΜΑΡΚΕΤ	[to soópermarket]	*supermarket*
28	ΤΟ ΒΟΥΝΟ	[to voonó]	*mountain*

The nominative case forms you would find in the dictionary for the words **ΛΕΩΦΟΡΕΙΩΝ**, **ΤΡΕΝΩΝ**, and **ΒΕΝΖΙΝΗΣ** are: **το λεωφορείο [to leoforío]** *bus* (n), **το τρένο [to tréno]** *train* (n), and **η βενζίνη [i venzíni]** *petrol/gas* (f). All three words are in the genitive case above (the first two are also in the plural). This case denotes possession and usually is translated by 'of', e.g. **σταθμός λεωφορείων [stathmós leoforíon]** *bus station* [lit. *station of buses*]. See also the notes in the **Grammar summary**.

Pronunciation tips

There are two words in the list of places above – **ΤΑΧΥΔΡΟΜΕΙΟ [tahiTHromío]** *post office* and **ΣΧΟΛΕΙΟ [sholío]** *school* – that use the sound of the letter χ **[h]** not mentioned yet. This sound, although it is almost similar to the **[h]** in **h**e, **h**ome, or **h**at, is less harsh in English than in Greek. Listen to the recordings or a native speaker using this sound in the above-mentioned or other words.

[to horió] 'The village' is a traditional Greek tavern.

▶ Διάλογος 1 [THiálogos 1] *Dialogue 1:* Πρέπει να πάμε στην πόλη [prépi na páme stin póli] *We have to go to town*

On the way back home from the market Mary asks **Ελπίδα** for some directions because she needs to go with John to the bank, the post office and a travel agency.

Mary   Συγνώμη, τι ώρα έχεις; Πρέπει να πάμε στην πόλη με τον John. Στην τράπεζα, στο ταχυδρομείο και σ'ένα ταξιδιωτικό γραφείο.
Ελπίδα   Μα είναι η πρώτη σας μέρα εδώ. Όλα σήμερα πρέπει να γίνουν;
Mary   Δυστυχώς. Πώς μπορούμε να πάμε εκεί;
Ελπίδα   Έχω χάρτη στο σπίτι. Και δεν είναι ανάγκη να πάτε στην πόλη. Η γειτονιά μας τα έχει όλα.

Mary   [signómi], [ti óra éhis]? [prépi na páme] [stin póli] [me ton John]. [stin trápeza] [sto tahiTHromío] [ke séna taksiTHiotikó grafío].
Excuse me, what time is it? We have to go into town with John. To the bank, the post office and a travel agency.

[elpíTHa] [ma íne] [i próti sas méra] [eTHó]. [óla símera] [prépi na yínoon]?
But it is your first day here. Does everything need to happen today?

Mary [THistihós]. [pos] [boroóme na páme ekí]?
Unfortunately. How can we get there?

[elpíTHa] [ého hárti] [sto spíti]. [ke THen íne anángi] [na páte] [stin póli]. [i yitoniá mas] [ta éhi óla] …
I've got a map at home. And it is not necessary to go into town. Our neighbourhood has got everything…

συγνώμη	[signómi]	I'm sorry/excuse me
πόλη	[póli]	town/city (f)
τράπεζα	[trápeza]	bank (f)
ταχυδρομείο	[tahiTHromío]	post office (n)
ταξιδιωτικό γραφείο	[taksiTHiotikó grafío]	travel agency (lit. travel office) (n)
μα	[ma]	but
πρώτη	[próti]	first (with f noun)
μέρα	[méra]	day (f)
όλα	[óla]	everything/all (n/pl)
σήμερα	[símera]	today
όλα πρέπει να γίνουν	[óla prépi na yínoon]	everything needs to happen
εκεί	[ekí]	there
χάρτη	[hárti]	map (m)
δεν είναι ανάγκη	[THen íne anángi]	it's not necessary
γειτονιά	[yitoniá]	neighbourhood (f)

Notes

- Do not confuse two words found in the last sentence of Dialogue 1: [hárti] is *map* whereas [hartí] is *paper*, and [póli] is *town* whereas [polí] means *much, a lot*. The spelling is also different in Greek: χάρτη – χαρτί and πόλη – πολύ.
- μα [ma] *but* is a synonym for αλλά [alá].
- The phrase είναι ανάγκη να... [íne anángi na]... *it is necessary to...* is synonymous with πρέπει να... [prépi na] *have to, must, is needed to*. This phrase was introduced in Dialogue 2, Unit 7.

ΣΤΑΥΡΟΣ & ΕΛΕΝΗ ΓΚΑΤΣΟΠΟΥΛΟΥ

'Paper town' – 'Hartopolis' is a stationery store.

📢 Διάλογος 2 [THiálogos 2] Dialogue 2:
Πού είναι η τράπεζα; [poo íne i trápeza]? Where is the bank?

Mary and John are on their way to the bank now. Although they have a map with them they are a little bit lost so they ask a passer-by.

John	Με συγχωρείτε, πού είναι η τράπεζα παρακαλώ;
Passer-by	Δε ξέρω. Δεν είμαι απο'δώ. Ρωτήστε στο περίπτερο.
John	Συγνώμη, πού είναι η Εθνική Τράπεζα παρακαλώ;
At kiosk	Ευθεία. Η τράπεζα είναι μόνο ένα τετράγωνο μακριά απ'εδώ.
Mary	Δεξιά ή αριστερά μας;
At kiosk	Αριστερά σας, όπως πάτε.
Mary	Ευχαριστούμε.
At kiosk	Παρακαλώ.

John	[me sinhoríte]. [poo íne i trápeza] [parakaló]?	*Excuse me. Where is the bank, please?*
Passer-by	[THe kséro]. [THen íme] [apo'THó]. [rotíste sto períptero].	*I don't know. I'm not from here. Ask at the kiosk.*
John	[signómi], [poo íne] [i ethnikí trápeza] [parakaló]?	*I'm sorry, where is the National Bank, please?*
At kiosk	[efthía]. [i trápeza] [íne móno éna tetrágono] [makriá ap'eTHó].	*Straight on. The bank is only one block from here.*
Mary	[THeksiá] [i aristerá mas]?	*On our right or on our left?*
At kiosk	[aristerá sas], [ópos páte].	*Your left, as you go.*
Mary	[efharistoóme].	*(We) thank you.*
At kiosk	[parakaló].	*You're welcome.*

με συγχωρείτε	[me sinhoríte]	*excuse me/pardon me* (pl/fml)
ρωτήστε	[rotíste]	*ask!* (pl/fml)
περίπτερο	[períptero]	*kiosk* (n)
εθνική	[ethnikí]	*national* (with f noun)
ευθεία	[efthía]	*straight* (on)
τετράγωνο	[tetrágono]	*block* (n)
δεξιά	[THeksiá]	*right*
αριστερά	[aristerá]	*left*
όπως πάτε	[ópos páte]	*as you go* (pl/fml)
παρακαλώ	[parakaló]	*you're welcome*

Note

Remember that the word **παρακαλώ [parakaló]** has more than one meaning. In the same dialogue you find it as 'please' and 'you're welcome'. In the following dialogue you will see a third meaning 'How can I help you?' said by a shop assistant when you enter a store or by a bank clerk. **[parakaló]** can also mean 'hello' when answering the phone. A very important word, isn't it?

▶ Διάλογος 3 [THiálogos 3] *Dialogue 3:* Στην τράπεζα [stin trápeza] *At the bank*

John and Mary finally find the bank and now they are trying to cash some traveller's cheques.

Teller	Παρακαλώ!
John	Καλημέρα σας. Θέλω ν'αλλάξω μερικές ταξιδιωτικές επιταγές.
Teller	Σε τι νόμισμα είναι; Μπορώ να τις δω;
John	Ορίστε. Πόσο έχει η λίρα Αγγλίας σήμερα; Είμαι τυχερός;
Teller	Έτσι νομίζω.
Mary	Μας λέτε πως να πάμε στο ταχυδρομείο από' δω;
Teller	Αυτό είναι εύκολο. Το ταχυδρομείο είναι ακριβώς δίπλα μας. Μόλις βγείτε από την τράπεζα, είναι στ'αριστερά σας.

Teller	[parakaló]!	*Please! (How can I help you?)*
John	[kaliméra sas]. [thélo nalákso] [merikés taksiTHiotikés epitayés].	*Good morning. I'd like to cash some traveller's cheques.*
Teller	[se ti nómizma íne]? [boró na tis THo]?	*In what currency? Can I see them?*
John	[oríste]. [póso éhi] [i líra anglías] [símera]? [íme tiherós]?	*Here you are. What is the exchange rate for the pound sterling today? Am I lucky?*
Teller	[étsi nomízo].	*I think so (lit. so I think).*
Mary	[mas léte] [pos na páme] [sto tahiTHromío] [apo'THó]?	*Can you tell us how to get to the post office from here?*

Teller [aftó íne éfkolo]. [to tahi-   *That's easy. The post*
THromío] [íne akrivós THípla   *office is right next to us.*
mas]. [mólis vyíte] [apó tin   *As soon as you come out*
trápeza] [íne staristerá sas].   *of the bank it's on your left.*

The word Αγγλίας [anglías] is in the genitive case here. You already
know the nominative and accusative form, which is Αγγλία [anglía].
Λίρα Αγγλίας literally means 'pound of England'.

ν'αλλάξω	[nalákso]	to change
μερικές	[merikés]	some (f/pl)
επιταγές	[epitayés]	cheques (f/pl)
νόμισμα	[nómizma]	currency (n)
μπορώ να τις δω;	[boró na tis THo]?	Can I see them?/ May I see them?
ορίστε	[oríste]	here you are!
πόσο έχει;	[póso éhi]?	How much is it?
λίρα	[líra]	pound (f)
Αγγλίας	[anglías]	(of) England (f/gen.)
σήμερα	[símera]	today
τυχερός	[tiherós]	lucky (with m noun)
έτσι	[étsi]	so
νομίζω	[nomízo]	I think
μας λέτε;	[mas léte]?	(Can you) tell us? (pl/fml)

Notes

- **Ορίστε!** [oríste]! *Here you go! Here it is!* can be used when you
  offer something to someone. Do you also remember **να!** [na] *here!*
  from Unit 10 when you show or give something to someone?
- Do not confuse the two different uses of **δω** [THo] in this
  dialogue. In the phrase [**boró na tis THo**] it means 'see' and in the
  phrase [**apo'THó**] it means 'here' being the contracted form of
  εδώ [eTHó].

Language rules

1 Συγνώμη! [signómi]! *Excuse me!*

This is an important word when you want to apologize, or attract the
attention of someone. You can always use **με συγχωρείς** [**me
sinhorís**] informally or **με συγχωρείτε** [**me sinhoríte**] formally.

Λυπάμαι [lipáme] *I'm sorry* or λυπάμαι πολύ [lipáme polí] *I'm very sorry* can be used if you have made a serious mistake or to give condolences to someone.

[signómi], [me sinhorís], and [me sinhoríte] can all be used for the phrase 'excuse me, where is the...?' Bear in mind that you should remember the gender of the noun you want to use. Look at the examples below:

Masculine nouns

> Πού είναι ο σταθμός λεωφορείων; [poo íne o̲ stathmós leoforíon]? *Where is the bus station?*
> Πού είναι ο τηλεφωνικός θάλαμος; [poo íne o̲ tilefonikós thálamos]? *Where is the telephone booth?*

Feminine nouns

> Πού είναι η πλατεία; [poo íne i̲ platía]? *Where is the square?*
> Πού είναι η πλαζ [poo íne i̲ plaz]? *Where is the beach?*

Neuter nouns

> Πού είναι το περίπτερο; [poo íne to̲ períptero]?
> *Where is the kiosk?*
> Πού είναι το σούπερμαρκετ; [poo íne to̲ soópermarket]?
> *Where is the supermarket?*

▶ 2 Η πρώτη σας μέρα [i próti sas méra] *Your first day*

Let's learn some ordinal numbers now:

1 [éna]	→	**1st**	πρώτος [prótos] (m) / πρώτη [próti] (f) / πρώτο [próto] (n)
2 [THío]	→	**2nd**	δεύτερος [THéfteros] (m) / δεύτερη [THéfteri] (f) / δεύτερο [THéftero] (n)
3 [tría]	→	**3rd**	τρίτος [trítos] (m) / τρίτη [tríti] (f) / τρίτο [tríto] (n)
4 [tésera]	→	**4th**	τέταρτος [tétartos] (m) / τέταρτη [tétarti] (f) / τέταρτο [tétarto] (n)
5 [pénde]	→	**5th**	πέμπτος [pémptos] (m) / πέμπτη [pémpti] (f) / πέμπτο [pémpto] (n)

The three forms are used with masculine, feminine, and neuter nouns correspondingly, e.g. **πρώτος σταθμός [prót<u>o</u>s stathmós]** *first station* (m), **πρώτη τράπεζα [prót<u>i</u> trápeza]** *first bank* (f), and **πρώτο σχολείο [prót<u>o</u> sholío]** *first school* (n).

3 Ευθεία [efthía]! *Straight!*

When giving or understanding directions the following words are very important. Try to learn them by heart:

←	↑	→
αριστερά [aristerá] *left*	**ευθεία** [efthía] *straight*	**δεξιά** [THeksiá] *right*
στ'αριστερά [staristerá] *on the left*	**ευθεία μπροστά** [efthía brostá] *straight ahead*	**στα δεξιά** [sta THeksiá] *on the right*
στ'αριστερά σου [staristerá soo] *on your left* (infml)	**ίσια** [ísia] *straight ahead*	**στα δεξιά σου** [sta THeksiá soo] *on your right* (infml)
στ'αριστερά σας [staristerá sas] *on your left* (fml)		**στα δεξιά σας** [sta THeksiá sas] *on your right* (fml)

4 Ακριβώς δίπλα μας [akrivós THípla mas] *Right next to us*

Specifying where a place is becomes important, too. Study the words in the box opposite:

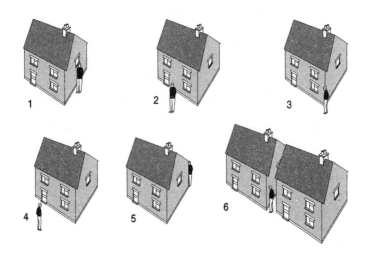

1 δίπλα στο(ν)/στη(ν)	[THípla sto(n)] or [THípla sti(n)]	next to
2 μποστά από	[brostá apó]	in front of
3 στη γωνία	[sti gonía]	in/at/on the corner
4 απέναντι από	[apénandi apó]	across from/opposite
5 πίσω από	[píso apó]	behind
6 μεταξύ	[metaksí]	between

5 Όπως πάτε... [ópos páte]... The way you go... As you go...

You need to use a number of verbs when giving directions. The most frequent ones are the following. There are two columns in Greek to show 'you – singular or informal' and 'you – plural or formal'.

You (sing/infml)	You (pl/fml)	
πήγαινε [píyene]!	πηγαίνετε [piyénete]!	Go!
στρίψε [strípse]!	στρίψτε [strípste]!	Turn!
βγες [vyes]!	βγείτε [vyíte]!	Get off! Get out!
συνέχισε [sinéhise]!	συνεχίστε [sinehíste]!	Continue!
σταμάτησε [stamátise]!	σταματήστε [stamatíste]!	Stop!
περπάτησε [perpátise]!	περπατήστε [perpatíste]!	Walk!
οδήγησε [oTHíyise]!	οδηγήστε [oTHiyíste]!	Drive!

ℹ 1 Η τράπεζα [i trápeza] The bank

An essential stop when visiting Greece is always the bank. You will be able to find a bank even in remote areas. Usual banking hours are Monday to Thursday from 8:00 to 14:00 and Friday from 8:00 to 13:30, although in many resorts there are currency exchanges which stay open until late, some of them operating even at weekends. Simply check your options in the place you are visiting. Some travel agencies also offer foreign exchange, with a higher commission, of course.

ΕΘΝΙΚΗ ΤΡΑΠΕΖΑ ΤΗΣ ΕΛΛΑΔΟΣ

National Bank of Greece.

Most bank employees speak English. In case you find yourself in a 'tricky' situation, use some of the phrases you have learnt in this unit. The clerk might ask you for your **διαβατήριο [THiavatírio]** *passport* in order to process your request. You can always present it with **ορίστε! [oríste]!** *Here it is!* just to impress!

2 Το ταχυδρομείο [to tahiTHromío] *The post office*

'ELTA' is the public post office in Greece.

This is probably another essential stop when visiting Greece. Post office hours are usually the same as banking hours, so simply ask about them where you are. Important vocabulary here is: **γράμμα [gráma]** *letter (n)*, **γραμματόσημο [gramatósimo]** *stamp (n)*, **φάκελος [fákelos]** *envelope (m)*, **κάρτα [kárta]** *card (f)*. A typical request is **ένα γραμματόσημο για Αγγλία/ Αμερική, παρακαλώ!** **[éna gramatósimo] [yia anglía]/ [amerikí] [parakaló]!** *A stamp for England/America, please!* Of course, you might be given four or five different stamps for that, but this is a different story... You can add **απλό [apló]** *surface mail*, **εξπρές [exprés]** *express mail*, or **συστημένο [sistiméno]** *registered mail*.

3 Στ'αριστερά σας [staristerá sas] *On your left*

You are probably accustomed to reading maps and road signs when travelling to places, rather than asking for directions. Of course, monolingual signs or confusing road signs create the necessity of asking directions on the spot.

Key vocabulary here can include: **αριστερά [aristerá]** *left*, **δεξιά [THeksiá]** *right*, **ίσια [ísia]** or **ευθεία [efthía]** *straight (on)*. The words **πάνω [páno]** *up* or **κάτω [káto]** *down* are also important. **Εδώ [eTHó]** *here* or **εδώ πέρα [eTHó péra]** *over here* and **εκεί [ekí]** *there* or **εκεί πέρα [ekí péra]** *over there* are often used as well. Do not hesitate to ask again when in doubt or when you want to double-check the information received.

Practice makes perfect

▶ **1** Listen to the recording and tick the appropriate square with the direction for each place.

	i [aristerá]	ii [efthía]	iii [THeksiá]
a			
b			
c			
d			
e			
f			

2 Can you match the words on the left with the translations on the right? Cover the transliteration column and try to work only with the Greek script for more challenge!

a	το φαρμακείο	[to farmakío]	i	restaurant
b	το θέατρο	[to théatro]	ii	beach
c	το εστιατόριο	[to estiatório]	iii	discotheque
d	η τουαλέτα	[i tooaléta]	iv	train station
e	η πλαζ	[i plaz]	v	pharmacy
f	η δισκοθήκη	[i THiskothíki]	vi	river
g	ο ποταμός	[o potamós]	vii	toilet
h	ο σταθμός	[o stathmós leoforíon]	viii	theatre
	λεωφορείων		ix	bus station
i	ο σταθμός τρένων	[o stathmós trénon]		

3 You see some Greek signs. Can you match them with their appropriate meaning?

a	ΤΗΛΕΦΩΝΟ	i	AIRPORT
b	ΤΑΧΥΔΡΟΜΕΙΟ	ii	SUPERMARKET
c	ΣΧΟΛΕΙΟ	iii	PHARMACY
d	ΑΕΡΟΔΡΟΜΙΟ	iv	POST OFFICE
e	ΑΣΤΥΝΟΜΙΑ	v	MUSEUM
f	ΦΑΡΜΑΚΕΙΟ	vi	TELEPHONE
g	ΜΟΥΣΕΙΟ	vii	POLICE
h	ΣΟΥΠΕΡΜΑΡΚΕΤ	viii	SCHOOL

4 Look at the pictures below and try to match the different kinds of shops with their Greek signs. Three new words have been added for you. Will you be able to guess them correctly?

i ΒΙΒΛΙΟΠΩΛΕΙΟΝ   iv ΣΟΥΠΕΡΜΑΡΚΕΤ   vii ΚΡΕΟΠΩΛΕΙΟΝ
ii ΑΡΤΟΠΟΙΕΙΟΝ   v ΠΕΡΙΠΤΕΡΟ   viii ΤΑΧΥΔΡΟΜΕΙΟ
iii ΚΟΜΜΩΤΗΡΙΟ   vi ΦΑΡΜΑΚΕΙΟ   ix ΤΑΞΙΔΙΩΤΙΚΟ
    ΓΡΑΦΕΙΟ

5 You are talking to a bank clerk [*tamías*]. Complete the dialogue using the information in *italics*.

[tamías]   [parakaló]!
you   a *I'd like to change some traveller's cheques.*
[tamías]   [se ti nómizma íne]?
you   b *They are in Pounds Sterling.*
[tamías]   [polí oréa]. [i líra símera] [éhi penínda evró] [i mía].
you   c *I'm lucky today. I like that. Here you go!*

▶ 6 Listen again to Dialogue 3 of this unit and fill in the blanks. Choose the missing words from the box.

Clerk   [parakaló]!
John   [kaliméra sas]. [thélo] a _____ [merikés taksiTHiotikés] b _____.
Clerk   [se ti c _____ [íne]? [boró na tis THo]?
John   [oríste]. [póso éhi i] d _____ [anglías] [símera]? [íme tiherós]?
Clerk   [étsi nomízo].
Mary   [mas] e ___ [pos na páme] [sto] f _____ [apo'THó]?
Clerk   [aftó íne] g _____. [to] h _____ [íne akrivós THípla mas]. i _____ [vyíte] [apó tin trápeza] [íne staristerá sas].

[líra]	[tahiTHromío]	[nalákso]	[epitayés]	[éfkolo]	[léte]
	[mólis]	[nómizma]			

▶ **7 You are staying with a friend. He is showing you the area where he lives on a map. Listen to the recording and before reading the text, tick the buildings and places on the map as you hear them mentioned.**

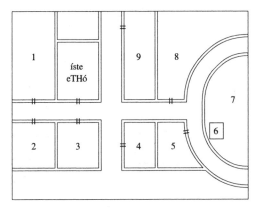

[to spíti moo] [íne eTHó] [sti gonía]. [THípla moo] [íne to soópermarket] [ke apénandi i eklisía]. [ipárhi mía megáli platía] [éna tetrágono makriá]. [i platía éhi éna períptero]. [apénandi apó to períptero] [íne to farmakío]. [to tahiTHromío íne] [píso apó to farmakío].

8 Can you match the numbers in the map above with the names of the places (a–f below)? Three of the numbers will not have a match.

1	2	3	4	5	6	7	8	9

a πλατεία [platía] **b** περίπτερο [períptero] **c** ταχυδρομείο [tahiTHromío] **d** φαρμακείο [farmakío] **e** εκκλησία [eklisía] **f** σούπερμαρκετ [soópermarket]

Mini test

a What are the words for 'post office', 'bank', 'hotel', and 'museum'?

b How can you say 'left – straight on – right'? There are more than three words in Greek. Can you remember them all?

c What are the Greek expressions for 'excuse me' or 'I'm sorry'? Again, there were more than two.

d You see some signs outside some buildings. ΝΟΣΟΚΟΜΕΙΟ, ΕΣΤΙΑΤΟΡΙΟ, ΠΑΡΚΙΝ, ΓΚΑΡΑΖ, ΠΡΑΤΗΡΙΟ ΒΕΝΖΙΝΗΣ, ΑΕΡΟΔΡΟΜΙΟ. What do they mean?

e What are the opposite words for [kondá], [apénandi], [soópermarket], [aristerá], [ekí] ?

f If you are in a bank, can you say the following? 'Can you tell us what the exchange rate is?', 'I've got some traveller's cheques.', 'Where can I change them?', 'I have Pounds Sterling and American Dollars.'

Πάμε καλά! [páme kalá]! You are ready now to move on to Unit 12. Take a short break first. This unit was a little longer… **Θα σε δω εκεί! Γεια σου! [tha se THo ekí]! [yiásoo]!**

πάμε για ψώνια!

let's go shopping!

In this unit you will learn
- how to describe in more detail what you want to buy
- how to ask about prices and sizes
- how to say more colours in Greek
- how to read some common signs and public notices
- more about word order

Before you start

- Revise Unit 5 before you start this unit. We hope you like this method of revising past units, actively drawing upon past and present knowledge of your Greek, and at the same time checking 'old' materials with 'new' insights.

- You might have already been compiling lists of words that are important to you. Another way of learning this personalized vocabulary is to use index cards. On the front of the card you can write down the word you would like to learn. On the back of the card you can write information about the word, e.g. the translation into English, the Greek spelling, possible opposites, synonyms, family words, phrases that include this word, or anything else that is important to you. The possibilities are numerous. By flipping the card backwards and forwards and testing yourself on the information you will be able to memorize it better and faster.

Key words and phrases

There are a lot of phrases you'll hear and you can use when you're out shopping in Greece. Here are some of them:

Παρακαλώ!	[parakaló]!	How can I help you?
Να σας βοηθήσω σε κάτι;	[na sas voithíso se káti]?	Can I help you with something?
Μόνο βλέπω.	[móno vlépo].	Just looking.
Έχετε αυτό σε μαύρο;	[éhete aftó se mávro]?	Have you got this in black?
Τι νούμερο φοράτε;	[ti noómero foráte]?	What size do you take (lit. wear)?
Μπορώ να το δοκιμάσω;	[boró na to THokimáso]?	Can I try it on?
Πού είναι το δοκιμαστήριο;	[poo íne to THokimastírio]?	Where is the fitting/ changing room?
Είναι λίγο μικρό/ μεγάλο.	[íne lígo mikró/ megálo].	It's a bit small/big.
Θα το πάρω.	[tha to páro].	I'll take it.
Μπορώ να πληρώσω με λίρες/ δολάρια/επιταγή;	[boró na pliróso me líres]/ [THolária]/ [epitayí]?	Can I pay in pounds/ dollars/by cheque?

Recognizing public signs and notices when you're in the street is also extremely important. Below you'll see some signs and notices. Look at the pictures on pages 149–50 and try to become familiar with most of them. Don't hesitate to come back to them whenever you find it necessary.

The corresponding Greek signs are:

a	ΚΤΥΠΗΣΤΕ ΤΟ ΚΟΥΔΟΥΝΙ [ktipíste to kooTHoóni]	*Ring the bell*
b	ΑΝΟΙΚΤΟ or ΑΝΟΙΚΤΑ [aniktó] or [aniktá]	*Open*
c	ΚΛΕΙΣΤΟ or ΚΛΕΙΣΤΑ [klistó] or [klistá]	*Closed*
d	ΕΚΠΤΩΣΕΙΣ [ekptósis]	*Sales*
e	ΤΑΜΕΙΟ(Ν) [tamío(n)]	*Cashier*
f	ΠΕΡΙΜΕΝΕΤΕ ΣΤΗ ΣΕΙΡΑ [periménete sti sirá]	*Queue this side/ Wait in queue*
g	ΜΗ ΠΑΤΑΤΕ ΤΟ ΓΡΑΣΙΔΙ [mi patáte to grasíTHi]	*Don't step on the lawn/ grass*
h	ΧΑΛΑΣΜΕΝΟ or ΕΚΤΟΣ ΛΕΙΤΟΥΡΓΙΑΣ [halazméno] or [ektós litoorgías]	*Broken/Out of order*
i	ΑΠΑΓΟΡΕΥΕΤΑΙ ΤΟ ΚΑΠΝΙΣΜΑ [apagorévete to kápnizma]	*No smoking (lit. smoking is forbidden)*
j	ΕΞΟΔΟΣ [éksoTHos]	*Exit*
k	ΕΙΣΟΔΟΣ [ísoTHos]	*Entrance*
l	ΩΘΗΣΑΤΕ [othísate]	*Push*
m	ΕΛΞΑΤΕ [élksate]	*Pull*
n	ΑΝΔΡΩΝ [andrón]	*Men*
o	ΓΥΝΑΙΚΩΝ [yinekón]	*Women*
p	ΤΟΥΑΛΕΤΕΣ [tooalétes]	*Toilets*

You will see the English signs for WC and STOP everywhere in Greece.

Pronunciation tips

The sound **β** [**v**] is one of the very few sounds not mentioned yet in the last eleven units. You have come across several Greek words with this sound, e.g. **μπράβο** [**brávo**] *bravo*, **νουβέλα** [**noovéla**] *novel*, **βουνό** [**voonó**] *mountain*, and **βράδυ** [**vráTHi**] *evening*. The corresponding sound in English is [**v**] as in **v**ast, **v**et, and **v**olcano.

'Vardavas': A chain of optical stores in Greece.

'Vasilopoulos': A chain of supermarkets in Greece.

▶ Διάλογος 1 [THiálogos 1] *Dialogue 1*

On the way to the travel agency Mary sees a summer dress in the window of a store. She asks John to stop.

Υπάλληλος	Γεια σας! Να σας βοηθήσω σε κάτι;
Mary	Θέλω να δω το φόρεμα που έχετε στη βιτρίνα.
Υπάλληλος	Ποιο απ'όλα; Το κόκκινο, το πράσινο ή το μπλε;
Mary	Το μπλε. Υπάρχει στο μέγεθός μου;
Υπάλληλος	Μία στιγμη, να δω. Τι νούμερο φοράτε; 38, 40;
Mary	Το σαράντα είναι καλύτερο. Έχετε άλλα χρώματα;
Υπάλληλος	Ένα λεπτό! Μια στιγμή!

[ipálilos]	[yiásas]! [na sas voithíso se káti]?	Hello! Can I help you with anything?
Mary	[thélo na THo] [to fórema poo éhete] [sti vitrína].	I'd like to see the dress you have in the window.
[ipálilos]	[pio apóla]? [to kókino], [to prásino] [i to ble]?	Which one? The red, the green or the blue one?
Mary	[to ble]. [ipárhi] [sto mégethos moo]?	The blue one. Is there one in my size?
[ipálilos]	[mía stigmí, na THo]. [ti noómero foráte]? [triánda októ], [saránda]?	One moment, let me see. What size do you wear? 38, 40?
Mary	[to saránda] [íne kalítero]. [éhete ála hrómata]?	40 is better. Have you got any other colours?
[ipálilos]	[éna leptó]! [mía stigmí]!	Just a minute! Just a moment!

να σας βοηθήσω;	[na sas voithíso]?	Can I help you? (pl/fml)
κάτι	[káti]	something/anything
φόρεμα	[fórema]	dress (n)
βιτρίνα	[vitrína]	shop window (f)
ποιο;	[pio]?	which? (with n nouns)
κόκκινο	[kókino]	red (n)
πράσινο	[prásino]	green (n)
μπλε	[ble]	blue (m/f/n)
υπάρχει	[ipárhi]	there is
μέγεθος	[mégethos]	size (n)
στιγμή	[stigmí]	moment (f)
φοράτε	[foráte]	you wear/you are wearing (pl/fml)
λεπτό	[leptó]	minute (n)

- Remember that **Να σας βοηθήσω σε κάτι;** [**na sas voithíso se káti**]? can also be substituted by **παρακαλώ;** [**parakaló**]?
- Both **μέγεθος** [**mégethos**] and **νούμερο** [**noómero**] mean 'size'. **Νούμερο** [**noómero**] also means 'number'.
- The word [**pio**] means 'which' when spelled **ποιο** and 'further' when spelt **πιο**. For example: **Ποιο βιβλίο;** [**pio vivlío**]? *Which book?* and **πιο κάτω** [**pio káto**] *further down*. There is a difference in the Greek spelling but not in the sound. The word **ποιο** is shown in its neuter form here. Also read the notes in the **Grammar summary** about interrogative pronouns.

▶ **Διάλογος 2 [THiálogos 2]** *Dialogue 2*

John takes the opportunity to look for some shoes to buy.

John	Πόσο κάνουν αυτά τα παπούτσια;
Υπάλληλος	Όλα εδώ είναι με έκπτωση είκοσι τοις εκατό.
John	Μπορώ να τα δοκιμάσω;
Υπάλληλος	Βέβαια. Καθίστε σ'αυτό το σκαμπό. Τι νούμερο βάζετε;
John	Σαράντα τέσσερα. Φέρτε μου ένα ζευγάρι με κορδόνια κι'ένα παντόφλες, παρακαλώ.
Υπάλληλος	Παντοφλέ εννοείτε, έτσι δεν είναι;
John	Ναι, ναι! Συγνώμη.

John	[póso kánoon] [aftá ta papoótsia]?	*How much are these shoes?*
[ipálilos]	[óla eTHó] [íne me ékptosi] [íkosi tis ekató].	*Everything here has a 20% reduction.*
John	[boró na ta THokimáso]?	*Can I try them on?*
[ipálilos]	[vévea], [kathíste] [saftó to skambó]. [ti noómero vázete]?	*Of course, take a seat on this stool. What size are you (lit. what number do you put)?*
John	[saránda tésera]. [férte moo] [éna zevgári mávro] [me korTHónia] [kéna pandófles], [parakaló].	*44. Bring me a black pair with laces and one pair of slippers, please.*
[ipálilos]	[pandoflé enoíte], [étsi THen íne]?	*Slip-ons (loafers) you mean, don't you?*
John	[ne], [ne]! [signómi].	*Yes, yes! I'm sorry.*

αυτά	**[aftá]**	*these* (n/pl)
παπούτσια	**[papoótsia]**	*shoes* (n/pl)
έκπτωση	**[ékptosi]**	*reduction* (f)
Μπορώ να τα δοκιμάσω;	**[boró na ta THokimáso]**	*Can I try them on?*
καθίστε!	**[kathíste]!**	*Sit! Take a seat!* (pl/fml)
σκαμπό	**[skambó]**	*stool* (n)
νούμερο	**[noómero]**	*number, size* (n)
βάζετε	**[vázete]**	*you wear* (lit. put) (pl/fml)
φέρτε	**[férte]!**	*Bring!* (pl/fml)
ζευγάρι	**[zevgári]**	*pair* (n)
κορδόνια	**[korTHónia]**	*shoe laces* (n/pl)
παντόφλες	**[pandófles]**	*slippers* (f/pl)

παντοφλέ	[pandoflé]	*slip-ons (loafers)* (n)
εννοείτε	[enoíte]	*you mean* (pl/fml)
έτσι δεν είναι;	[étsi THen íne]? *Isn't that so?*	

Notes

* **Ζευγάρι [zevgári]** *pair* is an important word in Greek. Some possible pairs are: ζευγάρι κάλτσες [zevgári káltses] *pair of socks*, ζευγάρι παπούτσια [zevgári papoótsia] *pair of shoes* and ζευγάρι γυαλιά [zevgári yialiá] *pair of glasses*.

* Do not confuse the word [pandófles] *slippers* with [pandoflé] *slip-ons (loafers)* – they sound almost the same.

* Έτσι δεν είναι; [étsi THen íne]? is an important phrase when you want to verify information. Please note the examples: Είμαι τυχερός, έτσι δεν είναι; [íme tiherós] [étsi THen íne]? *I'm lucky, am I not?*, Ξέρω ελληνικά, έτσι δεν είναι; [kséro eliniká] [étsi THen íne]? *I know Greek, don't I?*, Μπορώ να σε δω, έτσι δεν είναι [boró na se THo] [étsi THen íne]? *I can see you, can't I?*, Δεν θέλεις να πας, έτσι δεν είναι; [THen thélis na pas] [étsi THen íne]? *You don't want to go, do you?*

▶ Διάλογος 3 [THiálogos 3] Dialogue 3

Mary sees a very nice shirt for John and starts talking to the shop assistant.

Mary	Ποια είναι η τιμή γι'αυτό το πουκάμισο;
Υπάλληλος	Πάει με το μέγεθος.
John	Μ'αρέσει πολύ αυτό το ριγέ αλλά και το καρώ είναι πολύ όμορφο. Ποιο σ'αρέσει περισσότερο, Mary;
Mary	Δεν ξέρω. Μ'αρέσει το καρώ αλλά το ριγέ μ'αρέσει περισσότερο.
John	Κι'εγώ το ίδιο. Μπορώ να το δοκιμάσω, παρακαλώ;
Υπάλληλος	Ναι. Πηγαίνετε στο δοκιμαστήριο, εκεί πέρα.

Mary	[pia íne i timí] [yi'aftó to pookámiso]?	*What's the price of this shirt?* (lit. for this shirt)
[ipálilos]	[pái me to mégethos].	*It goes according to size.*
John	[marési polí] [aftó to riyé] [alá ke to karó] [íne polí ómorfo]. [pio sarési perisótero], [Mary]?	*I like this striped one a lot but the checked one is also very nice. Which one do you like better, Mary?*

Mary	[THen kséro]. [marési to karó] [alá to riyé] [marési perisótero].	*I don't know. I like the checked one but I like the striped one more.*
John	[ki'egó] [to íTHio]. [boró na to THokimáso], [parakaló]?	*Me, too. Can I try it on, please?*
[ipálilos]	[ne]. [piyénete sto THokimastírio] [ekí péra].	*Yes. Go to the changing room, over there.*

τιμή	[timí]	*price* (f)
πουκάμισο	[pookámiso]	*shirt* (n)
μεσαίο	[meséo]	*medium, middle* (n)
ριγέ	[riyé]	*striped* (m/f/n)
καρώ	[karó]	*checked* (m/f/n)
όμορφο	[ómorfo]	*nice, beautiful* (n)
περισσότερο	[perisótero]	*more* (n)
ίδιο	[íTHio]	*same* (n)
δοκιμαστήριο	[THokimastírio]	*changing room* (n)
εκεί	[ekí]	*there*
πέρα	[péra]	*over*

Notes

* Do not confuse the new words **μεσαίο [meséo]** *medium size* with **μουσείο [moosío]** *museum*, or **περισσότερο [perisótero]** *more* with **ποδόσφαιρο [poTHósfero]** *football*. Of course, if you check the Greek spelling you'll see that it is different in all four words.
* **[ki'egó to íTHio]** is an expression meaning 'me, too' or 'likewise'. The literal translation would be 'and I the same'.

Language rules

1 Να σας βοηθήσω; [na sas voithíso]? *Can I help you?*

The above literally means 'to you help?'. You were also introduced to **να σας συστήσω! [na sas sistíso]!** *Let me introduce you!*, which again literally means 'to you introduce'. In both cases there is a verb omitted from the Greek phrases. The full and complete version would be: **Μπορώ να σας βοηθήσω; [boró na sas voithíso]?** *Can I help you?* and **Θέλω να σας συστήσω! [thélo na sas sistíso]!** *I want to introduce you!* Equally, Mary in Dialogue 1 says **Θέλω να δω το φόρεμα. [thélo na THo to fórema].** *I want to see the dress.* By omitting the verb **θέλω [thélo]**, we can turn the statement into the question **Να δω το φόρεμα; [na THo to fórema]?** *May I see the dress?*

2 Το κόκκινο, το πράσινο... [to kókino], [to prásino]... *The red, the green...*

Do you still remember the colours of the rainbow? Let's revise them for you: **μωβ** [mov], **μπλε** [ble], **πράσινο** [prásino], **κίτρινο** [kítrino], **πορτοκαλί** [portokalí], **κόκκινο** [kókino]. You should also remember **μαύρο** [mávro] and **άσπρο** [áspro]. Some more colours include: **καφέ** [kafé] *brown*, **ροζ** [roz] *pink*, **μπεζ** [bez] *beige*, **γαλάζιο** [yalázio] *sky blue*. **Σκούρο** [skoóro] *dark* and **ανοικτό** [aniktó] *light* are two important words that can be used with colours, e.g. **σκούρο πράσινο** [skoóro prásino] *dark green* and **ανοικτό μπλε** [aniktó ble] *light blue*.

The colours **μωβ, μπλε, πορτοκαλί, καφέ, ροζ, μπεζ** have only one form for masculine, feminine or neuter nouns, whereas **πράσινο, κίτρινο, κόκκινο, μαύρο, άσπρο** change with gender – here they are neuter with the ending -ο. The ending in the nominative singular becomes -ος for masculine, i.e. **πράσινος**, and -η for feminine, i.e. **πράσινη**.

Learning tip: Link up the study of colours with actual items connected to you, e.g. the colour of your hair, the colour of your car, etc.

3 Κάτι; [káti]? *Anything?*

There are some important word pairs in English that can be helpful to learn in Greek. You will be agreeably surprised to realize that these words do not have different forms in statements and questions in Greek. The word pairs are: something – anything?, someone – anyone?, etc. Note the examples below or have a look at the infinitive pronouns in the **Grammar summary** at the back of the book.

Θέλω κάτι. [thélo káti]. *I want something.*
Θέλεις κάτι; [thélis káti]? *Do you want anything?*
Κάποιος είναι εδώ. [kápios íne eTHó]. *Someone is here.*
Κάποιος είναι εδώ; [kápios íne eTHó]? *Is anyone here?*

The word **κάτι** [káti] has only one form, whereas the word **κάποιος** [kápios] is the masculine form, **κάποια** [kápia] is the feminine form, and **κάποιο** [kápio] the neuter form, as they relate to a person – you will probably have realized by now that some words for people can be neuter in Greek: **αγόρι** [agóri] *boy*, **κορίτσι** [korítsi] *girl*.

4 Αυτό το πουκάμισο [aftó to pookámiso]
This shirt

It has been mentioned on several occasions that you need to learn the gender (masculine/feminine/neuter) of Greek nouns. This applies also to the form of the words for 'this/that' and 'these/those' which have to agree with the gender of the noun they refer to. Look at the examples below:

Masculine (nominative)	Feminine	Neuter
αυτός ο άντρας [aftós o ándras] *this man*	αυτή η γυναίκα [aftí i yinéka] *this woman*	αυτό το παιδί [aftó to peTHí] *this child*
αυτοί οι άντρες [aftí i ándres] *these men*	αυτές οι γυναίκες [aftés i yinékes] *these women*	αυτά τα παιδιά [aftá ta peTHiá] *these children*
Note the difference between 'this/that' and 'these/those'.		
εκείνος ο άντρας [ekínos o ándras] *that man*	εκείνη η γυναίκα [ekíni i yinéka] *that woman*	εκείνο το παιδί [ekíno to peTHí] *that child*
εκείνοι οι άντρες [ekíni i ándres] *those men*	εκείνες οι γυναίκες [ekínes i yinékes] *those women*	εκείνα τα παιδιά [ekína ta peTHiá] *those children*

In these examples the article *the* **ο** [o], **η** [i], **το** [to], and **οι** [i] and **τα** [ta] cannot be left out in Greek. The literal translation is 'this **the** man', 'this **the** woman', etc. Simply learn it this way! **με αυτό τον τρόπο!** [me aftó ton trópo]!

5 Καθίστε! [kathíste]! *Have a seat!*

You had a list of frequent verbs for giving directions in note 5 in the previous unit. Those verbs were in the imperative form, which is used when we request or order something from someone. In this unit you have seen [**kathíste**]! *Sit down!*, [**férte**]! *Bring!* and [**piyénete**]! *Go!*. Let's make a short list with two columns for the Greek words in singular and plural.

sing/infml	pl/fml	
κάθισε! [káthise]!	καθίστε! [kathíste]!	*Sit down! Have a seat!*
φέρε! [fére]!	φέρτε! [férte]!	*Bring!*
πήγαινε! [píyene]!	πηγαίνετε! [piyénete]!	*Go!*
έλα! [éla]!	ελάτε! [eláte]!	*Come!*
μίλησε! [mílise]!	μιλήστε! [milíste]!	*Speak!*
πάρε! [páre]!	πάρτε! [párte]!	*Take!*

6 Σειρά λέξεων στα ελληνικά [sirá lékseon sta eliniká] *Word order* (lit. *order of words*) *in Greek*

This is a touchy subject! We have left it towards the end of the book because it often does not match English word order, which is in a way more rigid because the position of the word in English defines its role in the sentence. All the different endings and the forms of root words make Greek word order more flexible in what comes first and what follows next. In the previous eleven units we had some examples to illustrate this. You might even have wondered about the English translation of certain sentences. Don't worry! Look at it as a new game and all new games have new rules to follow. Of course, you are always at liberty to understand some, follow some, and break some. This is what makes this new game exciting. Put on a smile whenever you catch yourself making a language blunder! This is usually how young children react when we correct them in their early learning. Leave age and inhibitions behind you. We are all young at heart. This way, learning Greek will become an enjoyable and rewarding experience for you.

The next three units will touch upon this subject of word order in Greek with some examples. Until then, move forward and keep the right attitude, OK?

ℹ️ Ψώνια στην Ελλάδα [psónia stin eláTHa] *Shopping in Greece*

Unfortunately, Greece is no longer the shopping paradise it was in the 1960s and 1970s. Prices have gone up and you have to look closely for bargains. This is not to say though that foreign currencies don't enjoy some 'privileges' in Greece. And some local products can still be a bargain but perhaps only a little harder to find.

There are many jewellery stores that offer **ασήμι [asími]** *silver* and **χρυσό [hrisó]** *gold* in traditional or modern designs in all price ranges. **Γούνες [goónes]** *furs*, **δερμάτινα [THermátina]** *leather items, e.g. shoes, bags, etc.*, and **φλοκάτες [flokátes]** *flokati rugs* and **χαλιά [haliá]** *rugs* are also available in all tourist shopping areas. Popular souvenirs include **πήλινα [pílina]** *pottery*, **κεραμικά [keramiká]** *ceramics*, and **αγαλματίδια [agalmatíTHia]** *statues*. And for those who want to bring back a taste of Greece there are several alcoholic beverages, such as **κρασί [krasí]** *wine*, **ούζο [oózo]** *ouzo*, and **Μεταξά κονιάκ [metaxá koniák]** *Metaxa brandy*.

Ναι, ναι! [ne], [ne]! *Of course, yes!*

In Dialogue 2 there is a repetition of the word **[ne]** *yes*. This is a common way in Greek to emphasize a statement. If you pay close attention, you will realize that it is used with many words thus forming idiomatic expressions. Look at the examples below:

> **ναι [ne]** *yes* → **ναι, ναι [ne], [ne]!** *Of course, yes!* (Unit 12)
>
> **βέβαια [vévea]** *sure* → **βέβαια, βέβαια! [vévea], [vévea]!** *definitely sure!*
>
> **γρήγορα [grígora]** *fast* → **γρήγορα, γρήγορα! [grígora], [grígora]!** *extremely fast!*
>
> **βλέπω [vlépo]** *I see* → **βλέπω, βλέπω! [vlépo], [vlépo]!** *I do see!*
>
> **έλα!** *come!* → **έλα, έλα! [éla], [éla]** *Come on! Move!*
>
> **πρωί [proí]** *morning* → **πρωί, πρωί [proí], [proí]** *very early in the morning*
>
> **χαίρετε [hérete]** *hello* → **χαίρετε, χαίρετε [hérete], [hérete]** *hello, hello to you!*

As you can see, the repeated version denotes more emphasis and gives more urgency to the situation. Listen to native speakers using it and whenever you feel comfortable with those expressions, use them in certain instances yourself.

More about Greek names

The typical question to ask someone's name is – **Πώς σε/σας λένε; [pos se/sas léne]?** *What's your (infml/fml) name?* The typical answer is **Με λένε... [me léne]...** *My name is ....*

Greeks love to shorten names. Some examples of this are: **Κώστας** **[kóstas]** and **Ντίνος** **[dínos]** – short forms for **Κωνσταντίνος** **[konstandínos]** *Constantine*. **Άρης** **[áris]** is a short form for **Αρίσταρχος** **[arístarhos]** *Aristarhos*, **Αριστοτέλης** **[aristotélis]** *Aristotle* and other similar names. **Γιάννα** **[yiána]** is a short form for **Ιωάννα** **[ioána]** *Joanna* and **Λένα** **[léna]** is a short form for **Ελένη** **[eléni]** *Helen*.

They also like to use a diminutive form for their names by changing the endings. The ending **-άκης** **[-akis]** is used for male names such as **Κώστας** **[kóstas]** → **Κωστάκης** **[kostákis]** *(lit. little Constantine)*, **Γιάννης** **[yiánis]** → **Γιαννάκης** **[yianákis]** *(lit. little John)*, **Πέτρος** **[pétros]** → **Πετράκης** **[petrákis]** *(lit. little Peter)*. The equivalent ending for female names is **-ούλα** **[-oóla]** as in **Τασία** **[tasía]** → **Τασούλα** **[tasoóla]** *[lit. little Anastasia]*, or **Άννα** **[ána]** → **Αννούλα** **[anoóla]** *(lit. little Anna)*. The ending **[-oóla]** is part of many other female nicknames such as **Κούλα** **[koóla]**, **Λούλα** **[loóla]**, **Νούλα** **[noóla]**, **Σούλα** **[soóla]**, **Ρούλα** **[roóla]** or **Τούλα** **[toóla]**. There are so many possibilities!

The diminutive form is also used with other words in a similar way to the English ending '-let' as in 'book – booklet'. You might hear **καφεδάκι** **[kafeTHáki]** instead of **καφέ** **[kafé]** without the person denoting any lesser quantity of coffee. Another example is **νεράκι** **[neráki]** instead of **νερό** **[neró]** *water*, which could mean 'some water' but again does not indicate the quantity.

Sometimes the diminutive form is surprising, for example when a young man or young woman is addressed as **παιδάκι** **[peTHáki]** *(lit. little child)*. Here it is used as a term of endearment rather than literally. Be careful when using these forms and use them only when you feel you have grasped the real use in context.

Practice makes perfect

1 Can you match the words on the left with their counterparts on the right?

a	[káltses]	**i**	[mávro]
b	[zevgári]	**ii**	[noómero]
c	[áspro]	**iii**	[eTHó]
d	[skoóro]	**iv**	[papoótsia]
e	[mégethos]	**v**	[aniktó]
f	[ekí]	**vi**	[yialiá]

2 **Rearrange these lines to make a dialogue. You can work with the transliteration or the Greek script column.**

a [THistihós] [éhoome móno skoóro kafé].

b [ne], [thélo na THo] [aftó to fórema].

c [anikto kafé] [i bez]?

d [lipáme], [antipathó] [ta skoóra hrómata].

e [na sas voithíso se káti]?

f [ti hróma sas arési]?

a Δυστυχώς, έχουμε μόνο σκούρο καφέ.

b Ναι. Θέλω να δω αυτό το φόρεμα.

c Ανοικτό καφέ ή μπεζ;

d Λυπάμαι, αντιπαθώ τα σκούρα χρώματα.

e Να σας βοηθήσω σε κάτι;

f Τι χρώμα σας αρέσει;

3 **Can you translate the dialogue from Exercise 2 into English?**

4 **Match the pictures (a) to (d) with the phrases (i) to (iv) below. Use the column with the transliteration or the Greek script.**

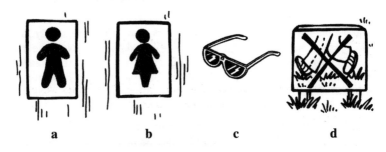

a   b   c   d

i [i maría théli na pái tooaléta].

ii [prépi nagoráso éna zevgári yialiá].

iii [thélo na páo vólta* tóra].

iv [o THimítris éhi anángi na pái tooaléta].

i Η Μαρία, θέλει να πάει τουαλέτα.

ii Πρέπει ν'αγοράσω ένα ζευγάρι γυαλιά.

iii Θέλω να πάω βόλτα τώρα.

iv Ο Δημήτρης έχει ανάγκη να πάει τουαλέτα.

*πάω βόλτα [páo vólta] *I go for a walk.*

5 **Can you translate the four sentences from Exercise 4 into English?**

6 Look at the pictures and match them with the key words below.

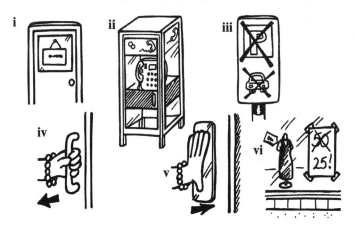

i   ii   iii

iv   v   vi

a sales   **d** push
b telephone   **e** pull
c no parking   **f** closed

7 Cryptolexis or 'hidden words' is a fun game. How many words can you recognize? They read across, down, up and backwards!

E	A	N	O	I	K	T	O
K	E	E	T	A	T	A	Π
E	Δ	Ω	O	N	O	M	A
I	Ω	Σ	O	T	K	E	N
Γ	P	A	Σ	I	Δ	I	T
K	Λ	E	I	Σ	T	O	A

▶ 8 **Listen again to Dialogue 3 of this unit and fill in the blanks. If you don't have the recording, choose the missing words from the box below. Three words are used twice.**

Mary [pia íne i] **a**_____ [yi'aftó to] **b** _____ ?
[ipálilos] [pái me to mégethos]. [pénde hiliáTHes to mikró], [éksi hiliáTHes to] **c** _____ [ki'eftá to megálo].
John [marési polí] [aftó to] **d** _____ [alá ke to] **e** _____ [íne polí ómorfo]. [pio sarési], **f** _____ [Mary]?
Mary [THen kséro]. [marési to] **e** _____ [alá to] **d** _____ [marési] **f** _____.
John [ki'egó] [to íTHio]. [boró na to] **g** _____, [parakaló]?
[ipálilos] [ne]. [piyénete sto] **h** _____ [ekí] **i** _____.

[pookámiso]	[perisótero]	[timí]	[karó]	[THokimáso]
[riyé]	[THokimastírio]	[meséo]	[péra]	

Mini test

a Look at the public signs and notices in **Key words and phrases** at the beginning of this unit. How many do you recognize when you cover the English translation?
b You see the signs **ΑΝΔΡΩΝ** and **ΓΥΝΑΙΚΩΝ** on bathroom doors. Which is which?
c You see the sign **ΕΛΞΑΤΕ** on a door. Will you pull or push?
d Is the sign **ΕΚΤΟΣ ΛΕΙΤΟΥΡΓΙΑΣ** a 'good' sign?
e Exits are usually marked in Greek. How do they read: **ΕΙΣΟΔΟΣ** or **ΕΞΟΔΟΣ**?
f What are the synonyms or opposite words for **[stigmí]**, **[mégethos]**, **[aniktó ble]**, **[mávro]**, **[skoóro]**, **[skambó]**?
g Έτσι δεν είναι [étsi THen íne]? How is it used in Greek?
h Name four new colours.
i How easy is it to translate Dialogue 3 if you hide the English translation?

OK! Θα σε δω στην επόμενη ενότητα. Γεια σου! [okei]! [tha se THo stin epómeni enótita]. [yiásoo]!

Τρένο ή πούλμαν;

train or coach?

In this unit you will learn
- how to make travel enquiries
- how to find out about public transport
- how to make travel arrangements
- about the days of the week
- about types of transport
- how to say the twelve months and four seasons

Before you start

- Revise Unit 6 before you start this unit. If you did the first **Revision test** for Units 1 to 5, you can do it again and compare your result to the first time you took it.

- Starting with Unit 11, you will have realized that the units are a little longer and include one more dialogue and perhaps more notes and explanations. Continue to apply your learning routines as you have in the last 12 units. You can also proceed with smaller chunks and take more frequent breaks. One break can be after the **Pronunciation tips**, a second one after the third dialogue, and the third break after the cultural notes. Of course, you are the one who will decide the amount and the frequency of your breaks. Always remember that language learning relies on persistence, patience, frequent revision, and real application. So, go for it!

Key words and phrases

To make travel enquiries, you can ask:

Θέλω μερικές πληροφορίες για ...
[thélo merikés pliroforíes yia]...
I'd like some information about...

... τον Πόρο/την Αθήνα/το Ναύπλιο/τα Γιάννενα.
... [ton póro]/[tin athína]/[to náfplio]/[ta yiánena].
... Poros Island/Athens/Nafplio/Ioannina.

Τι ώρα φεύγει/έρχεται/φτάνει;
[ti óra] [févyi]/[érhete]/[ftáni]?
What time does it leave/come/arrive?

To ask if you can book a seat, say:

Μπορώ να κάνω κράτηση/κρατήσεις;
[boró na káno] [krátisi]/[kratísis]?
Can I make a reservation/reservations?

Μία θέση/δύο θέσεις για το τρένο στις πέντε/στις οκτώ.
[mía thési]/[THío thésis] [yia to tréno] [stis pénde]/[stis októ].
One seat/two seats on the five/eight o'clock train.

Ένα εισιτήριο/δύο εισιτήρια για...
[éna isitírio]/[THío isitíria] [yia]...
One ticket/two tickets for ...

Ένα εισιτήριο απλό/δύο εισιτήρια μ'επιστροφή.
[ena isitírio apló]/THío isitíria mepistrofí].
One single ticket/two return tickets.

To ask about the method of payment:

Παίρνετε πιστωτικές κάρτες/ταξιδιωτικές επιταγές/ λίρες Αγγλίας;
[pérnete] [pistotikés kártes]/[taksiTHiotikés epitayés]/ [líres anglías]?
Do you take credit cards/traveller cheques/Pounds Sterling?

Πόσο κάνει το εισιτήριο; Πόσο κάνουν τα εισιτήρια;
[póso káni to isitírio]? [póso kánoon ta isitíria]?
How much is the ticket? How much are the tickets?

To ask how to get to a place, say:

Πώς μπορώ να πάω στο(ν)/στη(ν) ...
pos boró na páo] [sto(n)]/[sti(n)] ...?
How can I get to ...?

Πώς μπορούμε να πάμε από ... στο(ν)/στη(ν) ...
[pos boroóme na páme apó] ... [sto(n)]/[sti(n)] ... ?
How can we get from ... to ...?

A possible answer would be:

Μπορείτε να πάτε με το λεωφορείο/το αεροπλάνο/το πλοίο.
[boríte na páte me] [to leoforío]/[to aeropláno]/[to plío].
You can go by bus/plane/ship.

The word lists below are very important. Come back to them as often as needed. You will soon realize that many words are quite similar in both languages, e.g. [**tréno**] *train* or [**taksí**] *taxi*. Some of them are of course new, e.g. [**plío**] *ship*. Let's go over them now:

Μέσα συγκοινωνίας	**[mésa singinonías]**	*Types of transport*
το τρένο	[to tréno]	*train*
το αεροπλάνο	[to aeropláno]	*airplane*
το αυτοκίνητο	[to aftokínito]	*car*
το λεωφορείο	[to leoforío]	*bus*
το ταξί	[to taksí]	*taxi*
η μοτοσυκλέτα	[i motosikléta]	*motorcycle*
το μετρό	[to metró]	*underground*
η βάρκα	[i várka]	*boat*
το πλοίο	[to plío]	*ship*
Χρήσιμες λέξεις για το ταξίδι	**[hrísimes léksis yia to taksíTHi]**	*Useful words when travelling*
ο χάρτης	[o hártis]	*map*

ο πίνακας δρομολογίων	[o pínakas THromoloyíon]	*timetable*
το τελωνείο	[to telonío]	*customs*
οι αποσκευές	[i aposkevés]	*luggage* (pl)
η βαλίτσα	[i valítsa]	*suitcase*
το διαβατήριο	[to THiavatírio]	*passport*

Pronunciation tips

There are still two sounds in the Greek language that have not been mentioned yet, i.e. τζ [tz] and γ [y] or [g]. You have met the sound [tz] in a past unit in the word τζαμαρία [tzamaría] *conservatory/winter garden*. The closest sound to [tz] in English is probably the letter [j] in words like *Jim, jam, join*, or the soft sound [g] in words like *gem* or *gene*. You will be presented with the sound [y] in Unit 14.

'Coral gem' is a travel agency. Can you write 'gem' with Greek letters?

'Tzimas' pastry shop

▶ Διάλογος 1 [THiálogos 1] *Dialogue 1*

Mary and John finally arrive at the travel agency after their shopping spree at the store.

Υπάλληλος	Ναι, παρακαλώ;
John	Θέλουμε μερικές πληροφορίες για την Αίγινα αυτό το Σαββατοκύριακο και για τη Θεσσαλονίκη την άλλη εβδομάδα.
Υπάλληλος	Μάλιστα. Λοιπόν, για την Αίγινα έχει φέρυμποτ ή ιπτάμενα κάθε μέρα, όλη την ημέρα.
John	Πόσο κάνουν τα εισιτήρια;
Υπάλληλος	Μόνο πήγαινε ή και μ'επιστροφή;
John	Και μ'επιστροφή. Το Σάββατο πήγαινε και την Κυριακή έλα.
Υπάλληλος	Άστε με να δω.

[ipálilos]	[ne], [parakaló]?	*Yes, please?*
John	[théloome merikés pliroforíes] [yia tin éyina] [aftó to savatokíriako] [ke yia ti thesaloníki] [tin áli evTHomáTHa].	*We'd like some information about Aegina this weekend and Thessaloniki next week.*
[ipálilos]	[málista]. [lipón], [yia tin éyina] [éhi féribot] [i iptámena] [káthe méra] [óli tin iméra].	*Yes, sure, well, there are ferryboats or flying dolphins to Aegina every day, all day long.*
John	[póso kánoon] [ta isitíria]?	*How much are the tickets?*
[ipálilos]	[móno píyene] [i kai mepistrofí]?	*Just one way* (lit. to go) *or round trip?*
John	[ke mepistrofí]. [to sávato píyene] [ke tin kiriakí] [éla].	*Round trip. Leaving on Saturday and returning on Sunday.*
[ipálilos]	[áste me na THo].	*Let me see.*

πληροφορίες	**[plirofories]**	*information* (f/pl)
Αίγινα	**[éyina]**	*the island of Aegina in the Saronic Gulf* (f)
Σαββατοκύριακο	**[savatokíriako]**	*weekend* (n)
Θεσσαλονίκη	**[thesaloníki]**	*Thessaloniki* (f)
εβδομάδα	**[evTHomáTHa]**	*week* (f)
μάλιστα	**[málista]**	*Yes, sure! Of course!*
λοιπόν	**[lipón]**	*well*
φέρυμποτ	**[féribot]**	*ferryboat* (n)
ιπτάμενα	**[iptámena]**	*flying dolphins, hydrofoils* (n/pl)
κάθε	**[káthe]**	*every*
εισιτήρια	**[isitíria]**	*tickets* (n/pl)
πήγαινε	**[píyene]**	*go* (here: *one way*)
επιστροφή	**[epistrofí]**	*return* (here: *round trip*) (f)
Σάββατο	**[sávato]**	*Saturday* (n)
Κυριακή	**[kiriakí]**	*Sunday* (f)

Notes

- In Greek you can ask for μία πληροφορία [mía pliroforía] *one single piece of information* but also for μερικές πληροφορίες [merikés pliroforíes] *some information*. This noun has a singular and plural form in Greek.
- You might hear the word 'day' as μέρα [méra] or ημέρα [iméra] and the word 'week' as βδομάδα [vTHomáTHa] or εβδομάδα [evTHomáTHa]. Both forms are interchangeable.

- Do not confuse the two translations of the word 'well'. You already know **καλά [kalá]** in phrases like **είμαι πολύ καλά [íme polí kalá]** *I'm very well* and now the new word **λοιπόν [lipón]** found in this dialogue.

▶ Διάλογος 2 [THiálogos 2] *Dialogue 2*

Mary gets some information about Thessaloniki.

Mary	Μπορείτε να μας πείτε και για την Θεσσαλονίκη τώρα;
Υπάλληλος	Αμέ! Πώς θέλετε να πάτε; Με αεροπλάνο, τρένο ή πούλμαν;
Mary	Με αεροπλάνο φυσικά! Κάθε πότε έχει αεροπλάνο; Υπάρχουν συχνές πτήσεις;
Υπάλληλος	Τώρα το καλοκαίρι ναι. Υπάρχει η Ολυμπιακή βεβαια αλλά και η Κρόνος, Μάνος, και Ετζίαν πετούν εκεί. Οι ιδιωτικές εταιρείες είναι πιο φθηνές από την Ολυμπιακή αλλά δεν πετούν τόσο συχνά.
Mary	Ένα λεπτό! Δε καταλαβαίνω τίποτα! Πέστε μου πάλι … πότε φεύγει, πότε φθάνει;

Mary	[boríte na mas píte] [ke yia tin thesaloníki] [tóra]?	*Could you tell us also about Thessaloniki now?*
[ipálilos]	[amé]! [pos thélete na páte]? [me aeropláno], [tréno] [i poólman]?	*Sure! How would you like to go? By plane, train or coach?*
Mary	[me aeropláno fisiká]! [káthe póte éhi aeropláno]? [ipárhoon sihnés ptísis]?	*By plane of course! How often is there a flight* (lit. plane)? *Are there frequent flights?*
[ipálilos]	[tóra to kalokéri] [ne]. [ipárhi i olimbiakí vévea] [alá ke i krónoos], [mános], [ke etzían] [petoón ekí]. [i iTHiotikés eteríes] [íne pio fthinés] [apó tin olimbiakí] [alá THen petoón] [tóso sihná].	*Now during the summer, yes. There is Olympic Airways but also Cronus, Manos, and Aegian fly there. The private companies are cheaper than Olympic Airways but they don't fly so often.*
Mary	[éna leptó]! [THen katalavéno típota]! [péste moo páli] … [póte févyi], [póte ftháni]?	*Just a minute! I don't understand anything! Tell me again… when does it leave, when does it arrive?*

Μπορείτε να μας πείτε;	[boríte na mas píte]?	Can you tell us? (pl/fml)
αμέ!	[amé]!	Sure!
κάθε πότε;	[káthe póte]?	How often?
συχνές	[sihnés]	frequent (f/pl)
πτήσεις	[ptísis]	flights (f/pl)
καλοκαίρι	[kalokéri]	summer (n)
Ολυμπιακή	[olimbiakí]	Olympic Airways (f)
πετούν	[petoón]	they fly
ιδιωτικές	[iTHiotikés]	private (f/pl)
εταιρείες	[eteríes]	companies (f/pl)
φθηνές	[fthinés]	cheap (f/pl)
πιο ... από	[pio ... apó]	more ... than
αλλά	[alá]	but
τόσο	[tóso]	so
συχνά	[sihná]	often
καταλαβαίνω	[katalavéno]	I understand
τίποτα	[típota]	nothing
πέστε μου	[péste moo]	tell me (pl/fml)
πάλι	[páli]	again
φεύγει	[févyi]	it leaves
φθάνει	[ftháni]	it arrives

Notes

- Do not confuse the sounds of the words **φθηνό** [**fthinó**] *cheap* and **φθάνει** [**ftháni**] *it arrives*. They can also be heard as **φτηνό** [**ftinó**] and **φτάνει** [**ftáni**].
- **από** [**apó**] *from* has a second meaning in this dialogue. It can be translated as 'than' when comparing things.
- **κάθε πότε;** [**káthe póte**]? is synonymous with **πόσο συχνά;** [**póso sihná**]? found in the next dialogue. Both mean 'how often?'. Do not confuse the word **πότε;** [**póte**]? *when?* with the word **ποτέ** [**poté**] *never*. Another interesting expression is **πότε-πότε** [**póte**]-[**póte**] meaning 'sometimes' and is synonymous with **μερικές φορές** [**merikés forés**] which you already know.

▶ Διάλογος 3 [ΤΗιálogos 3] *Dialogue 3*

Mary wants to find out how often Olympic Airways flies to Thessaloniki and gets some information about the city.

Mary	Πόσο συχνά πετάει η Ολυμπιακή και πόση ώρα κάνει το ταξίδι;
Υπάλληλος	Η Ολυμπιακή έχει πέντε πτήσεις κάθε μέρα. Το ταξίδι είναι μόνο σαράντα πέντε λεπτά.

Mary	Πώς μπορούμε να πάμε στο κέντρο της πόλης;
Υπάλληλος	Με ταξί ή με λεωφορείο. Είναι περίπου μισή ώρα. Σε ποιό ξενοδοχείο μένετε;
John	Δεν ξέρουμε ακόμα. Μπορούμε να κάνουμε κράτηση μαζί σας;
Υπάλληλος	Ναι, βέβαια. Τώρα αμέσως μπορώ να δω τιμές και διαθεσιμότητα για σας στο κομπιούτερ.
John	Ωραία! Ας δούμε!

Mary	[póso sihná] [petái i olimbiakí] [ke pósi óra] [káni to taksíTHi]?	*How often does Olympic Airways fly and how long is the trip?*
[ipálilos]	[i olimbiakí éhi] [pénde ptísis] [káthe méra]. [to taksíTHi] [íne móno] [saránda pénde leptá].	*Olympic Airways has five flights every day. The trip is only 45 minutes.*
Mary	[pos boroóme na páme] [sto kéndro tis pólis]?	*How can we get to the centre of the city?*
[ipálilos]	[me taksí] [i me leoforío]. [íne perípoo misí óra]. [se pio ksenoTHohío ménete]?	*By taxi or by bus. It's about half an hour. Which hotel are you staying at?*
John	[THen kséroome akóma]. [boroóme na kánoome krátisi] [mazí sas]?	*We don't know yet. Can we make a reservation with you?*
[ipálilos]	[ne vévea]. [tóra amésos] [boró na THo timés] [ke THiathesimótita] [yia sás] [sto kompioóter].	*Yes, of course. I can check prices and availability for you right away on the computer.*
John	[oréa]! [as THoóme]!	*Nice! Let's see!*

πόσο συχνά;	**[póso sihná]?**	*How often?*
πόση ώρα;	**[pósi óra]?**	*How long? (lit. how much time?)*
ταξίδι	**[taksíTHi]**	*trip* (n)
κέντρο	**[kéndro]**	*centre* (n)
περίπου	**[perípoo]**	*about/approximately*
ξενοδοχείο	**[ksenoTHohío]**	*hotel* (n)
ακόμα	**[akóma]**	*still/yet*
κράτηση	**[krátisi]**	*reservation* (f)
αμέσως	**[amésos]**	*immediately*
τιμές	**[timés]**	*prices* (f/pl)

διαθεσιμότητα	[THiathesimótita]	*availability* (f)
για σας	[yia sas]	*for you* (pl/fml)
κομπιούτερ	[kompioóter]	*computer* (n)
Ας δούμε!	[as THoóme]!	*Let's see!*

Notes

• The word **ώρα [óra]** has some interesting and idiomatic uses. In this dialogue, the phrase **πόση ώρα [pósi óra]**? means 'how long?' compared to **τι ώρα είναι; [ti óra íne]**? 'what **time** is it?', and **στις πέντε η ώρα [stis pénde i óra]**. 'at five o'clock'.

• You might have noticed that **με ταξί [me taksí]** *by taxi* and **μεταξύ [metaksí]** *between* sound alike! You are right! Be sure to stress the word **ταξί [taksí]** *taxi* on the last syllable, otherwise you change the meaning to **τάξη [táksi]** which means 'order' or 'classroom'. Other words including **[taksí]** are **ταξίδι [taksíTHi]** *trip* or **ταξιδιωτικό γραφείο [taksiTHiotikó grafío]** *travel agency.*

• The word **[pio]** has two different meanings as stated in the previous unit. Here you see in Dialogue 2 **πιο φθηνές [pio fthinés]** *cheaper (lit.* more *cheap)*, and in Dialogue 3 **Σε ποιο ξενοδοχείο [se pio ksenoTHohío]** *at/in* which *hotel?* **Ποιο;** *which?* has more than one form depending on the gender of the noun it refers to. Also check in the **Grammar summary**.

• **για σας [yia sás]** means 'for you'. Does it sound like **γεια σας [yiá sas]** *hello* to you? You are right. Take notice that the stress and the spelling are different in both expressions. It's best if you can ask a native speaker to demonstrate both to you.

Language rules

1 Σειρά λέξεων στα ελληνικά [sirá lékseon sta eliniká] *Word order in Greek*

Let's start from where we left off in the last unit. As mentioned there, the different word endings make Greek word order more flexible in the sense of what comes first and what can follow. You will often hear the same statement said differently by different speakers because they will start with the part of their statement they would like to emphasize more. Note the examples below:

Είμαι κουρασμένος σήμερα. [íme koorazménos símera] OR
Κουρασμένος σήμερα είμαι. [koorazménos símera íme] OR
Κουρασμένος είμαι σήμερα. [koorazménos íme símera].

All three versions are possible and mean 'I am tired today'. In English, the only other possible word order would be 'Today, I'm tired.' with the Greek equivalent **Σήμερα είμαι κουρασμένος. [símera íme koorazménos]**. In English we put the stress on different words by changing the tone of our voice in order to put more emphasis on a particular part of the sentence. In Greek you are generally allowed to change the word order because the sentence function is shown by the word endings, whereas in English the standard word order is subject-verb-object. A simple but important piece of advice here is for you to keep the word order that you are most familiar with, which most of the time is the most common one in Greek as well. That's easy, isn't it? More notes and explanations will follow in the next unit.

2 Αυτό το Σαββατοκύριακο [aftó to savatokíriako] *This weekend*

It literally means 'this the weekend'. Note 4 in the previous unit provided you with further explanations. The word **Σαββατοκύριακο [savatokíriako]** *weekend* is a combination of the two words **Σάββατο [sávato]** *Saturday* and **Κυριακή [kiriakí]** *Sunday*. Are you ready now for the rest of the days?

Δευτέρα	[THeftéra]	*Monday*
Τρίτη	[tríti]	*Tuesday*
Τετάρτη	[tetárti]	*Wednesday*
Πέμπτη	[pémpti]	*Thursday*
Παρασκευή	[paraskeví]	*Friday*

All days are feminine except Saturday, which is neuter, e.g. **η Δευτέρα [i THeftéra]** but **το Σάββατο [to sávato]**. We therefore use **την [tin]** with the days of the week (except Saturdays) in the following phrases:

> **Πάμε στην Αθήνα <u>την</u> Τρίτη! [páme stin athína <u>tin</u> tríti]!**
> *Let's go to Athens <u>on</u> Tuesday!*
> **Τι κάνεις <u>την</u> Τετάρτη; [ti kánis <u>tin</u> tetárti]?**
> *What are you doing <u>on</u> Wednesday?*

We use **το [to]** only for Saturday and the word for 'weekend':

> **Πάμε στην Πάτρα <u>το</u> Σάββατο! [páme stin pátra <u>to</u> sávato]!**
> *Let's go to Patras <u>on</u> Saturday!*
> **Τι κάνεις <u>το</u> Σαββατοκύριακο; [ti kánis <u>to</u> savatokíriako]?**
> *What are you doing <u>on</u> the weekend?*

The following are also important:

προχθές	[prohthés]	*the day before yesterday*
εχθές	[ehthés]	*yesterday*
σήμερα	[símera]	*today*
αύριο	[ávrio]	*tomorrow*
μεθαύριο	[methávrio]	*the day after tomorrow*

Notes

- For the phrases 'the day before yesterday' and 'the day after tomorrow' Greeks use only two single words προχθές [prohthés] and μεθαύριο [methávrio]. Easy, right?
- You might hear different pronunciations for the word 'yesterday', i.e. [ehthés], [ehtés], [htés] or [hthés]. If possible, try to listen to a native speaker pronouncing those words. Similarly, you may hear [prohthés], [prohtés] or [proktés].

3 Την άλλη εβδομάδα [tin áli evTHomáTHa]
Next week

This literally means 'the other week'. You can substitute the word άλλη [áli] *next* with επόμενη [epómeni] *following*, or προηγούμενη [proigoómeni] *previous*. Some basic words here are:

ημέρα – ημέρες [iméra]–[iméres]	*day – days*
εβδομάδα – εβδομάδες [evTHomáTHa] – [evTHomáTHes]	*week – weeks*
μήνας – μήνες [mínas]–[mínes]	*month – months*
χρόνος – χρόνια [hrónos]–[hrónia]	*year – years*

Below is a list of the four seasons τέσσερις εποχές [téseris epohés] with their corresponding months μήνες [mínes]. Come back to this list whenever necessary.

Ο ΧΕΙΜΩΝΑΣ [o himónas] *Winter*	Η ΑΝΟΙΞΗ [i ániksi] *Spring*	ΤΟ ΚΑΛΟΚΑΙΡΙ [to kalokéri] *Summer*	ΤΟ ΦΘΙΝΟΠΩΡΟ [to fthinóporo] *Autumn*
Δεκέμβριος [THekémvrios]	Μάρτιος [mártios]	Ιούνιος [ioónios]	Σεπτέμβριος [septémvrios]

Ιανουάριος	Απρίλιος	Ιούλιος	Οκτώβριος
[ianooários]	[aprílios]	[ioólios]	[októvrios]
Φεβρουάριος	Μάϊος	Αύγουστος	Νοέμβριος
[fevrooários]	[máios]	[ávgoostos]	[noémvrios]

Not in written but in spoken Greek you may hear different versions of the months. Note: [THekémvris], [yenáris], [flevráris], [mártis], [aprílis], [máis], [ioónis], [ioólis], [ávgoostos], [septémvris], [októvris], [noémvris].

English translations were not included for the names of the months. We believe you won't make any mistakes as the sounds are quite familiar, aren't they?

We use τον [ton] with the names of the months because they are all masculine gender.

What is the name of this store?

Note that the final [s] is dropped as they are in the accusative case when used in a phrase with [ton].

Πάμε στην Αθήνα τον Μάρτιο! [páme stin athína ton mártio]!
Let's go to Athens in March!

Τι κάνεις τον Απρίλιο; [ti kánis ton aprílio]?
What are you doing in April?

It's a little bit more challenging with the names for the four seasons as they have different genders: **το χειμώνα** [to himóna] *in the winter*, **την άνοιξη** [tin ániksi] *in the spring*, **το καλοκαίρι** [to kalokéri] *in the summer*, and **το φθινόπωρο** [to fthinóporo] *in autumn*.

4 Δεν καταλαβαίνω τίποτα! [THen katalavéno típota]! *I don't understand a thing!*

Τίποτα [típota] usually means 'nothing' in statements and 'anything' in questions. Look at the examples:

Δε θέλω τίποτα. [THe thélo típota]. *I want nothing.**

Θέλεις τίποτα; [thélis tipota]? *Do you want anything?*

*Double negation is possible in Greek! Δε θέλω τίποτα [THe thélo típota] literally means 'I don't want nothing'!

The word καταλαβαίνω [katalavéno] *I understand* is important as it helps you to tell someone that you don't understand. Some useful phrases in this context are:

Δεν καταλαβαίνω τίποτα! [THen katalavéno típota]!
I don't understand anything!
Καταλαβαίνω πολύ λίγο! [katalavéno polí lígo]!
I understand very little!
Μίλα πιο σιγά! [míla pio sigá]! or Μιλήστε πιο σιγά!
[milíste pio sigá]! *Speak slower!* (infml + fml)
Μιλάς γρήγορα! [milás grígora]! or Μιλάτε γρήγορα!
[miláte grígora]! *You speak fast!* (infml + fml)
Πες το ξανά! [pésto ksaná]! or Πέστε το ξανά! [pésteto ksaná]!
Say it again! (infml + fml)
Τι εννοείς; [ti enoís]? or Τι εννοείτε; [ti enoíte]?
What do you mean? (infml + fml)
Τι; [ti]? *What?* (infml)
Πώς; [pos]? *How?*
Ορίστε; [oríste]? *What?* (fml) / *What did you say? / I beg your pardon?*

Remember the word ορίστε [oríste] can have three meanings: Ορίστε! [oríste]! *Here it is!*, Ορίστε; [oríste]? *What did you say?*, and when answering the phone Ορίστε; [oríste]? *Hello?*

ⓘ Λεωφορείο, ταξί και αεροπλάνο [leoforío], [taksí], [ke aeropláno] *Bus, taxi and aeroplane*

You will probably arrive by plane either in Athens or directly on an island, if that is your destination. In popular tourist spots flights arrive and depart at all hours even late at night or very early in the morning all through the summer. Private airlines have taken over some of the monopoly of the Greek airline Olympic Airways and several destinations are provided with even more flights nowadays. From the airport you can either take a taxi or a bus to your hotel, the centre of town or a destination out of town.

When taking a taxi enquire in advance (**Πόσο κάνει για...; [póso káni yia]... ?** *How much is it to ...?*) about the approximate amount to be charged and make sure that the taxi meter is turned on – a travel tip that is valid in all travel destinations around the world. Do not be surprised if the driver picks up other passengers to share the ride with you, provided of course that there is enough space. You won't share the cost of the journey though. Unfortunately, this is a very common practice, especially in Athens.

The public bus company KTEL runs buses within the town or through towns and villages. Tickets are purchased at kiosks close to bus stops or stations and need to be validated on the bus. Exceptions are buses that run on islands. Here you have conductors on the bus that sell and validate tickets. Be prepared for crowding at busy times. Remember that the concept of personal space is not the same in Greece as it is in England or America.

Time in the Greek context

Even though things have changed and Greeks no longer have ample free time to spend, the concept of time itself is somewhat different in Greece. Especially in the summer, when temperatures are high, everything naturally slows down. When making appointments or checking timetables you need to know that they are not necessarily kept to the minute, so give yourself ample time when travelling in order not to miss any ship or plane. When meeting Greek friends for dinner remember that an evening out in Greece starts around 9 p.m. at the earliest, so you might actually start eating at 10 p.m.! Sit back, slow down, relax, and enjoy your vacation!

Practice makes perfect

1 **Below is a list of basic time phrases. Can you say them in Greek? Some new words are: δεκαπενθήμερο [THeka-penthímero]** *fortnight,* **αιώνας [eónas]** *century* **(nom. case) and αιώνα [eóna]** *century* **(acc. case). The first one has been done for you.**

There are: υπάρχουν [ipárhoon]:

365 days in a year   **a**   365 ([triakósies eksínda pénde]) [iméres se éna hróno].

12 months in a year   **b** _____

52 weeks in a year   **c** _____

7 days in a week   **d** _____

2 weeks in a fortnight   **e** _____

24 hours in a day   **f** _____

60 minutes in an hour   **g** _____

100 years in a century   **h** _____

2 You look at a Greek calendar to check when you will be able to meet your friend. On Monday, Wednesday and Thursday you are not available. (a) What dates are those days? (b) Can you tell her the days you can meet?

Κυριακή 21.5.2000	Πέμπτη 25.5.2000
Δευτέρα 22.5.2000	Παρασκευή 26.5.2000
Τρίτη 23.5.2000	Σάββατο 27.5.2000
Τετάρτη 24.5.2000	Κυριακή 28.5.2000

3 Five days are listed below. Four names have been erased. (a) Can you write them back in? (b) The word σήμερα [símera] has lost its related words (yesterday, the day before yesterday, etc.)! Can you rectify that, too?

Tip: You can use transliteration or Greek script. It's up to you now!

8	9	10	11	12
		Τετάρτη [tetárti]		
		σήμερα [símera]		

4 Can you match the illustrations below with the names of the four seasons?

a ΧΕΙΜΩΝΑΣ [himónas]   c ΚΑΛΟΚΑΙΡΙ [kalokéri]
b ΑΝΟΙΞΗ [ániksi]   d ΦΘΙΝΟΠΩΡΟ [fthinóporo]

i  ii iii iv

5 Can you match the six illustrations with the sentences below? You can cover the transliteration and work with the Greek script alone.

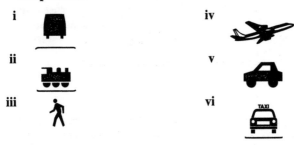

i
ii
iii

iv
v
vi

a [poté THen páo sti THooliá me to aeropláno]!
  Ποτέ δεν πάω στη δουλειά με το αεροπλάνο!
b [marési na pérno to tréno sihná].
  Μ'αρέσει να παίρνω το τρένο συχνά.
c [polés forés to taksí THen íne éfkolo stin athína].
  Πολλές φορές το ταξί δεν είναι εύκολο στην Αθήνα.
d [ipárhoon siníthos polá aftokínita stin yitoniá mas].
  Υπάρχουν συνήθως πολλά αυτοκίνητα στην γειτονιά μας.
e [merikés forés páo me ta pόTHia sto sholío].
  Μερικές φορές πάω με τα πόδια στο σχολείο.
f [sheTHόn poté THen pérno to leoforío].
  Σχεδόν ποτέ δεν παίρνω το λεωφορείο.

6 Can you translate the sentences from Exercise 5 into English?

7 You have now become more familiar with Greek letters. Look at the two advertisements below and try to make out their messages.

Κυρίες και κύριοι οι...
«PET SHOP BOYS»
Τετάρτη 28 και Πέμπτη 29 Ιουνίου
στο Θέατρο Λυκαβητού

Κάθε πρωί **στις**
7:00

▶ 8 A travel agent is telling you about the days of some flights to ΡΟΔΟΣ [róTHos] *Rhodes*, ΣΑΝΤΟΡΙΝΗ [santoríni] *Santorini* and ΗΡΑΚΛΕΙΟ [iráklio] *Iraklio*. Listen to the recording and tick the correct days for each destination.

	ΔΕΥΤΕΡΑ	ΤΡΙΤΗ	ΤΕΤΑΡΤΗ	ΠΕΜΠΤΗ	ΠΑΡΑΣΚΕΥΗ	ΣΑΒΒΑΤΟ
ΡΟΔΟΣ						
ΣΑΝΤΟΡΙΝΗ						
ΗΡΑΚΛΕΙΟ						

9 Complete the dialogue using the information in italics.

[ipálilos]	[parakaló]! [ti thélete]?
You	**a** *I'd like some information please. Are there any boats to Aegina?*
[ipálilos]	[fisiká]. [ipárhoon féribot] [ke iptámena THelfínia].
You	**b** *Which is faster? And which is cheaper?*
[ipálilos]]	[ta féribot] [íne pio ftiná] [ke ta THelfínia pio grígora].

You	c When does the next flying dolphin leave?
[ipálilos]	[se mía óra].
You	d How much is it?
[ipálilos]	[apló] [i mepistrofí]?
You	e Round trip for me.

▶ 10 **Listen again to Dialogue 3 of this unit and fill in the blanks. If you don't have the recordings, choose the missing words from the box below. One word is used twice.**

Mary	[póso sihná] a _____ [i olimbiakí]? [ke pósi óra] [káni to] b _____?
[ipálilos]	[i olimbiakí éhi] [pénde] c _____ [káthe méra]. [to] b _____ [íne móno] [saránda pénde leptá].
Mary	[pos boroóme na páme] [sto] d _____ [tis pólis]?
[ipálilos]	[me taksí] [i me] e _____ [íne perípou misí óra]. [se pio ksenoTHohío ménete]?
John	[THen kséroome] f _____. [boroóme na kánoome] g _____ [ksenoTHohíoo] [mazí sas]?
[ipálilos]	[ne vévea]. [tóra] h _____ [boró na THo timés] [ke THiathesimótita] [yia sás] [sto kompioóter].
John	[oréa]! i _____!

[kéndro]	[petái]	[krátisi]	[akóma]	[ptísis]	[taksíTHi]
	[amésos]	[leoforío]	[as THoóme]		

Mini test

a Can you name seven different types of transport?

b You want to go to a travel agency. How do you ask for directions?

c What are the words for 'single ticket' and 'return ticket'?

d What are the words for 'reservation', 'seat', and 'information' in Greek?

e The questions 'What time does it leave/come/arrive?' are very important. Do you remember them?

f You see the following sign: **ΠΛΗΡΟΦΟΡΙΕΣ**. What does it mean?

g Name five useful travel words.

Εντάξει; [endáksi]? Γεια σου τώρα! [yiásoo tóra]!

κράτηση
ξενοδοχείου
hotel reservation

In this unit you will learn
- how to enquire about rooms
- how to make hotel reservations
- how to talk about hotel facilities
- some hotel signs and notices

Before you start

- How is your revision coming along? You should revise Unit 7 now before you start this unit. Are you following some of the learning tips provided for you in previous units? Don't forget that what matters here is what works best for you. It's good if you have put some colour in your book. It's also good if you have bought and used some index cards. It's probably ideal if you spend a considerable amount of your time listening to the recordings and becoming more familiar with Greek signs and notices.

- We have also suggested the creation of word lists of personal interest. Of course these lists can be considerably different from learner to learner but personalizing your learning will make all the difference and it will be more fun. Remember that what finally matters is enjoying your learning and achieving some rewarding results while you practise Greek.

- Also remember that this book puts more emphasis on listening and speaking skills than on writing and reading skills. So, if you are able to understand and speak basic Greek and are familiar with some public signs and notices, your goals have been successfully achieved.

Take a short break now, revise Unit 7 and then come back here to start this unit. [tha se THo se lígo]!

Key words and phrases

It's best to book your accommodation before you arrive in Greece. Some options include staying in a ξενοδοχείο [ksenoTHohío] *hotel*, πανσιόν [pansión] *small hotel*, or δωμάτιο [THomátio] *(privately let) room*.

Here are some typical questions:

Μήπως έχετε δωμάτιο/δωμάτια; [mípos éhete THomátio/THomátia]?
   Do you have a room/any rooms?
Τι δωμάτιο θέλετε; [ti THomátio thélete]?
   What kind of room do you want?
Για πόσο καιρό; [yia póso keró]? *For how long?*
Για πόσες μέρες; [yia póses méres]? *For how many days?*
Πόσο καιρό θα μείνετε; [póso keró tha mínete]?
   How long will you stay?
Μπορείτε να συμπληρώσετε αυτό το έντυπο; [boríte na simblirósete aftó to éndipo]? *Can you fill in this form?*

Here are some typical answers:

Θέλω ένα μονόκλινο/δίκλινο/τρίκλινο. [thélo] [éna monóklino] / [THíklino] / [tríklino]. *I would like a single room/double room/ triple room.*

Για μία μέρα/τρεις/τέσσερις/έξι μέρες. [yia mía méra] / [tris]/[téseris]/[éksi] [méres]. *For one day/ three/four/six days.*

Καλή διαμονή! [kalí THiamoní]! Καλή παραμονή! [kali paramoní! *Have a nice stay!*

Λυπάμαι/δυστυχώς είμαστε γεμάτοι. [lipáme] / [THistihós] [ímaste yemáti]. *I'm sorry / unfortunately we are fully booked.*

The illustration below has some important items associated with hotels:

Masculine nouns

Χώρος υποδοχής	[hóros ipoTHohís]	*reception area*
λογαριασμός	[logariazmós]	*bill*
όροφος	[órofos]	*floor*

Feminine nouns

| ρεσεψιόν | [resepsión] | *reception desk* |
| βαλίτσα | [valítsa] | *suitcase* |

αποσκευή	[aposkeví]	(piece of) luggage
τηλεόραση	[tileórasi]	TV
χύτρα	[hítra]	kettle

Neuter nouns

κλειδί	[kliTHí]	key
ασανσέρ	[asansér]	lift/elevator
έντυπο	[éndipo]	form
ντους	[dooz]	shower
μπάνιο	[bánio]	bathroom
πιστολάκι μαλλιών	[pistoláki malión]	hair-dryer

Some important signs and notices you might find are:

Στο ασανσέρ [sto asansér] *In the lift/elevator*

3ος ΟΡΟΦΟΣ	[trítos órofos]	3rd floor
2ος ΟΡΟΦΟΣ	[THéfteros órofos]	2nd floor
1ος ΟΡΟΦΟΣ	[prótos órofos]	1st floor
ΗΜΙ: ΗΜΙΟΡΟΦΟΣ	[imiórofos]	Mezzanine
ΙΣ: ΙΣΟΓΕΙΟΝ	[isóyion]	Ground Floor
ΥΠ: ΥΠΟΓΕΙΟΝ	[ipóyion]	Basement

Στην πόρτα [stin pórta] *On the door*

| ΩΘΗΣΑΤΕ | [othísate] | Push |
| ΕΛΞΑΤΕ | [élksate] | Pull |

Στο δρόμο [sto THrómo] *In the street*

Look out for the sign **ΕΝΟΙΚΙΑΖΟΝΤΑΙ ΔΩΜΑΤΙΑ [eni-kiázonde THomátia]** *Rooms to let/for rent*. You might be able to see the room and haggle over the price!

Pronunciation tips

The Greek language has 25 different sounds. Believe it or not you have been introduced to all of them except **[y]** or soft **[g]** so far. As you were reminded in previous units, most sounds are more or less similar to English sounds. Some examples include **[k]**, **[l]**, **[m]** which are not difficult to reproduce, or **[h]** and **[r]** which are a little softer in English. You were also reminded to refer directly to the **Pronunciation guide** at the beginning of the book. In every **Pronunciation tips** section you also had authentic visuals with the sounds in question so you could start making associations between sound, spelling and pronunciation. You could also check the section of the **Greek alphabet** at the back of the book to see further examples and associations with the sounds presented in each unit.

Some of you might have put less effort into these sections, but paid more attention to the recordings or native speakers. Do not forget that by nature some of us are more visual learners and some of us more auditory learners. Some of us need detailed explanations and some of us are happy with a short answer and want to move on. This is why individual learning takes many different forms.

Let's go back to our sounds! The Greek letter γ can produce two different sounds: [y] approximately as in 'yield' and [y] as in 'yes'. If possible, you should listen to the recordings or Greek speakers to detect the fine nuances of these two sounds.

Would you like to take a short break now before you move on to the dialogues?

▶ Διάλογος 1 [THiálogos 1] *Dialogue 1*

John and Mary choose a hotel.

Υπάλληλος	Υπάρχει το Μακεδονία Παλλάς, το Βεργίνα, ή και το Καψής. Για πόσες μέρες το θέλετε;
John	Για δύο μέρες. Πιθανώς στο κέντρο της πόλης με θέα τη θάλασσα.
Υπάλληλος	Αυτό είναι εύκολο, αλλά το ξέρουμε την ημέρα που γίνεται η κράτηση.
Mary	Θέλουμε να κάνουμε την κράτηση από τώρα μαζί σας. John, εσύ τι λες;
John	Ναι, ναι. Συμφωνώ.
Υπάλληλος	Ωραία. Σας ενδιαφέρει;

[ipálilos]	[ipárhi] [to makeTHonía palás], [to veryína] [i ke to kapsís]. [yia póses méres] [to thélete]?	*There is the Macedonian Palace, the Vergina or even the Capsis. For how many days would you like it* (i.e. the hotel)?
John	[yia THío méres]. [pithanós] [sto kéndro tis pólis] [me théa ti thálasa].	*For two days. Probably in the city centre with a view of the sea.*
[ipálilos]	[aftó íne éfkolo], [alá to kséroome] [tin iméra] [poo yínete i krátisi].	*That's easy, but we know it on the day* (lit. we won't know until) *when we make the reservation* (lit. when the reservation takes place).

Mary	[théloome] [na kánoome] [tin krátisi] [apó tóra] [mazí sas]. John, [esí ti les]?	*We'd like* (lit. we want) *to make the reservation with you now. John, what do you think* (lit. say)*?*
John	[ne], [ne]. [simfonó].	*Yes, of course. I agree.*
[ipálilos]	[oréa]. [sas enTHiaféri]?	*Fine. Are you interested?*

για πόσες μέρες;	**[yia póses méres]?**	*For how many days? For how long?*
πιθανώς	**[pithanós]**	*likely, probably*
θέα	**[théa]**	*view* (f)
γίνεται	**[yínete]**	*it takes place / it happens*
τι λες;	**[ti les]?**	*What do you think* (lit. say)*?* (sing/infml)
δίκλινο	**[THíklino]**	*double room* (n)
ξεκινούν	**[ksekinoón]**	*they start*
Σας ενδιαφέρει;	**[sas enTHiaféri]?**	*Are you interested?* (lit. Does it interest you?) (pl/fml)

Notes

- Σας ενδιαφέρει; [sas enTHiaféri]? *Are you interested?* is related to ενδιαφέρον [enTHiaféron] *interesting* found in a previous unit, remember? Με ενδιαφέρει [me enTHiaféri] *I am interested* has an alternative form ενδιαφέρομαι [enTHiaférome] also meaning 'I am interested'. The full forms of με ενδιαφέρει [me enTHiaféri] follow the forms of the verb με λένε [me léne] in Unit 5 and the full forms of ενδιαφέρομαι [enTHiaférome] follow the forms of the verb κάθομαι [káthome] in Unit 9. Similar to μ'αρέσει – μ'αρέσουν [marési] – [marésoon], μ'ενδιαφέρει [menTHiaféri] means 'I am interested in one thing/person' and μ'ενδιαφέρουν [menTHiaféroon] 'I am interested in many things/people'.

- και [ke] has been found with more than one meaning so far. Apart from *and* it also means ή και [i ke] *or even* in this dialogue. Sometimes it is translated as *too* και η Μαρία [ke i maría] *Maria, too* or 'both' και ο Γιάννης και η Μαρία [ke o yiánis ke i maría] *both John and Mary*. Also, in the next dialogue you will find και τα τρία ξενοδοχεία [ke ta tría ksenoTHohía] *all three hotels* translating και [ke] as *all*. When telling the time it can be translated as *past*: Μια και πέντε [mía ke pénde] *five past one*.

- **δύσκολο [THískolo]** *difficult* is the opposite of **εύκολο [éfkolo]** *easy*. If you cannot do something **τώρα [tóra]** *now* you can say **σε λίγο [se lígo]** *in a little while*.
- **Τι λες; [ti les]?** (sing/infml) and **Τι λέτε; [ti léte]?** (pl/fml) *What do you think?* (lit. what do you say?) are important phrases. **Συμφωνείς; [simfonís]?**

▶ Διάλογος 2 [THiálogos 2] *Dialogue 2*

The travel agent describes the hotel facilities and services.

Υπάλληλος	Όλα τα δώματια έχουν μπάνιο ή ντους και κεντρική θέρμανση με air condition παντού το καλοκαίρι. Υπάρχουν μονόκλινα, δίκλινα και τρίκλινα με τηλέφωνο και τηλεόραση. Επίσης υπάρχει καφετέρια, εστιατόριο και πάρκιν.
Mary	Έχετε κανένα προσπέκτους, κανένα φυλλάδιο;
Υπάλληλος	Ναι, φυσικά. Εδώ μπορείτε να δείτε και τα τρία ξενοδοχεία.
Mary	Πώς μπορούμε να κάνουμε κράτηση;
Υπάλληλος	Με πιστωτική κάρτα ή μία μικρή προκαταβολή.

[ipálilos]	[óla ta THomátia] [éhoon bánio i dooz] [ke kendrikí thérmansi] [me er kondísion pandoó to kalokéri]. [ipárhoon monóklina], [THíklina] [ke tríklina] [me tiléfono ke tileórasi]. [epísis ipárhi kafetéria], [estiatório ke párkin].	*All rooms have a bath or shower and central heating with air conditioning everywhere in the summer. There are single rooms, double rooms and triple rooms with a telephone and television. There is also a coffee shop, a restaurant and a car park.*
Mary	[éhete kanéna prospéktoos], [kanéna filáTHio]?	*Have you got any prospectus, any booklet?*
[ipálilos]	[ne], [fisiká]. [eTHó boríte na THíte] [ke ta tría ksenoTHohía].	*Yes, of course. Here you can see all three hotels.*
Mary	[pos boroóme na kánoome krátisi]?	*How can we make a reservation?*
[ipálilos]	[me pistotikí kárta] [i mía mikrí prokatavolí].	*With a credit card or a small deposit.*

κεντρική	[kendrikí]	*central*
θέρμανση	[thérmansi]	*heating* (f)
air condition		Greek way of saying *air conditioning*
παντού	[pandoó]	*everywhere*
μονόκλινα	[monóklina]	*single rooms* (n/pl)
δίκλινα	[THíklina]	*double rooms* (n/pl)
τρίκλινα	[tríklina]	*triple rooms* (n/pl)
προσπέκτους	[prospéktoos]	*prospectus* (n)
φυλλάδιο	[filáTHio]	*booklet* (n)
πιστωτική κάρτα	[pistotikí kárta]	*credit card* (f)
προκαταβολή	[prokatavolí]	*deposit, down payment* (f)

Notes

- [er kondísion], τηλέφωνο [tiléfono], καφετέρια [kafetéria], πάρκιν [párkin], προσπέκτους [prospéktoos], and κάρτα [kárta] are words which are similar in English. That means that they are easy to remember.

- παντού [pandoó] means 'everywhere'. Πουθενά [poothená] is 'nowhere' and κάπου [kápoo] is 'somewhere'. Κάπου-κάπου [kápoo-kápoo] is an idiomatic expression meaning 'sometimes' which is a synonymous with μερικές φορές [merikés forés] or the idiomatic πότε-πότε [póte-póte].

- 'Air condition' is the Greek way of saying 'air conditioning'. Κεντρική θέρμανση [kendrikí thérmansi] *central heating* can be substituted with κεντρικός κλιματισμός [kendrikós klimatismós] meaning 'central air conditioning'. Κλίμα [klíma] stands for 'climate' in Greek.

▶ Διάλογος 3 [THiálogos 3] *Dialogue 3*

They decide to go ahead with the hotel reservation.

Mary	Θέλουμε να κάνουμε μία κράτηση στο Καψής.
Υπάλληλος	Ωραία. Μία κράτηση για δύο μέρες στο Καψής. Τι ημερομηνία είναι το πρώτο βράδυ;
Mary	Έντεκα του μήνα, ημέρα Τετάρτη.
Υπάλληλος	Να δω. Ναι, δε βλέπω πρόβλημα αυτή την ημερομηνία. Ένα λεπτό να κάνω την κράτηση. Έντεκα Ιουνίου, για δύο μέρες, με θέα τη θάλασσα.
Mary	Ακριβώς. Κανένα πρόβλημα!
Mary	[théloome] [na kánoome]	*We want to make a*

[ipálilos]	[mía krátisi] [sto kapsís].	reservation at the Capsis.
[ipálilos]	[oréa]. [mía krátisi] [yia THío méres] [sto kapsís]. [ti imerominía] [íne to próto vráTHi]?	Good. A reservation for two days at the Capsis. What date is the first night?
Mary	[éndeka too mína], [iméra tetárti].	On the 11th of the month, Wednesday.
[ipálilos]	[na THo]. [ne], [THe vlépo próvlima] [aftí tin imerominía]. [éna leptó] [na káno tin krátisi]. [éndeka iooníoo] [yia THío méres] [me théa ti thálasa].	Let me see. Yes, I don't see any problem on this date. Just a minute so I can make the reservation. June 11th for two days with a sea view.
Mary	[akrivós]. [kanéna próvlima]!	Exactly. No problem!

ημερομηνία	[imerominía]	date (f)
πρόβλημα	[próvlima]	problem (n)
ακριβώς	[akrivós]	exactly
κανένα πρόβλημα!	[kanéna próvlima]!	No problem!

Note

κανένα [kanéna] is an important word. Although the easiest translation is usually 'no' as in κανένα πρόβλημα [kanéna próvlima] no problem, if you look up the word in the dictionary, you will find several different translations according to context and use. Κανένα [kanéna] is the word for the neuter gender, κανείς [kanís] or κανένας [kanénas] are the words for the masculine gender and καμία [kamía] for the feminine gender.

Language rules

1 Σειρά λέξεων [sirá léxeon] Word order

At the end of some units you are greeted with the phrase Θα σε δω στην επόμενη ενότητα [tha se THo stin epómeni enótita] I'll see you in the next unit. Σε [se] means 'you' and comes before the verb in Greek. This is a small 'anomaly' if you consider that the rest of the words follow the same word order in both languages.

Another difference in the word order can be detected with the order of adjectives, which in Greek can actually come before or after the noun they modify. Again, this is something not possible in English. Note the examples: [éna spíti mikró] or [éna mikró spíti] both meaning 'a small house', [**mía ómorfi yinéka**] or [**mía yinéka ómorfi**] both meaning 'a beautiful woman', or [**éna éfkolo taxíTHi**] or [**éna taxíTHi éfkolo**] both meaning 'an easy trip'. The second options are not as common but still possible.

2 Σας ενδιαφέρει; [sas enTHiaféri]? *Are you interested?*

Did you read the notes about this at the end of Dialogue 1? [**enTHiaféron**]? [**me enTHiaféri**], [**me enTHiaféroon**], and [**enTHiaférome**] can all be used to express interest. Let's see the full forms of all three verbs below:

με/σε/τον/την/το/μας/σας/τους/τις/τα ενδιαφέρει
[me]/[se]/[ton]/[tin]/[to]/[mas]/[sas]/[toos]/[tis]/[ta] [enTHiaféri]
it interests me/you/her/it/us/you/them

με/σε/τον/την/το/μας/σας/τους/τις/τα ενδιαφέρουν
[me]/[se]/[ton]/[tin]/[to]/[mas]/[sas]/[toos]/[tis]/[ta]
[enTHiaféroon]
they interest me/you/him/her/it/us/you/them.

BUT

ενδιαφέρο**μαι**	[enTHiafér**ome**]	*I am interested*
ενδιαφέρ**εσαι**	[enTHiafér**ese**]	*you are interested*
ενδιαφέρ**εται**	[enTHiafér**ete**]	*he/she/it is interested*
ενδιαφερ**όμαστε**	[enTHiafer**ómaste**]	*we are interested*
ενδιαφέρ**εστε**	[enTHiafér**este**]	*you are interested*
ενδιαφέρ**ονται**	[enTHiafér**onde**]	*they are interested*

Note some examples below:

Σας ενδιαφέρει το σινεμά; [sas enTHiaféri to sinemá]?
Are you interested in the cinema?
Σας ενδιαφέρουν το σινεμά και το θέατρο; [sas
enTHiaféroon to sinemá ke to théatro]? *Are you interested in
the cinema and the theatre?*
Ενδιαφέρεστε για το σινεμά; [enTHiaféreste yia to sinemá]?
Are you interested in the cinema?
Ενδιαφέρον, αλλά δεν ενδιαφέρομαι! [enTHiaféron],
[alá THen enTHiaférome]! *Interesting, but I am not interested!*
Σε ενδιαφέρει η Μαρία; [se enTHiaféri i maría]?
Are you interested in Mary?

3 Πόσες μέρες; [póses méres]? *How many days? How long?*

You probably remember **Πόσο κάνει; [póso káni]?** *How much is it?* **Πόσο κάνουν; [póso kánoon]?** *How much are they?*, or **Πόσο χρονών είσαι; [póso hronón íse]?** *How old are you?* It's best if you remember these words in context. Note some other examples:

> **Πόσο καιρό; [póso keró]?** *How long?* in **Πόσο καιρό κάνει το τρένο; [póso keró káni to tréno]?**
> *How long does the train take?*

> **Πόσο μακριά/κοντά; [póso makriá]/[kondá]?**
> *How far/close?* in **Πόσο μακριά/κοντά είναι το ξενοδοχείο; [póso makriá]/[kondá] [íne to ksenoTHohío]?**
> *How far/close is the hotel?*

ℹ Accommodation in Greece

The National Tourist Organization of Greece (NTOG) or **Ελληνικός Οργανισμός Τουρισμού (ΕΟΤ) [elinikós organizmós toorizmoó]**, spoken as **[eót]**, is probably your best source of information about accommodation in Greece if you have not booked a room before your arrival. It has several offices all over Greece in larger cities and tourist resorts, so please ask for the office closest to you. Many tourist guide books list a number of types of accommodation and they are frequently updated for accurate information. Local travel agencies will try to book a place for you but remember that they live on commission so prices can be a little higher.

Official prices are controlled by the NTOG and should always be displayed in the room showing all charges including taxes. Unless you are travelling with an organized tour, you will be required to leave your **διαβατήριο [THiavatírio]** *passport* with the reception desk or hotel owner. This is done in order to officially register your stay at the specific hotel with the local authorities and tax office. Once this is done, your papers will promptly be returned to you.

You can also stay at an organized camping site or rent a whole house for the summer but prior arrangements and bookings need to be made. Sleeping on the beach is prohibited, although you will see many sleeping bags during high season in popular destinations. Once again, try to make arrangements before your arrival. It will make all the difference in saving time, money and energy.

Practice makes perfect

1 A travel agent gave you a brochure of some travel services he provides. Can you match the jumbled English list below with the services in the brochure?

Ταξιδιωτικές Υπηρεσίες

i Αεροπορικά Εισιτήρια για Ελλάδα και Εξωτερικό

ii Ακτοπλοϊκά Εισιτήρια για τα νησιά

iii Κρατήσεις Ξενοδοχείων στην Ελλάδα

iv Εισιτήρια Τραίνων και Λεωφορείων

---

a Train and bus services

b Boat tickets

c Plane tickets

d Hotel accommodation

2 Look at the table below and listen to a receptionist telling you what facilities the rooms have. Tick the appropriate boxes for all three rooms.

	a	b	c	d	e	f	g	h
i ΔΩΜΑΤΙΟ 105								
ii ΔΩΜΑΤΙΟ 207								
iii ΔΩΜΑΤΙΟ 309								

3 You are booking a hotel room by phone. The receptionist asks 'Για πόσες μέρες;' or 'Για πόσο καιρό;' Tell him:

a one day
b three days
c four days

d six days
e one week
f a fortnight

▶ **4** You are calling the receptionist to complain about some things missing from or not working in your bathroom. Can you listen to the recording and tick all the items in question? Some new words have been translated for you.

New vocabulary: **το σαπούνι [to sapoóni]** *soap*, **το σαμπουάν [to sampooán]** *shampoo*, **η οδοντόβουρτσα [i oTHondóvoortsa]** *toothbrush*, **η οδοντόπαστα [i oTHondópasta]** *toothpaste*, **ο νιπτήρας [o niptíras]** *hand basin*, **η πετσέτα [i petséta]** *towel*

▶ **5** You are listening to Αγγελική [angelikí], Δέσποινα [THéspina] and Κώστας [kóstas] making reservations for their next summer vacation. Listen and tick the different types of rooms they are interested in.

	a μονόκλινο [monóklino]	b δίκλινο [THíklino]	c μπάνιο [bánio]	d ντους [dooz]	e θέα [théa]
i Αγγελική					
ii Δέσποινα					
iii Κώστας					

6 Complete the following dialogue using the information in italics.

Receptionist	[parakaló]! [boró na sas voithíso]?
You	**a** *Yes! Do you perhaps have any rooms?*
Receptionist	[ne]. [ti THomátio thélete]?
You	**b** *A double with a bathroom.*
Receptionist	[THistihós], [éhoome móno me dooz].
You	**c** *Can I see it? … Okay, I'll take it.*
Receptionist	[to THiavatírio sas parakaló].
You	**d** *Here it is. Where is the lift/elevator?*

7 You see some signs and notices around you. Can you match them with the English translations?

a ΗΜΙΟΡΟΦΟΣ   **i** Ground floor

b ΕΝΟΙΚΙΑΖΟΝΤΑΙ ΔΩΜΑΤΙΑ   **ii** Basement

c ΥΠΟΓΕΙΟΝ   **iii** Pull

d ΙΣΟΓΕΙΟΝ   ΩΘΗΣΑΤΕ   **iv** Mezzanine

e   **v** Push

f ΕΛΞΑΤΕ   **vi** Rooms to let

8 Monsterwords! Greeks speak fast, but not that fast! Can you separate the words in the following sentences and then translate them into English?

a [THistihósímasteyemáti]!   Δυστυχώςείμαστεγεμάτοι!

b [kalíTHiamoní]!   Καλήδιαμονή!

c [pósokeróthamínete]?   Πόσοκαιρόθαμείνετε;

d [yiaéksiméresimíaevTHomáTHa]?   Γιαέξιμέρεςήμιαεβδομάδα;

e [borítenasimplilóseteaftótoéndipo]?   Μπορείτενασυμπλη-
                                          ρώσετεαυτότοέντυπο;

f [theloómeénaTHíklinoparakaló].   Θέλουμεέναδίκλινο-
                                          παρακαλώ.

▶ **9 Listen again to Dialogue 3 of this unit and fill in the blanks. If you don't have the recordings, choose the missing words from the box below. Two words are used twice and one word is used three times!**

Mary	**a** _____ [na kánoome] [mía] **b** _____ [sto kapsís].
[ipálilos]	[oréa]. [mía] **b**_____ [yia THío méres] [sto kapsís], [ti] **c** _____ [íne to próto vráTHi]?
Mary	[stis éndeka too mína], [iméra] **d** _____.

[ipálilos] [na THo]. [ne], [THe vlépo] **e** _____ [aftí tin] **c**_____.
[éna leptó] [na káno tin] **b** _____ [éndeka iooníoo] [yia
THío méres] [me] **f**_____ [ti thálasa].

Mary [akrivós]. [kanéna] **e** _____!

[tetárti] [imerominía] [théloome] [krátisi] [théa] [próvlima]

Mini test

a Ask for a single or double room.
b Ask for a single room with bath and TV.
c Ask for a triple room with a sea view.
d **[to THomátio sas] [íne] [ston tríto órofo],** a receptionist says.
What is it in English?
e 'How much is the room per day? is what you want to say.
f Name five words related to accommodation.
g What are the pair words for: **[THistihós]**, **[pandoó]**,
[monóklino], **[dooz]**, **[othísate]**, **[mípos]**, **[ipóyion]**?

Συγχαρητήρια! **[sinharitíria]!** You've got only one more unit to go!
Take a short break and then proceed to complete this book. You've
done well so far. You can definitely make the last step. Θα σε δω
σύντομα! **[tha se THo síndoma]!** ... σύντομα ... **[síndoma]** ...
shortly Γεια σου τώρα! **[yiásoo tóra]!**

15

τον κατάλογο παρακαλώ!

the menu, please!

In this unit you will learn
- how to cope with a Greek menu
- how to order starters, main dishes and desserts
- how to order drinks
- how to understand a waiter's basic phrases
- words related to Greek food

Before you start

Revise Unit 8 before you start your last unit. Remember that you should continue the revision of all remaining units after the completion of Unit 15. If at this stage revision still leaves you with some unanswered questions, try to ask a Greek either at home or during your next visit to Greece. Of course, some native speakers might not be able to explain language nuances and they might tell you 'We just say so', or 'This is how we say it', or 'Don't ask why!' If you really want to have an explanation, locate a language tutor, and you might then receive a simple answer to a simple question. **Εντάξει; [endáksi]?** *OK?*

When you have finished revising Unit 8, move on to this interesting and important unit.

Key words and phrases

To attract the attention of a waiter or waitress, you can simply call out **παρακαλώ! [parakaló]!** You might see some Greeks raising their hands or snapping fingers but these 'advanced' methods are not recommended here! Older people still call out **γκαρσόν! [garsón]!** as in French, or even worse **παιδί! [peTHí]!** *hey, guy!* (lit. child) but of course this is not recommended either! The waiter/waitress might reply with **αμέσως! [amésos]!** *Right away!* or **έφτασα! [éftasa]!** *I'll be right there* (lit. *I arrived*).

First questions can be:

> **Τον κατάλογο, παρακαλώ! [ton katálogo parakaló]!**
> *The menu please!*
> **Μου/μας δίνετε... [moo/mas THínete]...**
> *Can you give me/us...*
> **Μου/μας φέρνετε... [moo/mas férnete] ...**
> *Can you bring me/us ...*
> **Φέρτε μου/μας ... [férte moo/mas]...**
> *Bring me/us ...*
> **Τι έχετε; [ti éhete]?**
> *What do you have?*
> **Μήπως έχετε...; [mípos éhete] ... ?**
> *Perhaps you have ...?*

The waiter/waitress can ask:

> **Είστε έτοιμος/έτοιμη/έτοιμοι; [íste étimos/étimi/étimi]?**
> *Are you ready?* (m/f/pl)
> **Τι θα πιείτε; [ti tha pyíte]?**
> *What will you drink?*

Τι θα φάτε; [ti tha fáte]?
What will you eat?
Τι θα πάρετε; [ti tha párete]?
What will you have (lit. *take*)*?*

Ordering meals you can say:

Μουσακά! [moosaká]!
Mousaka! (Note the stress on the final ά)
Μία μουσακά! [mia moosaká]!
A mousaka!
Μία μερίδα μουσακά! [mía meríTHa moosaká]!
A portion of mousaka!
Φέρτε μου μίαμερίδα μουσακά! [férte moo mía meríTHa moosaká]!
Bring me a portion of mousaka!

It is OK to give a direct order in Greek, without the necessity of saying 'please', or to use a modifying phrase like 'will you', 'would you', etc.

If you are not familiar with some of the dishes on the menu, the waiter/waitress might say **Ελάτε να δείτε! [eláte na THíte]!** *Come and see!* and take you back to the kitchen to show you and explain those dishes!

At the table:

Raising glasses, you can wish: **υγείαν! [iyían]!**, **Στην υγεία σου/σας! [stin iyía soo/sas]!** or simply **γειά σου! [yiásoo]!** or **γειά σας! [yiásas]!** Everything means 'Cheers!' (lit. health/your health/to your health).

Καλή όρεξη! [kalí óreksi]! (lit. *good appetite*) before starting to eat and **καλή χώνεψη! [kalí hónepsi]!** (lit. *good digestion*) at the end of your meal, can be heard. Of course, there is no English equivalent for the latter! You also need to know **το λογαριασμό, παρακαλώ! [to logariazmó parakaló]!** when you are ready to ask for the bill.

To understand the menu, you need to become familiar with the following words:

ΟΡΕΚΤΙΚΑ	**[orektiká]**	*appetizers, starters*
ΜΕΖΕΔΕΣ	**[mezéTHes]**	*small dishes*
ΛΑΔΕΡΑ	**[laTHerá]**	*food cooked in oil*
ΨΑΡΙΑ	**[psária]**	*fish*
ΨΗΤΑ	**[psitá]**	*grilled foods*
ΜΑΓΕΙΡΕΥΤΑ	**[mayireftá]**	*cooked foods that the restaurant always has ready to serve*

ΤΗΣ ΩΡΑΣ	[tis óras]	(lit. of the hour, meaning that the food is cooked while you wait)
ΣΑΛΑΤΕΣ	[salátes]	*salads*
ΓΛΥΚΑ	[gliká]	*desserts* (lit. sweets)
ΠΟΤΑ	[potá]	*beverages*

Beverages

ένα τσάϊ	[éna tsái]	a tea
ένα καφέ	[éna kafé]	a coffee
ένα χυμό	[éna himó]	a juice
ένα ούζο	[éna oózo]	an ouzo
ένα κρασί	[éna krasí]	a wine
ένα άσπρο	[éna áspro]	a white
ένα κόκκινο	[éna kókino]	a red
ένα ροζέ	[éna rozé]	a rosé
μία ρετσίνα	[mía retsína]	a resinated Greek wine
μία μπύρα	[mía bíra]	a beer
μία κόκα κόλα	[mía kóka kóla]	a coke
μία σόδα	[mía sóTHa]	a soda water

Utensils and dishes

ένα μαχαίρι	[éna mahéri]	a knife
ένα πηρούνι	[éna piroóni]	a fork
ένα κουτάλι	[éna kootáli]	a soup spoon
ένα κουταλάκι	[éna kootaláki]	a teaspoon
ένα πιάτο	[éna piáto]	a plate
ένα πιατάκι	[éna piatáki]	a saucer
ένα ποτήρι	[éna potíri]	a glass
ένα φλυτζάνι	[éna flitzáni]	a cup

Are you ready for the dialogues now? With all these key words and phrases you won't have any problems with the vocabulary in this unit. Right? Έτσι δεν είναι; [étsi THen íne]? Let's go! Πάμε! [páme]!

▶ Διάλογος 1 [THiálogos 1] *Dialogue 1:*
Αυτό είναι αλήθεια! [aftó íne alíthia]! *This is true!*

Back at home Άγγελος and Ελπίδα have made reservations at a taverna close by.

Ελπίδα	Ελάτε! Πάμε στην ταβέρνα του Πέτρου. Έχουμε κάνει κράτηση για τις εννιά το βράδυ.
John	Πολύ ωραία! Είμαι πολύ κουρασμένος και χρειάζομαι ένα καλό βραδινό.
Mary	Αυτό είναι αλήθεια! Ήταν μία πολύ κουραστική μέρα.

... [σε λίγο]

Σερβιτόρος	Καλησπέρα κ. Παππά. Γεια σας κα. Παππά. Πώς είστε; Έχω καιρό να σας δω.
Άγγελος	Είμαστε καλά αλλά πολύ απασχολημένοι. Πού είναι το τραπέζι μας σήμερα;

[elpíTHa]	[eláte]! [páme stin tavérna too pétroo]. [éhoome káni krátisi] [yia tis eniá to vráTHi].	*Come on! Let's go to Peter's taverna. We have made a reservation for nine o'clock in the evening.*
John	[polí oréa]! [íme polí koorazménos] [ke hriázome éna kaló vraTHinó].	*Very good! I'm very tired and I need a nice dinner.*
Mary	[aftó íne alíthia]! [ítan mía polí koorastikí méra].	*That's true! It was a very tiring day.*
	...[se lígo]	*... in a little while*
[servitóros]	[kalispéra kírie Pappá]. [yeia sas kiría Pappá]. [pos íste]? [ého keró na sas THo].	*Good evening Mr. Pappas. Good evening Mrs. Pappas. How are you? I haven't seen you for some time (lit. I have time to see you).*
[ángelos]	[ímaste kalá] [alá polí apasholiméni]. [poo íne to trapézi mas símera]?	*We are fine but very busy. Where is our table today?*

ταβέρνα	**[tavérna]**	*taverna, Greek restaurant* (f)
χρειάζομαι	**[hriázome]**	*I need*
αλήθεια	**[alíthia]**	*truth* (f)
αυτό είναι αλήθεια	**[aftó íne alíthia]**	*this is true* (lit. this is the truth)
κουραστική	**[koorastikí]**	*tiring* (f)
καιρό	**[keró]**	*time* (m)
έχω καιρό να...	**[ého keró na]** ...	*I haven't ... for some time*
απασχολημένοι	**[apasholiméni]**	*busy* (pl)

Notes

- **Αυτό είναι αλήθεια [aftó íne alíthia]** *that's true.* The opposite is **αυτό είναι ψέμα [aftó íne pséma]** *that's a lie.* You can also learn **αυτό είναι σωστό [aftó íne sostó]** *that's right* and **αυτό είναι λάθος [aftó íne láthos]** *that's wrong.*

- You realize that **κουρασμένος** [**koorazménos**] *tired* and **κουραστική** [**koorastikí**] *tiring* are words derived from the same root, don't you?

- Be careful with the phrase **έχω καιρό να ...** [**ého keró na**]... . Here it means 'It's been some time since ...' It literally means 'I've got some time to ...' or 'I have time to ...'.

- **Απασχολημέν<u>ος</u>** [**apasholimén<u>os</u>**], *απασχολημένη* [**apasholimén<u>i</u>**], *απασχολημέν<u>ο</u>* [**apasholimén<u>o</u>**] *busy* (m/f/n) is an important adjective. Keep in mind that Greek adjectives have different endings when they refer to the different genders. You can revise the notes in Unit 7 or go over the notes in the **Grammar summary**.

Petros tavern

▶ Διάλογος 2 [THiálogos 2] *Dialogue 2:* 'Ένα μπουκάλι νερό [éna bookáli neró] *A bottle of water*

They ask for the menu and about today's specials.

Άγγελος	Μας φέρνετε τον κατάλογο, κύριε Πέτρο.
Σερβιτόρος	Αμέσως. Να σας πω για τα πιάτα της ημέρας όμως. Σήμερα έχουμε παστίτσιο, αρνάκι με πατάτες στο φούρνο και γεμιστά.
Άγγελος	Φέρτε μας μία χωριάτικη σαλάτα, ένα τζατζίκι και δύο πατάτες τηγανιτές, ώσπου να δούμε τον κατάλογο.
Σερβιτόρος	Τι θα πιείτε;
Άγγελος	'Ένα μπουκάλι νερό κι'ένα άσπρο κρασί. 'Έχετε Ρομπόλα ή Μπουτάρι;

[ángelos]	[mas férnete ton katálogo] [kírie pétro].	*Could you bring us the menu, Mr. Peter?*
[servitóros]	[amésos]. [na sas po] [yia ta piáta tis iméras ómos]. [símera éhoome] [pastítsio],	*Right away. Let me tell you about today's specials though. Today*

[arnáki me patátes sto foórno] [ke yemistá]. — *we've got pastitsio, oven roasted lamb with potatoes, and stuffed (peppers and tomatoes).*

[ángelos]	[férte mas] [mía horiátiki saláta], [éna tzatzíki] [ke THío patátes tiganités] [óspoo na THoóme] [ton katálogo].	*Bring us a Greek salad, a tzatziki and two portions of chips until we see the menu.*
[servitóros]	[ti tha pyíte]?	*What will you drink?*
[ángelos]	[éna bookáli neró] [k'éna bookáli] [áspro krasí]. [éhete robóla i bootári]?	*A bottle of water and a bottle of white wine. Have you got Robolla or Boutari?*

μας φέρνετε;	[mas férnete]?	*(Will/could) you bring us?* (pl/fml)
να σας πω	[na sas po]	*let me tell you* (lit. to you tell)
πιάτα	[piáta]	*plates* (n/pl), *dishes*
πιάτα της ημέρα	[piáta tis iméras]	*today's specials* (lit. plates of the day)
όμως	[ómos]	*though, although*
παστίτσιο	[pastítsio]	*pastitsio* (n), *(layers of minced meat and macaroni, topped with béchamel sauce)*
αρνάκι	[arnáki]	*lamb* (n)
φούρνο	[foórno]	*oven* (m)
γεμιστά	[yemistá]	*stuffed (here: stuffed peppers and tomatoes)*
χωριάτικη σαλάτα	[horiátiki saláta]	*mixed Greek salad* (f) *with feta cheese*
τζατζίκι	[tzatzíki]	*tzatziki* (n) *(yogurt dip with garlic)*
δύο πατάτες	[THío patátes]	*two fried potatoes* (f/pl)
τηγανιτές	[tiganités]	(here: *two portions of chips*)
ώσπου	[óspoo]	*until*
τι θα πιείτε;	[ti tha pyíte]?	*What will you drink?* (pl/fml)
άσπρο κρασί	[áspro krasí]	*white wine* (n)
Ρομπόλα ή Μπουτάρι	[robóla i bootári]	brands of Greek white wine

ΜΑΓΕΙΡΕΥΤΑ

851.	Παστίτσιο	3.50€
852.	Μουσακάς	3.50€
853.	Τας κεμπάπ	5.00€
854.	Σουτζουκάκια...................................	4.70€
855.	Μοσχάρι στιφάδο	5.00€
856.	Μοσχάρι τυλιχτό (τυρί, σως μουστάρδας)...........	5.90€
857.	Μοσχάρι στάμνας	5.60€
858.	Κοτόπουλο κοκκινιστό (με μακαρόνια)	4.85€
859.	Κοτόπουλο λεμονάτο	4.85€
861.	Πιάτο ημέρας	
560.	Σούπα ημέρας	2.05€
864.	Γεμιστά (μόνο το καλοκαίρι)	3.25€

Greek dishes

▶ **Διάλογος 3 [THiálogos 3]** *Dialogue 3:*
**Μέχρι την επόμενη φορά! [méhri tin epómeni
forá]** *Until the next time!*

Everybody has enjoyed the main course and now they contemplate
dessert.

Σερβιτόρος	Πώς ήταν όλα; Να πάρω τα πιάτα;
Ελπίδα	Όλα ήταν ωραία. Τι γλυκά ή φρούτα έχετε, κύριε Πέτρο;
Σερβιτόρος	Έχουμε σπιτικό μπακλαβά ή καταΐφι. Επίσης φρούτα εποχής και όπως συνήθως κρεμ καραμελέ.
Ελπίδα	Τι θα πάρουμει Εγώ θέλω ένα μέτριο κι'ένα μπακλαβά.
Mary	Εγώ θα ήθελα φρούτα εποχής.
Άγγελος	Ένα σκέτο κι'ένα γλυκό για μας.
	... σε λίγο
Σερβιτόρος	Καληνύχτα σας. Σας ευχαριστούμε.
κ. Πέτρος	Καληνύχτα.
Άγγελος	Καληνύχτα κύριε Πέτρο. Μέχρι την επόμενη φορά!
Mary and John	Καληνύχτα!

[servitóros]	[pos ítan óla]? [na páro ta piáta]?	How was everything? Can I take the plates?
[elpíTHa]	[óla ítan oréa]. [ti gliká i froóta éhete], [kírie pétro]?	Everything was nice. What kind of sweets or fruit have you got, Mr Peter?
[servitóros]	[éhoome spitikó baklavá i kataífi]. [epísis froóta epohís] [ke ópos siníthos] [krem karamelé].	We have homemade baklava or kataifi. Also seasonal fruit and as usual crème caramel.
[elpíTHa]	[ti tha pároome]?	What will we have (lit. take)?
	[egó thélo éna métrio] [kéna baklavá].	I'd like a medium (Greek coffee) and one baklava.
Mary	[egó tha íthela] [froóta epohís].	I would like (some) seasonal fruit.
[ángelos]	[éna skéto] [kéna glikó] [yia mas].	One black and one sweet (coffee) for us.
	… [se lígo]	… in a little while
[servitóros]	[kaliníhta sas]. [sas efharistó].	Good night. Thank you.
[kírios pétros]	[kaliníhta].	Good night.
[ángelos]	[kaliníhta kírie pétro] [méhri tin epómeni forá]!	Good night, Mr Peter. Until the next time!
Mary and John	[kaliníhta]!	Good night!

ήταν	[ítan]	it was
Να πάρω τα πιάτα;	[na páro ta piáta]?	Shall I take the plates?
γλυκά	[gliká]	sweets (n/pl)
σπιτικό	[spitikó]	homemade (n)
μπακλαβά	[baklavá]	type of Greek pastry (m)
καταΐφι	[kataífi]	type of Greek pastry (n)
φρούτα εποχής	[froóta epohís]	seasonal fruit (lit. fruit of the season) (n/pl)
όπως συνήθως	[ópos siníthos]	as usual
κρεμ καραμελέ	[krem karamelé]	crème caramel
Μέχρι την επόμενη φορά!	[méhri tin epómeni forá]!	Until the next time!

Note

You can see the obvious association between **σπίτι [spíti]** *home* and **σπιτικό [spitikó]** *homemade*. If you want to eat homemade food, ask **Έχετε σπιτικό φαγητό; [éhete spitikó fayitó]?** *Do you have homemade food?* Also, do not confuse **γλυκά [gliká]** *desserts* with **γλυκό [glikó]** which is 'dessert' but also 'sweet coffee'.

Language rules

1 Τι θα πάρετε; [ti tha párete]? *What will you have?*

Unit 14 briefly mentioned the use of the word **θα [tha]** *will*. In this unit you were introduced to certain phrases including **[tha]** which is used to form the future tense in Greek:

Τι θα πιείτε; [ti tha pyíte]?	*What will you drink?*
Τι θα φάτε; [ti tha fáte]?	*What will you eat?*
Τι θα πάρετε; [ti tha párete]?	*What will you have?*
Τι θα πάρουμε; [ti tha pároome]?	*What will we have?*

As mentioned in the previous unit, in English, 'will' comes before the verb, which does not change its form. In Greek, **[tha]** comes before a *different* form of the root verb. Note the examples:

πίνω μπύρα [píno bíra]	*I drink beer* →
θα πιω μπύρα [tha pio bíra]	*I will drink beer*

Note: πιω *drink*, **πιο** *more* and **ποιο** *which* all sound **[pio]** in Greek! Only the spelling changes. Check on comments in the past units.

<u>τρώω</u> μουσακά [tró-o moosaká]	*I eat mousaka* →
θα <u>φάω</u> μουσακά [tha fáo moosaká]	*I will eat mousaka*
<u>παίρνω</u> κρασί [pérno krasí]	*I have* (lit. take) *wine* →
θα <u>πάρω</u> κρασί [tha páro krasí]	*I will have wine*

Some verbs, though, do not have a new form in the future, even in Greek. Note the following:

έχω [ého] *I have* → θα έχω [tha ého]	*I will have*
κάνω [káno] *I do* → θα κάνω [tha káno]	*I will do*
είμαι [íme] *I am* → θα είμαι [tha íme]	*I will be*

Now let's see the full form of one of them:

θα είμαι	[tha íme]	I will be
θα είσαι	[tha íse]	you will be
θα είναι	[tha íne]	he/she/it will be
θα είμαστε	[tha ímaste]	we will be
θα είσαστε/είστε	[tha ísaste/íste]	you will be
θα είναι	[tha íne]	they will be

2 Πώς ήταν όλα; [pos ítan óla]? *How was everything?*

ήταν **[ítan]** *was* is the past form of the verb **είμαι [íme]** *I am* that you already know. Do you remember all the forms of **[íme]**? Let's hope so because you have revised it at least a couple of times so far. If not, Unit 1 has all its forms. Look at the new forms below:

ήμουν	[ímoon]	I was
ήσουν	[ísoon]	you were
ήταν	[ítan]	he/she/it was
ήμασταν	[ímastan]	we were
ήσασταν	[ísastan]	you were
ήταν	[ítan]	they were

You might hear a slightly different form for this verb: **[ímoona]**, **[ísoona]**, **[ítane]**, **[ímastan]**, **[ísastan]**, **[ítane]**. These forms are less frequent but interchangeable.

Do not confuse the word **ήταν [ítan]**, which stands for both 'he/she/it was' and 'they were'.

By the way, **είμαι [íme]** is 'I am', **θα είμαι [tha íme]** is 'I will be', and **ήμουν [ímoon]** is 'I was'. **Ενδιαφέρον; [enTHiaféron]**?

Although it was not mentioned, some phrases presented in earlier units made use of the past tense. Some examples include: **Καλώς όρισες! [kalós órises]!** *Welcome!* (lit. well you came) **Χάρηκα! [hárika]!** *Pleased to have met you!* (lit. I was pleased/glad) **Καλώς σε/σας βρήκα! [kalós se/sas vríka]!** *Nice to be here!* (lit. nice I found you).

ℹ️ Πάμε στην ταβέρνα [páme stin tavérna]
Let's go to the taverna

There was a first mention of different meals in Unit 8. You read about them when you revised this unit earlier, **έτσι δεν είναι; [étsi THen íne]?** Eating out is a very informal business in Greece. There are many different names for restaurants according to the main dishes served. Neither **εστιατόριο [estiatório]** *restaurant* or **ταβέρνα [tavérna]** *taverna* have any clear distinction nowadays. **Εστιατόριο** used to be a more formal place than a **ταβέρνα**. Also a **ταβέρνα** used to be open only in the evening, whereas most of them are open now throughout the day. A **ταβέρνα** specializing in grilled meats is called **ψησταριά [psistariá]** or **χασαποταβέρνα [hasapotavérna]** from **χασάπης** meaning *butcher*. A taverna offering fish and seafood is called **ψαροταβέρνα [psarotavérna]** from **ψάρι [psári]** *fish*. A **μεζεδοπωλείο [mezeTHopolío]** or **ουζομεζεδοπωλείο [oozo-mezeTHopolío]** is an informal place serving **μεζέδες [mezéTHes]** *small dishes* with **ούζο [oózo]** *ouzo*.

Some Greek dishes and drinks are an acquired taste. No explanation can replace the real experience of a Greek restaurant or taverna. 'A new culture starts from the mouth' some people say. They might be right. Why don't you give it a try and remember to be open to new tastes and new ways of cooking. You might be pleasantly surprised! **Ελπίζω να σε δω σε καμιά ταβέρνα σύντομα! [elpízo na se THo se kamiá tavérna síndoma]!** *I hope to see you in a taverna soon!* **Τι λες; [ti les]?** *What do you say?*

Practice makes perfect

1 A waiter asks you '[*ti tha pyíte*]?' Look at the pictures and order …

▶ **2** Now listen to the recording to check that you placed your order correctly in Exercise 1. Listen again, and write your order in Greek script.

3 Would you be able to ask a waitress to bring you the following items from the illustration? If you don't remember all of them, match them with the words provided for you in the box.

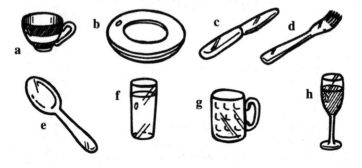

[potíri]	[flitzáni]	[mahéri]	[kootáli]
ποτήρι	φλυτζάνι	μαχαίρι	κουτάλι
[piáto]	[piroóni]	[potíri bíras]	[potíri yia krasí]
πιάτο	πιρούνι	ποτήρι μπύρας	ποτήρι για κρασί

4 A waiter asks you '[ti tha fáte]?' Translate your order into Greek.

a A Greek salad, tzatziki and chips.
b Roast lamb and potatoes.
c A portion of pastitsio and a portion of stuffed peppers and tomatoes.

5 Now you look at the menu (below) and you decide to order ...

a Schnitzel Hoffman
b Pork cutlet cooked in wine
c Beef Souvlaki
d Beefsteak with Gouda cheese

Can you find them in the menu and write down the number of each item?
Here is some vocabulary to help you:

μπιφτέκι	[biftéki]	beefsteak
μπριζόλα	[brizóla]	cutlet
μοσχαρίσιο	[mosharísio]	beef
χοιρινό	[hirinó]	pork

ΠΙΑΤΑ ΤΗΣ ΩΡΑΣ

€

301. Σνίτσελ Βιενουά	5.45
303. Σνίτσελ Χόφμαν (ζαμπόν, τυρί φούρνου)	6.00
311. Μπιφτέκι σχάρας	4.85
321. Φιλέτο σχάρας	8.65
371. Κοτόπουλο σχάρας	4.85
381. Μπριζόλα μοσχαρίσια γάλακτος	6.45
382. Μπριζόλα χοιρινή	5.00
383. Μπριζόλα χοιρινή (κρασάτη)	5.30
391. Σουβλάκι μοσχαρίσιο	6.30
392. Σουβλάκι χοιρινό	5.15
393. Σουβλάκι κοτόπουλο	4.85
881. Μπιφτέκι γεμιστό (τυρί γκούντα)	5.60
882. Παϊδάκια (μερίδα)	5.60
883. Συκώτι μοσχαρίσιο σχάρας	3.80
884. Συκώτι μοσχαρίσιο "Το Χωριό" (πράσινη πιπεριά, σκόρδο)	4.10

6 Try the following puzzle. If you get the answers right, the shaded vertical column spells out the word for a type of restaurant in Greek. Try it in Greek script if possible. If not, transliteration is OK [*ópos siníthos*]!

a What will you <u>eat</u> (pl/fml)? **e** bill
b wine   **f** Will you <u>bring</u> us?
c book   **g** salad
d water

▶ 7 Listen to the recording and tick what Άννα [ána], Σοφία [sofía], and Άρης [áris] order.

	a χωριάτικη [horiátiki]	b πατάτες [patátes]	c μπιφτέκι [biftéki]	d μουσακά [moosaká]	e κρασί [krasí]	f νερό [neró]
i Άννα						
ii Σοφία						
iii Άρης						

▶ 8 Listen again to Dialogue 3 of this unit and fill in the blanks. If you don't have the recording, choose the missing words from the box below. One word is used twice.

[servitóros]   [pos] **a** _____ [óla]? [na páro ta piáta]?
[elpíTHa]   [óla] **a** _____ [oréa]. [ti] **b** _____ [i froóta éhete], [kírie pétro]?
[servitóros]   [éhoome] **c** _____ [baklavá i kataífi]. **d** _____ [froóta epohís] [ke] **e** _____ [siníthos] [krem karamelé].

[elpíTHa]	[ti tha pároome]? [egó thélo éna métrio] [k'éna baklavá].
Mary	[egó tha íthela] [froóta epohís].
[ángelos]	[ke THío elinikoós] [yia más]. [éna] **f**_____ [k'énan] **g** _____.
	... [se lígo]
[servitóros]	[kaliníhta sas]. [sas efharistó].
[kírios pétros]	[kaliníhta].
[ángelos]	[kaliníhta kírie pétro]. [méhri tin epómeni forá]!
Mary and John	[kaliníhta]!

> [gliká] [epísis] [skéto] [ítan] [spitikó] [ópos] [glikó]

Mini test

a How do you ask for the menu or the bill?
b 'Can you bring/give me?' is what you want to say.
c A waitress said to you **[amésos]**, **[éftasa]!** What is that in English?
d **[ti tha pyíte]?** was the question. Give three possible answers.
e **[ti tha fáte]?** was the question. Give three possible answers.
f You've just dropped your knife – fork – plate – glass. Can you ask for new ones?
g You are looking at a menu. What do OPEKTIKA – MEZEΔEΣ – ΨΑΡΙΑ – ΨΗΤΑ – ΤΗΣ ΩΡΑΣ – ΓΛΥΚΑ mean in English?

> Congratulations on choosing *Teach Yourself Beginner's Greek* in your efforts to learn this beautiful and rich language. Aristarhos Matsukas, the author of this book, will be more than happy to hear your comments. Your comments and/or suggestions will help us to improve future editions.
>
> You can contact the author directly at the following e-mail address: aja14@web.de, or by writing c/o Teach Yourself, Hodder & Stoughton, 338 Euston Road, London NW1 3BH, England.
>
> Even though you have reached the end of the book, you should not close it, but instead continue your revision, starting with Unit 9 next time. Revise also anything you have highlighted in the book, or go over your index cards. Whatever you do, once again, **MΠΡΑΒΟ! [brávo]!**

There are three **Revision tests** in this course. You can take them as soon as you complete Units 5, 10 and 15 respectively but you can also take them later. You can always omit this section if tests make you apprehensive, although it can be a challenge for you to test yourself and see how well you remember the materials you have covered. You can add up the points to see your total mark and compare it if you redo the **Revision test** at a later time. More than 70% will be a satisfactory mark, whereas less than 70% might suggest some further revision. **Καλή τύχη! [kalí tíhi]!** *Good luck!*

Revision test 1

1 What greetings will you use at the following times? *(5 points)*

a 8:30   **d** 21:00
b 12:30   **e** 23:40
c 16:10

2 Can you fill in the speech bubbles below with greetings? *(10 points)*

3 There are some numbers missing from the boxes. Can you fill them in and write them in words: *(10 points)*

a	1	2		4	
b	6		8	9	
c			13		15
d		17	18		

4 A friend is showing some family pictures hanging on the wall. Match the phrases below with the pictures (You can work either with the transliteration or Greek script): *(10 points)*

i [o yiórgos] [ke i maría].	**i** Ο Γιώργος και η Μαρία
ii [i ikoyenía papá].	**ii** Η οικογένεια Παππά.
iii [i elpíTHa] [íne i aTHelfí moo].	**iii** Η Ελπίδα είναι η αδελφή μου.
iv [o papoós moo] [o yiánis].	**iv** Ο παππούς μου ο Γιάννης.
v [o ksáTHelfos ke i ksaTHélfi moo]	**v** Ο ξάδελφος και η ξαδέλφη μου.

5 Below is the layout of a house. Do you remember the words for each room? The first one has been done for you. *(6 points)*

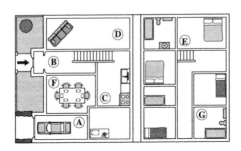

A [párkin]   E _____
B _____   F _____
C _____   G _____
D _____

6 Look at the car stickers below and name the countries and their corresponding languages. *(10 points)*

Symbol	Country	Language
USA	a	i
D	b	ii
F	c	iii
IT	d	iv
GR	e	v

7 Choose the correct forms of the Greek word for 'the' and 'in the'. *(10 points)*

a [íme apó] ___ [athína].   i [i]   ii [tin]   iii [stin]
b ___ [athína íne stin eláTHa].   i [i]   ii [tin]   iii [stin]
c ___ [lonTHíno íne stin anglía]. i [o]   ii [to]   iii [sto]
d [méno] ___ [lonTHíno].   i [o]   ii [to]   iii [sto]
e [méno] ___ [athína].   i [i]   ii [tin]   iii [stin]

8 Look at the Greek words below. What is their correct transliteration? *(5 points)*

a ΑΕΡΟΛΙΜΕΝΑΣ
  i [aepoliménas]   ii [aeroTHiménas] iii [aeroliménas]
b ΑΘΗΝΩΝ
  i [athinón]   ii [aTHinón]   iii [athnnón]
c ΕΛΕΥΘΕΡΙΟΣ
  i [elefTHérios]   ii [elefthérios]   iii [elethérios]
d ΒΕΝΙΖΕΛΟΣ
  i [benizélos]   ii [venizélos]   iii [venisélos]
e ΛΟΝΔΙΝΟ
  i [lonTHíno]   ii [lonthíno]   iii [loTHíno]
f ΠΑΡΙΣΙ
  i [parísi]   ii [papísi]   iii [parízi]

9 Can you solve the crossword puzzle below by translating the clues into Greek? The shaded vertical word spells out the word for *architect*. *(13 points)*

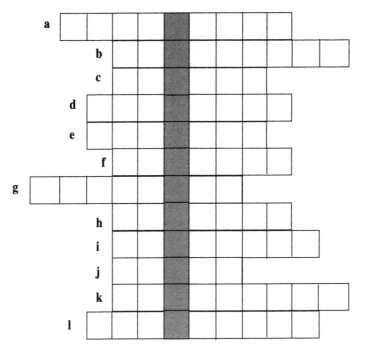

a writer **b** waitress **c** Athens **d** Good morning **e** doctor **f** USA **g** musician **h** father **i** I work **j** near **k** pianist **l** teacher

10 Complete the following dialogue using the information in italics: *(20 points)*

[yiánis]   [na sas sistíso] [apo'THó i maría].
You   **a** *Hi Maria! Pleased to meet you!*
[maría]   [ki'egó]. [apó poo íse]?
You   **b** *From the States. From New York. You?*
[maría]   [apó ta yiánena] [alá tóra méno stin athína]. [esí]?
You   **c** *I also live in Athens now. I am a children's book writer.*

Revision test 2

1 Some people tell you the times they work. Match the clock faces with the phrases below. *(10 points)*

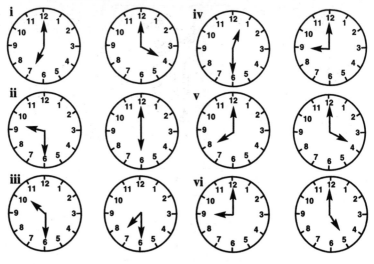

a [THoolévo apó tis októ méhri tis téseris].
b [i maría íne sto spíti apó tis eniámisí méhri tis éksi].
c [THen tró-o poté apó tis THoTHekámisi méhri tis eniá].
d [íme sti THooliá apó tis eftá méhri tis téseris].
e [THen marési na THoolévo apó tis eniá méhri tis pénde].
f [o yiórgos vlépi tileórasi apó tis THekámisi méhri tis eptámisi].

2 Can you translate the phrases in Exercise 1 into English? *(10 points)*

a _____
b _____
c _____
d _____
e _____
f _____

3 Match the phrases below with the illustrations opposite . *(10 points)*

a [i maría íne stin koozína ke mayirévi].
b [o yiánis íne ékso apó to spíti].
c [i mitéra moo vlépi polí tileórasi].
d [o patéras moo pánda THiavázi efimeríTHa].
e [o kóstas akoó-i moosikí óli tin iméra].
f [i eléni íne sto grafío apó tis eniá méhri tis mía].

4 **Can you translate the phrases in Exercise 3 into English?** *(10 points)*

a _____
b _____
c _____
d _____
e _____
f _____

5 **Look at the illustrations. Can you match the action phrases on page 218 with the jumbled illustrations below?** *(10 points)*

a [káno dooz]
b [tró-o proinó]
c [páo yia ípno]
d [ksipnáo stis eptá]
e [THiavázo sto kreváti]

f [páo sti THooliá]
g [févgo apó ti THooliá]
h [sikónome apó to kreváti]
i [etimázome yia THooliá]
j [etimázome yia ípno]

6 **Translate the phrases in Exercise 5 into English.** *(10 points)*

7 **Can you describe the following daily routine in Greek?** *(20 points)*

8 Match the list of Greek names with their English translations.
(10 points)

a [yiánis], **b** [eléni], **c** [ána], **d** [THimítris], **e** [ángelos], **f** [andónis],
g [yioryía], **h** [níkos], **i** [nióvi], **j** [elpíTHa]

i Jim, **ii** Anthony, **iii** Helen, **iv** Georgia, **v** Nick, **vi** Niobe, **vii** John,
viii Hope, **ix** Anne, **x** Angelos

**9 How many fruits, vegetables and herbs among other words
can you find in the word search below? Words read across, down
and backwards.** *(10 points)*

a	f	p	k	a	t	o
a	r	a	k	a	s	o
n	a	t	a	m	o	d
a	o	a	l	e	l	a
n	o	t	o	r	a	k
a	l	a	t	oo	r	f
s	a	m	r	o	o	h

Revision test 3

**1 You are at 33 Kerkiras Street. Tell people how many blocks
(counting inclusively) away places *a* to *e* on the map are.** *(5
points)*

2 Can you match the visuals below with the English headings?
(5 points)

i	underground	iii	restaurant	v	pastry shop
ii	closed	iv	ticket		

3 Match the illustrations with the phrases below. *(10 points)*

a [ta peTHiá miláne]
b [i maría prépi na THoolépsi]
c [pináo]

d [THen káthome spíti tóra]
e [THipsáo]
f [o yiórgos íne koorazménos]

4 How do people usually travel? Match the words below with the illustrations. *(10 points)*

a [me aeropláno]
b [me tréno]
c [me leoforío]

d [me plío]
e [me aftokínito]
f [me várka]

5 Do you remember the names of the months? Write them below. *(12 points)*

a _____ e _____ i _____
b _____ f _____ j _____
c _____ g _____ k _____
d _____ h _____ l _____

6 Can you list the days of the week? *(8 points)*

a _____ e _____
b _____ f _____
c _____ g _____
d _____

7 Looking at the menu below try to translate the different headings. Also say the names of the non-alcoholic beverages. *(10 points)*

ΠΙΑΤΑ ΤΗΣ ΩΡΑΣ

ΚΟΤΟΠΟΥΛΟ ΣΧΑΡΑΣ (370 γρ.*)		5,45€
(φιλέτο στήθος με λαχανικά, ρύζι, coca cola light)		
ΚΟΤΟΠΟΥΛΟ ΣΧΑΡΑΣ (350 γρ.*)		5,45€
(φιλέτο στήθος με σαλάτα εποχής, coca cola light)		
ΜΠΙΦΤΕΚΙ ΣΧΑΡΑΣ (340 γρ.*)		5,60€
(με σαλάτα εποχής, coca cola light)		
ΜΠΙΦΤΕΚΙ ΣΧΑΡΑΣ (360δ γρ.*)		5,60€
(με σπαγγέτι, coca cola light)		

*γρ. means grams.

ΑΝΑΨΥΚΤΙΚΑ

ΠΟΡΤΟΚΑΛΑΔΑ

0,70€

ΜΠΥΡΕΣ-ΚΡΑΣΙΑ

AMSTEL/AMSTEL LIGHT	1,00€
HEINEKEN	1,00€
MYTHOS	1,00€
ΜΑΚΕΔΟΝΙΚΟΣ ΛΕΥΚΟΣ	5,75€

8 Can you write in transliteration or Greek script the amounts in Euros for each number below? *(10 points)*

a 1000€ _____   d 350€ _____
b 2000€ _____   e 500€ _____
c 250€ _____

9 **Look at the visuals below and match them with the key words.**
(10 points)

i

Ανοίξτε το ραδιόφωνό σας!
σταθμός

ii

Καλοκαίρι
2000

ΒΙΒΛΙΟΠΩΛΕΙΑ
ΕΛΕΥΘΕΡΟΥΔΑΚΗΣ

iii

ΙΟΝΙΚΗ ΤΡΑΠΕΖΑ

iv

Τζόκερ Το Μεγάλο
Παιχνίδι

v

Ώρες Λειτουργίας
Τρίτη – Σάββατο: 10.00 – 14.00
Κυριακή: 11.00 – 14.00
Δευτέρα: κλειστά

a joker
b opening hours
c bank

d radio station
e bookstore

10 **Can you translate most of the information in the visuals in Exercise 9 into English? You now know almost everything!**
(20 points)

i _____

ii _____

iii _____

iv _____

v _____

the Greek alphabet

You can go through this section unit by unit, or in small batches of units together. In either case, you can revise the capital and small letters in question, their names, and their approximate equivalent sounds in English. You will also see a list of examples from the current or past units, which actually includes the letter in question. This new list has three columns: the word, its transliteration, and its translation. It can be utilized as a short memory quiz by covering one column and then guessing the other two. Obvious associations between sounds and spelling can gradually increase thus helping all learners who are interested in the Greek script.

Unit 1

Letter	Name	Equivalent sound in English
K κ	[kápa]	[k] as in *kit*
Λ λ	[lámTHa]	[l] as in *let*
M μ	[mi]	[m] as in *met*

A B Γ Δ E Z H Θ I K Λ M N Ξ O Π P Σ T Y Φ X Ψ Ω

κ λ μ

Examples

καλημέρα	[kaliméra]	*good morning*
καλησπέρα	[kalispéra]	*good evening*
καληνύχτα	[kaliníhta]	*good night*
πολύ	[polí]	*very / much*

χάρηκα	[hárika]	*pleased to have met you*
κάνεις	[kánis]	*you do*
καλά	[kalá]	*well*
Ελλάδα	[eláTHa]	*Greece*

Unit 2

Letter	Name	Equivalent sound in English
Π π	[pi]	[p] as in *pet*
Ρ ρ	[ro]	[r] as in *rest*
Σ σ/ς	[sígma]	[s] as in *set* or [z] as in *zip*

```
Α Β Γ Δ Ε Ζ Η Θ Ι Κ Λ Μ Ν Ξ Ο Π Ρ Σ Τ Υ Φ Χ Ψ Ω
              κ λ μ              π ρ σ
```

Examples

Παρίσι	[parísi]	*Paris*
Ρώμη	[rómi]	*Rome*
Βερολίνο	[verolíno]	*Berlin*
από	[apó]	*from*
εσύ	[esí]	*you*
είστε	[íste]	*you are*
Μαδρίτη	[maTHríti]	*Madrid*

Unit 3

Letter	Name	Equivalent sound in English
Ε ε	[épsilon]	[e] as in *met*
Ι ι	[yióta]	[i] as in *sit*
Ο ο	[ómikron]	[o] as in *lot*
Α α	[álfa]	[a] as in *raft*

```
Α Β Γ Δ Ε Ζ Η Θ Ι Κ Λ Μ Ν Ξ Ο Π Ρ Σ Τ Υ Φ Χ Ψ Ω
α       ε       ι κ λ μ       ο π ρ σ
```

Examples

σερβιτόρος	[servitóros]	*waiter*
γιατρός	[yiatrós]	*doctor*
δάσκαλος	[THáskalos]	*teacher*
συγγραφέας	[sigraféas]	*writer*
αρχιτέκτονας	[arhitéktonas]	*architect*
παιδιά	[peTHiá]	*children*
μόνο	[móno]	*only*
κοντά	[kondá]	*near*

Unit 4

Letter	Name	Equivalent sound in English
Θ θ	[thíta]	[th] as in **th**in
Δ δ	[THélta]	[TH] as in **th**is

A B Γ Δ E Z H Θ I K Λ M N Ξ O Π P Σ T Y Φ X Ψ Ω

α   δ ε   θ ι κ λ μ   o π ρ σ

Examples

διαμέρισμα	[THiamérizma]	*apartment*
καθιστικό	[kathistikó]	*sitting room*
δωμάτιο	[THomátio]	*room*
Λονδίνο	[lonTHíno]	*London*
δουλειά	[THooliá]	*work / job*
δουλεύω	[THoolévo]	*I work*
Αθήνα	[athína]	*Athens*

Unit 5

This unit had no pronunciation tips. Challenge yourself and try to write the following Greek words in capital letters. The first one has been done for you. If you find it difficult, consult the **Pronunciation guide** at the beginning of the book.

Αθήνα	ΑΘΗΝΑ	[athína]	*Athens*
γιαγιά	_____	[yiayiá]	*grandmother*
λεπτό	_____	[leptó]	*minute*
οικογένεια	_____	[ikoyénia]	*family*
ερώτηση	_____	[erótisi]	*question*

εσύ	_____	[esí]	_you_
παιδιά	_____	[peTHiá]	_children_
τριών	_____	[trión]	_three_
χρονών	_____	[hronón]	_years old_

The sound [i] is produced in Greek by three different individual letters and two two-letter combinations. The word 'family' above includes the two two-letter combinations. The sound [o] is produced in Greek by two different individual letters.

Cover the box below and see if you can find the five letters producing these two sounds, [i] and [o] from the list of words above.

```
Α Β Γ Δ Ε Ζ Η Θ Ι Κ Λ Μ Ν Ξ Ο Π Ρ Σ Τ Υ Φ Χ Ψ Ω
          η    ι              ο              υ              ω
```

Ηη [íta], **Ιι** [yióta], and **Υυ** [ípsilon] produce the sound [i] in Greek. **Οο** [ómikron] and **Ωω** [oméga] produce the sound [o] in Greek.

Unit 6

Letter	Name	Equivalent sound in English
Ψ ψ	[psi]	as in _laps_
Τ τ	[taf]	as in _tea_
ΤΣ τσ	[taf-sígma]	as in _sets_

```
Α Β Γ Δ Ε Ζ Η Θ Ι Κ Λ Μ Ν Ξ Ο Π Ρ Σ Τ Υ Φ Χ Ψ Ω
α     δ ε   η θ ι κ λ μ     ο π ρ σ τ υ     ψ ω
```

Examples

τώρα	[tóra]	_now_
τσάι	[tsái]	_tea_
ψωμί	[psomí]	_bread_
διψάτε;	[THipsáte]?	_are you thirsty?_
κορίτσι	[korítsi]	_girl_
τι	[ti]	_what_

Unit 7

Letter	Name	Equivalent sound in English
Ι ι	[yióta]	[i] as in *sit*
ΟΥ ου	[ómikron-ípsilon]	[oo] as in *cool*

Α Β Γ Δ Ε Ζ Η Θ Ι Κ Λ Μ Ν Ξ Ο Π Ρ Σ Τ Υ Φ Χ Ψ Ω
α   δ ε   η θ ι κ λ μ   ο π ρ σ τ υ   ψ ω

Examples

κουζίνα	[koozína]	*kitchen*
τους αρέσουν	[toos arésoon]	*they like*
τραπέζι	[trapézi]	*table*
λουτρό	[lootró]	*bathroom*
πρακτικό	[praktikó]	*practical*
κάνουν	[kánoon]	*they do*
δίκιο	[THíkio]	*right*
που	[poo]	*that*
γιαγιά μου	[yiayiá moo]	*my grandmother*

Unit 8

Letter	Name	Equivalent sound in English
Τ τ	[taf]	[t] as in *tea*
Λ λ	[lámTHa]	[l] as in *let*
Ν ν	[ni]	[n] as in *net*

Α Β Γ Δ Ε Ζ Η Θ Ι Κ Λ Μ Ν Ξ Ο Π Ρ Σ Τ Υ Φ Χ Ψ Ω
α   δ ε   η θ ι κ λ μ ν   ο π ρ σ τ υ   ψ ω

Examples

τι	[ti]	*what*
τελικά	[teliká]	*finally*
ψώνια	[psónia]	*shopping*
τρένο	[tréno]	*train*
σπάνια	[spánia]	*rarely*
λουτρό	[lootró]	*bathroom*

| θέλετε | [thélete] | you want |
| πεινάτε | [pináte] | you are hungry |

Unit 9

Letter	Name	Equivalent sound in English
ΜΠ μπ	[mi-pi]	[b] as in **b**oy or [mb] as in ti**mb**er
ΝΤ ντ	[ni-taf]	[d] as in **d**ay or [nd] as in e**nd**
ΓΚ γκ	[gáma-kápa]	[g] as in **g**o or [ng] as in E**ng**lish
ΓΓ	[gáma-gáma]	[ng] as in E**ng**lish
Ζ ζ	[zíta]	[z] as in **z**ip

The sounds **[b]**, **[d]**, and **[g]** appear at the beginning of a word whereas **[mb]**, **[nd]** and **[ng]** appear within a word. 'γγ' appears only within a word, never at the beginning, therefore we have not shown the capital above.

| A | B | Γ | Δ | E | Z | H | Θ | I | K | Λ | M | N | Ξ | O | Π | P | Σ | T | Y | Φ | X | Ψ | Ω |
| α | | | δ | ε | ζ | η | θ | ι | κ | λ | μ | ν | | ο | π | ρ | σ | τ | υ | | | ψ | ω |

Examples

μπράβο	[brávo]	bravo
έντεκα	[éndeka]	eleven
κοντά	[kondá]	near
Αγγλία	[anglía]	England
γκαρσονιέρα	[garsoniéra]	studio / bedsit
άντρας	[ándras]	man / husband
γκολ	[gol]	goal
κουζίνα	[koozína]	kitchen
μπάσκετ	[básket]	basketball
μπλουζ	[blooz]	blues
ετοιμάζω	[etimázo]	I prepare

Unit 10

Letter	Name	Equivalent sound in English
Φ φ	[fi]	[f] as in **f**it
P ρ	[ro]	[r] as in **r**est
T τ	[taf]	[t] as in **t**ea

А В Г Δ Е Z Н Θ I К Λ М N Ξ О П Р Σ Т Υ Φ Χ Ψ Ω
α   δ ε ζ η θ ι κ λ μ ν   ο π ρ σ τ υ φ   ψ ω

Examples

φρούτα	[froóta]	*fruit*
φρέσκα	[fréska]	*fresh*
προφορά	[proforá]	*pronunciation*
πορτοκάλι	[portokáli]	*orange*
ελεύθερες	[eléftheres]	*free*
τηλεόραση	[tileórasi]	*television*
φορές	[forés]	*times*
θέατρο	[théatro]	*theatre*

Unit 11

Letter	Name	Equivalent sound in English
Χ χ	[hi]	[h] as in *hit*
Ξ ξ	[ksi]	[ks] as in *banks* or *six*

А В Г Δ Е Z Н Θ I К Λ М N Ξ О П Р Σ Т Υ Φ Χ Ψ Ω
α   δ ε ζ η θ ι κ λ μ ν ξ ο π ρ σ τ υ φ χ ψ ω

Examples

ταχυδρομείο	[tahiTHromío]	*post office*
σχολείο	[sholío]	*school*
έξι	[éksi]	*six*
ξέρω	[kséro]	*I know*
χάρτης	[hártis]	*map*
λέξεις	[léksis]	*words*
με συγχωρείτε	[me sinhoríte]	*excuse me*
τυχερός	[tiherós]	*lucky*
λαχανικά	[lahaniká]	*vegetables*
έρχομαι	[érhome]	*I come*

Unit 12

Letter	Name	Equivalent sound in English
Β β	[víta]	[v] as in *vet*

A B Γ Δ E Z H Θ I K Λ M N Ξ O Π P Σ T Y Φ X Ψ Ω
α β   δ ε ζ η θ ι κ λ μ ν ξ ο π ρ σ τ υ φ χ ψ ω

Examples

μπράβο	[brávo]	*bravo*
νουβέλα	[noovéla]	*novel*
βουνό	[voonó]	*mountain*
βράδυ	[vráTHi]	*evening*
βοηθήσω	[voithíso]	*I help*
βιτρίνα	[vitrína]	*shop window*
βάζετε	[vázete]	*you put on*
βγείτε	[vyíte]	*you come out*

Unit 13

Letter	Name	Equivalent sound in English
Tζ τζ	[taf-zíta]	[tz] as in *jazz* or *gem*

Examples

τζαμαρία	[tzamaría]	*winter garden / conservatory*
τζαζ	[tzaz]	*jazz*

Unit 14

Letter	Name	Equivalent sound in English
Γ γ	[gáma]	[hy] as in *yield*, [y] as in *yes* or soft [g] as in *su**g**ar*

A B Γ Δ E Z H Θ I K Λ M N Ξ O Π P Σ T Y Φ X Ψ Ω
α β γ δ ε ζ η θ ι κ λ μ ν ξ ο π ρ σ τ υ φ χ ψ ω

Examples

ισόγειον	[isóyion]	*ground floor*
υπόγειον	[ipóyion]	*basement*
διάλογος	[THiálogos]	*dialogue*

επιταγή	[epitayí]	*cheque*
πηγαίνω	[piyéno]	*I go*
φεύγω	[févgo]	*I leave / I depart*
απαγορεύεται	[apagorévete]	*it is forbidden*
γυναίκα	[yinéka]	*woman*

Unit 15

This is our last unit. Some of you really wanted to learn the Greek script! Let's see if you have remembered the following features of the Greek alphabet. Come back to this section whenever you wish to check the reference tables.

Capital letters

1 There are 24 capital letters: Α, Β, Γ, Δ, Ε, Ζ, Η, Θ, Ι, Κ, Λ, Μ, Ν, Ξ, Ο, Π, Ρ, Σ, Τ, Υ, Φ, Χ, Ψ, Ω. Do you remember the names of all of them? You can always check the **Pronunciation guide** in the beginning of the book and listen to the recordings.

2 The following 10 letters are not in the English alphabet: Γ, Δ, Θ, Λ, Ξ, Π, Σ, Φ, Ψ, Ω. The remaining 14 are identical in both alphabets. Of course, you are reminded that some of them <u>look</u> the same but don't <u>sound</u> alike. Those letters are: Β, Η, Ρ, Χ.

Lower-case letters

1 There are 25 lower-case letters: α, β, γ, δ, ε, ζ, η, θ, ι, κ, λ, μ, ν, ξ, ο, π, ρ, σ/ς, τ, υ, φ, χ, ψ, ω. You know by now that there are two letters for 's' in Greek: σ and ς (only as a final "s").

2 The following 17 letters are not in the English alphabet: β, γ, δ, ε, ζ, θ, κ, λ, μ, ξ, π, σ/ς, τ, φ, χ, ψ, ω. Some of them are easy to remember, for instance β → b, ε → e, κ → k, τ → t.

Final remarks

If you are intrigued by the Greek alphabet, keep practising what you have learnt throughout this course. One suggestion is for you to test a group of words you know and see if you can write them in Greek or go over some of the authentic visuals and see if you can transliterate the Greek words or even translate them.

grammar summary

This grammar summary is intended mainly to act as a reference guide to the language used in the course. It is by no means a complete grammar, although some elements in this section do not appear in the course and are included for learners who wish to progress a little further.

You can skim through this section before you start Unit 1 and you can always refer back whenever you meet a new grammatical point in a unit and compare it with the notes here. Grammatical explanations in the **Language rules** section in the course are somewhat short and to the point, with some examples for practical application. Here the approach is different and more organized and systematic in terms of grouping grammatical points together.

The most important grammatical groups outlined in this section are: **Articles**, **Nouns**, **Adjectives**, **Adverbs**, **Pronouns**, **Prepositions** and **Verbs**. In most instances you will find tables to which the different groups belong, along with a few examples and direct references back to units.

1 Articles

The words *a*, *an* and *the* are called **articles** in English. *A* and *an* are called **indefinite articles** and *the* is called the **definite article**. All articles come before a noun. Greek articles have a lot more than three forms! This is because the nouns they define are divided into three genders: masculine (m), feminine (f) and neuter (n). The Greek words for *a*, *an* and *the* are therefore different for each gender. This is one of the reasons that all nouns in the course are given with their gender, i.e. (m), (f) or (n). In addition, each noun group has further forms in the singular and plural, so the articles have to agree with these, too.

Greek also has different endings for **nouns** and their articles (and adjectives – see below) when nouns are used in different ways within a sentence – for example, if they are the subject or the object of the sentence. These different forms of nouns are called **cases**. There are three main cases: nominative (nom) – the subject of the sentence; genitive (gen) – this shows possession, that something belongs to someone; and accusative (acc) – the object of the sentence. English grammar has lost virtually all examples of case. The English word 'who' is perhaps the only one that can actually illustrate this idea. It is 'who' in the nominative case, 'whose' in the genitive case and 'whom' in the accusative case. The following tables show the different forms of Greek articles.

Indefinite article *a/an*

	Masculine	**Feminine**	**Neuter**
(nom)	ένας [énas]	μία [mía]	ένα [éna]
(gen)	ενός [enós]	μίας [mías]	ενός [enós]
(acc)	έναν [énan]	μία [mía]	ένα [éna]

Definite article *the*

	Masculine	Singular **Feminine**	**Neuter**	**Masculine**	Plural **Feminine**	**Neuter**
(nom)	ο [o]	η [i]	το [to]	οι [i]	οι [i]	τα [ta]
(gen)	του [too]	της [tis]	του [too]	των [ton]	των [ton]	των [ton]
(acc)	το(ν) [to(n)]	τη(ν) [ti(n)]	το [to]	τους [toos]	τις [tis]	τα [ta]

Articles are often used with the preposition σε [se] *at, to, in, on*, creating compound definite articles in the genitive and accusative cases only. The words in the singular are: στου [stoo], στης [stis], στο(ν) [sto(n)], στη(ν) [sti(n)], and in the plural: στων [ston], στους [stoos], στις [stis], στα [sta]. These compound words cannot stand as two separate words, e.g. σε + του [se] + [too].

See also Units 1, 2 and 3 among others.

2 Nouns

The names of people and things are called **nouns**. As stated above, Greek nouns are divided into three genders, and each noun has a singular and plural form, and changes according to the role it plays in the sentence (its case) – nominative, genitive, accusative. When you look up nouns in a dictionary you will find them in the nominative singular form. You can usually tell their gender by their endings. Most masculine nouns end in **-ας [-as]**, **-ης [-is]** and **-ος [-os]**, most feminine nouns in **-α [-a]** and **-η [-i]**, and most neuter nouns in **-ι [-i]**, **-o [-o]** and **-μα [-ma]**. The course has introduced most nouns in the nominative case either in singular or plural. Some genitive and accusative forms have appeared in a few dialogues without any special mention. As a rule of thumb, remember that nouns in the nominative case come before the verb and indicate the subject of the sentence, nouns in the accusative case come after the verb and indicate the object. The genitive case is used to show possession. The different forms are set out below:

Masculine nouns

	Singular	Plural
(nom)	ο φίλος [o filos]	οι φίλοι [i fíli]
(gen)	του φίλου [too fíloo]	των φίλων [ton fílon]
(acc)	τον φίλο [ton fílo]	τους φίλους [toos fíloos]

Feminine nouns

	Singular	Plural
(nom)	η κουζίνα [i koozína]	οι κουζίνες [i koozínes]
(gen)	της κουζίνας [tis koozínas]	των κουζινών [ton koozinón]
(acc)	την κουζίνα [tin koozína]	τις κουζίνες [tis koozínes]

Neuter nouns

	Singular	Plural
(nom)	το βιβλίο [to vivlío]	τα βιβλία [ta vivlía]
(gen)	του βιβλίου [too vivlíoo]	των βιβλίων [ton vivlíon]
(acc)	το βιβλίο [to vivlío]	τα βιβλία [ta vivlía]

See also Units 1, 2, 3, 4 and 7 among others.

3 Adjectives

Adjectives are words which *describe* people or things. They give more information about the noun they describe. Note: a car (noun), a big car (adjective-noun), a big red car (adjective-adjective-noun). The endings of adjectives change according to the noun they describe, i.e. masculine, feminine or neuter endings, singular or plural, nominative, genitive, accusative. Most adjectives have the same endings as the word **μεγάλος [megálos]** *big* below:

Singular

	Masculine	Feminine	Neuter
(nom)	μεγάλος [megálos]	μεγάλη [megáli]	μεγάλο [megálo]
(gen)	μεγάλου [megáloo]	μεγάλης [megális]	μεγάλου [megáloo]
(acc)	μεγάλο [megálo]	μεγάλη [megáli]	μεγάλο [megálo]

Plural

	Masculine	Feminine	Neuter
(nom)	μεγάλοι [megáli]	μεγάλες [megáles]	μεγάλα [megála]
(gen)	μεγάλων [megálon]	μεγάλων [megálon]	μεγάλων [megálon]
(acc)	μεγάλους [megáloos]	μεγάλες [megáles]	μεγάλα [megála]

See also Units 10, 11 and 12 among others.

4 Adverbs

Adverbs are words which usually describe *the way* things happen. Unlike adjectives, which give more information about the *nouns* they describe, adverbs give more information about the *verbs* they describe. Many Greek adverbs end in **-α [-a]** or **-ως [-os]**, something similar to the English ending *-ly* for many English adverbs. Some examples include: **γρήγορα [grígora]** *quickly*, **καλά [kalá]** *well, nicely*, **βέβαια [vévea]** of *course/surely*.

Many Greek adverbs are formed from their corresponding adjective. Notice the changes below: **γρήγορος [grígoros]** *fast, quick* → **γρήγορα [grígora]** *quickly*, **καλός [kalós]** *good, nice* → **καλά [kalá]** *nicely*, **βέβαιος [véveos]** *certain, sure* → **βέβαια [vévea]** *surely*. Unlike adjectives, adverbs have only one form. There is a small exception to this remark regarding a few adjectives which have two almost similar forms which are interchangeable in use. Some examples are **βέβαια** [vévea] and **βεβαίως** [vevéos] *of course, surely* and **σπάνια** [spánia] and **σπανίως** [spaníos] *rarely.*

Adverbs are often 'doubled up' for the purpose of emphasis. You can go over the notes on page 158, in Unit 12.

See also Unit 8.

5 Pronouns

Important and frequent words like *I, you, he* or *my, your, his* or *myself, yourself, himself* or *me, you, him* etc. are pronouns. Pronouns are grouped in several sub-categories: personal, reflexive, demonstrative, possessive, relative, interrogative and indefinite pronouns.

Personal pronouns

	Nominative		Genitive		Accusative	
	strong	**weak**	**strong**	**weak**	**strong**	**weak**
I	εγώ [egó]	–	εμένα [eména]	μου [moo]	εμένα [eména]	με [me]
you	εσύ [esí]	–	εσένα [eséna]	σου [soo]	εσένα [eséna]	σε [se]
he	αυτός [aftós]	τος [tos]	αυτού [aftoó]	του [too]	αυτόν [aftón]	τον [ton]
she	αυτή [aftí]	τη [ti]	αυτής [aftís]	της [tis]	αυτή(v) [aftí(n)]	τη(v) [ti(n)]
it	αυτό [aftó]	το [to]	αυτού [aftoó]	του [too]	αυτό [aftó]	το [to]
we	εμείς [emís]	–	εμάς [emás]	μας [mas]	εμάς [emás]	μας [mas]
you (pl)	εσείς [esís]	–	εσάς [esás]	σας [sas]	εσάς [esás]	σας [sas]
they	αυτοί [aftí]	τοι [ti]	αυτών [aftón]	τους [toos]	αυτούς [aftoós]	τους [toos]
	αυτές [aftés]	τες [tes]			αυτές [aftés]	τις/τες [tis/tes]
	αυτά [aftá]	τα [ta]			αυτά [aftá]	τα [ta]

Personal pronouns have both a strong and a weak form in the genitive and accusative cases.

Most Greek verbs like **έχω [ého]** *I have* take the nominative form of the personal pronoun, which is not absolutely necessary as it is in English, because the ending of the verb itself shows who is the subject. Some verbs like **μου αρέσει [moo arési]** *I like* or **με λένε [me léne]** *I am called* take the accusative form of the personal pronoun. All strong forms are used for the purpose of emphasis in Greek. Actually it is possible to use both the strong and weak form for extra emphasis. E.g. **εμένα μου αρέσει το ράδιο [eména moo arési to ráTHio]** *I (I) like the radio* or **εμένα με λένε Δημήτρη [eména me léne THimítri]** *I (I) am called Dimitri*.

Check also Units 2, 3 and 5.

Reflexive pronouns

Words like *myself, yourself*, etc. are reflexive pronouns. They are not as common in Greek as in English and they usually appear only in the accusative form with prepositions, e.g. **με τον εαυτό μου [me ton eaftó moo]** <u>with</u> *myself*, **για τον εαυτό της [yia ton eaftó tis]** <u>for</u> *herself*, **στον (σε + τον) εαυτό τους [ston eaftó toos]** <u>to</u> *themselves*.

Demonstrative pronouns

	Masculine	Feminine	Neuter
this	αυτός [aftós]	αυτή [aftí]	αυτό [aftó]
these	αυτοί [aftí]	αυτές [aftés]	αυτά [aftá]
that	εκείνος [ekínos]	εκείνη [ekíni]	εκείνο [ekíno]
those	εκείνοι [ekíni]	εκείνες [ekínes]	εκείνα [ekína]
such a	τέτοιος [tétios]	τέτοια [tétia]	τέτοιο [tétio]
such + pl	τέτοιοι [tétyi]	τέτοιες [téties]	τέτοια [tétia]
so much	τόσος [tósos]	τόση [tósi]	τόσο [tóso]
so many	τόσοι [tósi]	τόσες [tóses]	τόσα [tósa]

- The different forms in the singular and plural for **αυτός**, **εκείνος** and **τόσος** are identical with the adjective **μεγάλος, -η, -ο** as shown in the previous paragraph in this section.
- The demonstrative pronouns **αυτός** and **εκείνος** need the corresponding article for the noun in use, e.g. αυτός **ο** άντρας [aftós o ándras] *this man*, εκείνη **η** γυναίκα [ekíni i yinéka] *that woman*, αυτά **τα** παιδιά [aftá ta peTHiá] *these children*.

Possessive pronouns

my	μου [moo]
your (sing/infml)	σου [soo]
his	του [too]
her	της [tis]
its	του [too]
our	μας [mas]
your (pl/fml)	σας [sas]
their	τους [toos]

Possessive pronouns have only one form in Greek. They always come *after* the noun they modify, whereas in English they come before the noun. In Greek, the noun is accompanied by its corresponding article, e.g. **το σπίτι μου [to spíti moo]** *my house*, **τα σπίτια μας [ta spítia mas]** *our houses*, **ο φίλος της [o fílos tis]** *her friend*, **οι φίλοι τους [i fíli toos]** *their friends*.

These words are called possessive pronouns in Greek grammar and possessive adjectives in English grammar!

Check also Unit 5.

Relative pronouns

The words below are the most common relative pronouns in Greek.

who	που [poo]
which	που [poo]
that	που [poo]
whatever	ό,τι [óti]

Interrogative pronouns

Question words like *what? who? how? where?* are interrogative pronouns. Some have only one form, some more than one for m/f/n use.

what?	τι; [ti]?
where?	πού; [poo]?
how?	πώς; [pos]?
why?	γιατί; [yiatí]?
when?	πότε; [póte]?

	Masculine	Feminine	Neuter
who? which?	ποιος; [pios]?	ποια; [pia]?	ποιο; [pio]?
how much?	πόσος; [pósos]?	πόση; [pósi]?	πόσο; [póso]?
which ones?	ποιοι; [pii]?	ποιες; [pies]?	ποια; [pia]?
how many?	πόσοι; [pósi]?	πόσες; [póses]?	πόσα; [pósa]?

Indefinite pronouns

Words like *each one*, *everyone*, *someone*, *no-one*, etc. are indefinite pronouns. Some have only one form, some more than one for m/f/n use.

all, everything	όλα [óla] + plural
something, anything?	κάτι [káti]
nothing, anything?	τίποτα [típota]
every, each	κάθε [káthe]

	Masculine	Feminine	Neuter
everyone (m/f/n)	καθένας [kathénas]	καθεμία [kathemía]	καθένα [kathéna]
everybody (m/f/n) + (pl)	όλοι [óli]	όλες [óles]	όλα [óla]
some (pl)	μερικοί [merikí]	μερικές [merikés]	μερικά [meriká]
someone, something (m/f/n)	κάποιος [kápios]	κάποια [kápia]	κάποιο [kápio]
one, one (person) (m/f/n)	κανείς [kanís]	καμία [kamía]	κανένα [kanéna]
no-one, nothing (m/f/n)	κανένας [kanénas]	καμία [kamía]	κανένα [kanéna]

6 Prepositions

Prepositions in English are such words as *between*, *from*, *in*, *by*, *for*, *with*, etc. All corresponding Greek prepositions have only one form. The word following Greek prepositions will sometimes be followed by a noun in the genitive or more often in the accusative case. Some frequent prepositions are:

Genitive		
εναντίον	[enandíon]	*against*
μεταξύ	[metaxí]	*between*
υπέρ	[ipér]	*in favour, for*

Accusative		
από	[apó]	*from*
για	[yia]	*for, to, over*
με	[me]	*with, by*
χωρίς	[horís]	*without*
μετά	[metá]	*after*
μέχρι	[méhri]	*until*
πριν	[prin]	*before*
προς	[pros]	*towards*
σε	[se]	*to, in, on, at (place)*
στις	[stis]	*at (time)*

There are also some two-word prepositions. All of them are followed by nouns in the accusative.

Accusative		
πάνω από	[páno apó]	*over, above*
κάτω από	[káto apó]	*underneath, below*
μπροστά από	[brostá apó]	*in front of*
πίσω από	[píso apó]	*behind*
κοντά σε	[kondá se]	*close to*
δίπλα σε	[THípla se]	*next to*
γύρω από	[yíro apó]	*around from*
μέσα σε	[mésa se]	*inside*
έξω από	[ékso apó]	*outside, out of*

7 Verbs

Words that indicate action, being, or feeling are called verbs. **Κάνω** [**káno**] *I do*, **μιλάω** [**miláo**] *I speak* or **μένω** [**méno**] *I live* are three examples from the several verbs this course includes.

Remember that a dictionary will list these three verbs, and all others, using the I-form of the verb. This is the main form used for reference to Greek verbs (as the infinitive form in English – to do, to speak, to live, etc. – does not exist in Greek) as well as for the I-form in the present tense. Verb tenses refer to different points in time, such as the present, the future and the past. This course relies mostly on present tense, touches on the future and past tenses, and introduces some forms after the word **να** [**na**] and imperatives.

Also, remember that personal pronouns, words like *I, he, they*, etc. in English, are not necessary in Greek because of the change in the verb ending. So, **κάνω** can be seen as **κάν-** (the verb stem which remains unchanged) and -ω (the verb ending which tells you whether *I, he, they*, etc. is performing the action). There are two verb endings in Greek for the I-form: -ω [-o] and μαι [-me], e.g. περιμένω [periméno] *I wait* and κάθομαι [káthome] *I sit*. The course introduces you to the main verb groups (or conjugations – there are two main conjugations) in both the active voice (verbs ending in -ω) and the passive voice (verbs ending in -ομαι/-αμαι).

The present tense for the main verb groups found in the course are set out below. Once you memorize the different endings, you will be confident enough to use them in context. Remember that the majority of Greek verbs fall into the first conjugation.

Present tense

Active voice

1st Conjugation

έχω	[ého]	*I have*
έχεις	[éhis]	*you have*
έχει	[éhi]	*he/she/it has*
έχουμε	[éhoome]	*we have*
έχετε	[éhete]	*you have*
έχουν	[éhoon]	*they have*
θέλω	[thélo]	*I want*
θέλεις	[thélis]	*you want*
θέλει	[théli]	*he/she/it wants*
θέλουμε	[théloome]	*we want*
θέλετε	[thélete]	*you want*
θέλουν(ε)	[théloon(e)]	*they want*

Check also Units 1, 2, 3.

2nd Conjugation

Group A		
πεινάω/πεινώ	[pináo/pinó]	*I am hungry*
πεινάς	[pinás]	*you are hungry*
πεινά(ει)	[piná(-i)]	*he/she/it is hungry*
πεινάμε	[pináme]	*we are hungry*
πεινάτε	[pináte]	*you are hungry*
πεινούν(ε)	[pinoón(e)]	*they are hungry*

Group B

μπορώ	[boró]	I can
μπορείς	[borís]	you can
μπορεί	[borí]	he/she/it can
μπορούμε	[boroóme]	we can
μπορείτε	[boríte]	you can
μπορούν(ε)	[boroón(e)]	they can

Both groups in the second conjugation include verbs always stressed on the last syllable in their main form.

Passive voice

χαίρομαι	[hérome]	I am glad
χαίρεσαι	[hérese]	you are glad
χαίρεται	[hérete]	he/she/it is glad
χαιρόμαστε	[herómaste]	we are glad
χαίρεστε	[héreste]	you are glad
χαίρονται	[héronde]	they are glad
λυπάμαι	[lipáme]	I am sorry
λυπάσαι	[lipáse]	you are sorry
λυπάται	lipáte]	he/she/it is sorry
λυπόμαστε	[lipómaste]	we are sorry
λυπάστε	[lipáste]	you are sorry
λυπούνται	[lipoónde]	they are sorry

All verbs in the passive voice end in **-μαι [-me]**.

Future tense

The future tense in Greek is formed with the particle **θα [tha]** (equivalent to *will* in English) and the verb. Some verbs do not change their form in the future tense, but most do. Below you see a list of verbs belonging to both groups:

Verbs without any different form in the future

θα είμαι [tha íme] *I will be*, θα έχω [tha ého] *I will have*, θα ξέρω [tha kséro] *I will know* and θα πάω [tha páo] *I will go*.

Verbs with a different form in the future

Most verbs belong to this sub-group. Examples are:

δίνω → θα δώσω	[tha THóso]	*I will give*
θέλω → θα θελήσω	[tha thelíso]	*I will want*
μένω → θα μείνω	[tha míno]	*I will stay*
παίρνω → θα πάρω	[tha páro]	*I will take*
στέλνω → θα στείλω	[tha stílo]	*I will send*
φέρνω → θα φέρω	[tha féro]	*I will bring*
φεύγω → θα φύγω	[tha fígo]	*I will leave*

Verbs with an irregular form in the future

Some verbs have a completely new form in the future. Examples are:

βλέπω → θα δω	[tha THo]	*I will see*
έρχομαι → θα έρθω	[tha értho]	*I will come*
ζω → θα ζήσω	[tha zíso]	*I will live*
τρώω → θα φάω	[tha fáo]	*I will eat*
χαίρομαι → θα χαρώ	[tha haró]	*I will be glad*

The different endings for *I, he/she/it, you,* etc. are the same as those in the present tense. Below are two verbs **έχω** and **στέλνω** with their full forms in the future:

θα έχω	[tha ého]	*I will have*
θα έχεις	[tha éhis]	*you will have*
θα έχει	[tha éhi]	*he/she it will have*
θα έχουμε	[tha éhoome]	*we will have*
θα έχετε	[tha éhete]	*you will have*
θα έχουν	[tha éhoon]	*they will have*
θα στείλω	[tha stílo]	*I will send*
θα στείλεις	[tha stílis]	*you will send*
θα στείλει	[tha stíli]	*he/she/it will send*
θα στείλουμε	[tha stíloome]	*we will send*
θα στείλετε	[tha stílete]	*you will send*
θα στείλουν	[tha stíloon]	*they will send*

Here again is the full table for **είμαι [íme]**, the verb *to be*:

θα είμαι	[tha íme]	*I will be*
θα είσαι	[tha íse]	*you will be*
θα είναι	[tha íne]	*he/she/it will be*
θα είμαστε	[tha ímaste]	*we will be*
θα είσαστε/είστε	[tha ísaste]	*you will be*
θα είναι	[tha íne]	*they will be*

The imperative form

The imperative is a form of the verb you can use to request, tell or order someone to do something, e.g. 'Come here!', 'Stop!', 'Don't speak!', 'Turn left!', 'Go now!'. This form is very frequent and important in everyday language. Remember that since Greek has two 'you' forms (informal–singular and formal–plural) as many other languages including German, French or Spanish, you need to learn two individual words for the imperatives.

These are some of the verbs presented in Unit 11.

(sing/infml)	**(pl/fml)**	
πήγαινε [píyene]!	πηγαίνετε [piyénete]!	*Go!*
στρίψε [strípse]!	στρίψτε [strípste]!	*Turn!*
θγες [vyes]!	θγείτε [vyíte]!	*Get off! Get out!*
συνέχισε [sinéhise]!	συνεχίστε [sinehíste]!	*Continue!*
σταμάτησε [stamátise]!	σταματήστε [stamatíste]!	*Stop!*
περπάτησε [perpátise]!	περπατήστε [perpatíste]!	*Walk!*
οδήγησε [oTHíyise]!	οδηγήστε [oTHiyíste]!	*Drive!*

Other tenses

This course intentionally has not introduced the learner to other verb tenses with the exception of Unit 15 which outlined the past tense of the verb 'to be'. Rarely, some verbs appeared in different tenses but those were few instances and no grammatical mention was made. Two examples to illustrate this are: **καλώς σας βρήκα! [kalós sas vríka]!** *Nice to have met you!* and **έχω κάνει κράτηση [ého káni krátisi]** *I have made a reservation* (present perfect).

Here again is the table for the past form of the verb **είμαι** *to be*:

ήμουν	[ímoon]	*I was*
ήσουν	[ísoon]	*you were*
ήταν	[ítan]	*he/she/it was*
ήμασταν	[ímastan]	*we were*
ήσασταν	[ísastan]	*you were*
ήταν	[ítan]	*they were*

Here is the past tense of **έχω** *I have*:

είχα	[íha]	*I had*
είχες	[íhes]	*you had*
είχε	[íhe]	*he/she/it had*
είχαμε	[íhame]	*we had*
είχατε	[íhate]	*you had*
είχαν	[íhan]	*they had*

For interested learners, the *Teach Yourself Greek* complete course introduces all main verb tenses.

key to the exercises

Unit 1

1 **a** [kaliméra] **b** [kalispéra] **c** [kaliníhta]
2 **a** iii **b** v **c** i **d** ii **e** iv
3 **a** i **b** iii **c** ii **d** iv
4 a, c, e, b, d
5 **a** i **b** iii **c** i **d** ii
6 **a** [i] **b** [o] **c** [o] **d** [o] **e** [i] **f** [i]
7 **a** [sas] **b** [o] **c** [i] **d** [polí] **e** [stin] **f** [se] **g** [me]
8

k	a	l	i	m	e	r	a
a	b	o	p	s	t	i	n
l	b	o	o	t	h	i	o
a	y	i	a	s	o	o	t
p	e	r	i	m	e	n	o

Mini test

1 **a** [yiásoo], **b** [ti kánis]?, **c** [ti kánis eTHó sto aeroTHrómio]?,
d [efharistó], **e** [yiásas], **f** [kaliméra] - [kaliníhta], **g** [héro polí]
2 **a** [yia], **b** [yiásoo], **c** [yiásas], **d** [yia/yiásoo]

Unit 2

1 **a** [eláTHa] Ελλάδα (**i**) [eliniká] ελληνικά **b** [ispanía]
Ισπανία (**ii**) [ispaniká] ισπανικά **c** [italía] Ιταλία (**iii**)
[italiká] ιταλικά **d** [galía] Γαλλία (**iv**) [galiká] γαλλικά
e [anglía] Αγγλία (**v**) [angliká] αγγλικά.
2 **a** iv, **b** ii, **c** iii, **d** i

3 **a** [íne apó tin thesaloníki]. *He/she is from Thessaloniki.* **b** [alá
  tóra méno stin pátra]. *But now I live in Patras.* **c** [miláo italiká
  ke líga ispaniká]. *I speak Italian and a little Spanish.* **d** [i
  athína íne stin eláTHa]. *Athens is in Greece.* **e** [ke to parísi stin
  galía]. *And Paris in France.*
5 **a** ii, **b** iii, **c** ii, **d** ii, **e** i, **f** ii
6 **a** [italía] Ιταλία, **b** [anglía] Αγγλία, **c** [ispanía] Ισπανία,
  d [galía] Γαλλία, **e** [yermanía] Γερμανία
7 **a** [apó], **b** [óhi], **c** [egó], **d** [esí], **e** [óhi], **f** [alá]

Mini test

a [apó poo íse]? or [apó poo íste]? **b** [poo ménis tóra]? or [poo
ménete tóra]? **c** [íme apó to Cardiff] [alá tóra méno sto
Manchester]. **d** [angliká], [galiká], [ispaniká], [yermaniká],
[eliniká], [italiká] **e** [lonTHíno], [rómi], [athína] **f** [ne] – [óhi],
[póli] – [hóra], [eliniká] – [angliká], [maTHríti] – [parísi], [egó]
[esí], [emís] – [aftí] or [aftés] or [aftí]

Unit 3

1 **b** [esí], **c** [aftí]/[aftés]/[aftá], **d** [egó], **e** [aftós], **f** [aftí], **g** [emís],
  h [aftí]/[aftés]/[aftá]
2 **a** [THen miláme yermaniká]. **b** [THen kséro ton ángelo].
  c [THen ksérete tin ána]. **d** [THen periméni tris fíloos]. **e** [THen
  ménoon sta yiánena]. **f** [THen íme apó tin amerikí]. **g** [THen íne
  apó tin italía].
3 **a** [ménete stin yermanía]? **b** [aftí íne apó tin afstralía]? **c** [kséris
  líga eliniká]? **d** [aftés periménoon THío fíloos]? **e** [milás
  angliká]? **f** [THen miláte ispaniká]? **g** [íste apó tin anglía]?
4 **a** [yiatrós] γιατρός, **b** [THaskála] δασκάλα, **c** [nosokóma]
  νοσοκόμα, **d** [sigraféas] συγγραφέας, **e** [servitóros]
  σερβιτόρος, **f** [arhitéktonas] αρχιτέκτονας
5 **a** iv, **b** v, **c** i, **d** ii, **e** iii
6 **a** ii, **b** i, **c** ii, **d** iii, **e** ii
7 **a** [íme servitóra. THen íme pianístria]. *I'm a waitress. I'm not a
  pianist.* **b** [THen íme sigraféas]. *I'm not a writer.* **c** [íste yiatrós]?
  [óhi], [íme moosikós]. *Are you a doctor? No, I'm a musician.*
  d [méno kondá stin thesaloníki]. *I live close to (near) Thessaloniki.*
  e [THen ímaste apó tin anglía]. *We are not from England.*
8 **a** [kséris], **b** [óhi], **c** [móno], **d** [poo], **e** [kondá], **f** [ne]

Mini test

a [ti THooliá kánis]? [ti THooliá kánete]? **b** e.g. [íme sigraféas].
c I'm a writer. **d** I live in Manchester. I live close to Manchester.
e [ángelos], [yiánis], [thomás], [dimítris] **f** [maría], [ána], [ioána]

g [yiatrós], [THáskalos], [nosokómos] *male nurse*, [servitóros] **h** what?, how/what?, where?, who/which/what? **i** [íse] is informal, [íste] is more formal. **j** [THen katalavéno]. See Exercise 2 in this unit for how to form negative sentences.

key to the exercises

Unit 4

1 a v, **b** iv, **c** i, **d** ii, **e** vi, **f** iii
2 a [kondá] κοντά *near* – [makriá] μακριά *far*, **b** [póli] πόλη *city* – [hóra] χώρα *country*, **c** [spíti] σπίτι *house* – [THiamérizma] διαμέρισμα *apartment/flat*, **d** [salóni] σαλόνι *living room* – [kathistikó] καθιστικό *sitting room*, **e** [koozína] κουζίνα *kitchen* – [trapezaría] τραπεζαρία *dining room*, **f** [mikró] μικρό *small* – [megálo] μεγάλο *big*
3 a iv, **b** ii, **c** i, **d** v, **e** iii
4 c, e, b, d, f, a
5 a [salóni], **b** [trapezaría], **c** [koozína], **d** [bánio], **e** [ipnoTHomátio], **f** [hol]
6 a [éna]/[miTHén]/[miTHén], **b** [éna]/[tría]/[tésera], **c** [éna]/[éksi]/[éksi], **d** [éna]/[éksi]/[eniá], **e** [éna]/[eptá]/[éna], **f** [éna], [eniá], [eniá]
7 a [spíti], **b** [garsoniéra], **c** [salóni], **d** [koozína], **e** [bánio], **f** [retiré] vertical: saloni
8 a [sálo], **b** [pósa], **c** [megálo], **d** [mazí], **e** [pénde], **f** [polí]

Mini test

a [bánio], [tooaléta], [vesé], **b** [tzamaría], [trapezaría], [ipnoTHomátio], [koozína], **c** [retiré], [THiamérizma], [garsoniéra], [katikía], **d** [méno se mía monokatikía sto lonTHíno], **e** [mikró], [makriá], [polikatikía], **f** [kathistikó], [tooaléta], [katikía], **g** [eptá]/[éksi]/[tésera]/ [pénde]/[éna]/[tría]/[októ], [miTHén]/[THío]/[tésera]/[eniá]

Unit 5

1 a iv, **b** ii, **c** i, **d** vi, **e** v, **f** iii
2 a vi, **b** ii, **c** iv, **d** iii, **e** v, **f** i
3 a iv, **b** iii, **c** i, **d** v, **e** ii
4 a 15, **b** 17, **c** 12, **d** 13, **e** 11, **f** 14
5 a 7849321, **b** 9904057
6 a [to THiamérizmá too], **b** [to spíti mas], **c** [o papoós toos], **d** [i mitéra tis], **e** [to THomátió moo], **f** [o ándras soo] or [o ándras sas] or [o sízigos soo] or [o sízigos sas]

7

p	a	p	o	o	s	y
a	n	p	l	h	c	i
m	y	i	n	e	k	a
e	o	a	e	n	a	y
k	o	r	i	t	s	i
k	m	i	t	e	r	a

8 **a** [ándras], **b** [ton], **c** [peTHiá], **d** [korítsi], **e** [níkos], **f** [hronón], **g** [THóTHeka], **h** [THéka], **i** [eptá], **j** [yiatí]

Mini test

a [patéras], [mitéra], [peTHí], [papoós], [yiayiá], [yios], [kóri], [egonós], [egoní], [aTHelfós], [aTHelfí], [(e)ksáTHelfos], [(e)ksaTHélfi]
b 11 [éndeka], 12 [THóTHeka], 14 [THekatésera], 17 [THekaeptá] or [THekaeftá], 19 [THekaeniá] or [THekaenéa], 20 [íkosi] **c** Any answer is possible here. Say it to a native speaker! **d** [póso hronón íse/íste]?
e Peter, Hope, Anthony, Niobe [from Greek mythology: the daughter of Tantalus], James, Helen. **f** [pos to léne] [sta eliniká]?

Unit 6

1 **a** iii, **b** v, **c** iv, **d** vi, **e** i, **f** ii
2 **a** iii, **b** v, **c** iv, **d** vi, **e** i, **f** ii
3 **a** iv, **b** v, **c** i, **d** iii, **e** ii
4 c, e, a, d, f, b
5 **a** [kondá soo]? [yiatí]?, **b** [angliká]? [egó], [thélo na miláo] [eliniká]!, **c** [yiatí óhi]? [kafé stin arhí]. [éna frapé] [yia ména].
6 **a** [ksanavlépo], **b** [psomí], **c** [lemonáTHa] **d** [tsái], **e** [himós], **f** [frapés], **g** [kóka kóla]
7 **a** [eláte], **b** [kanapé], **c** [karékla], **d** [pináte], **e** [éna], **f** [mía], **g** [éhis], **h** [yia], **i** [ména]

Mini test

a [kafés], [portokaláTHa], [tsái], [himós], [lemonáTHa], [frapés], [gála]
b [éla kondá moo] and [páme kondá too] **c** [éhete] [portokaláTHa i himó]? **d** [kathíste] or [páre mía karékla] **e** For example: 82 [ogTHónda THío], 15 [THekapénde], 56 [penínda éksi] **f** Unit 6 starts on page 64, and finishes on page 75. [apó eksínda tésera méhri evTHomínda pende].

Unit 7

1 **a** [mov], **b** [ble], **c** [prásino], **d** [kítrino], **e** [portokalí], **f** [kókino]
2 **a** [ble] + [áspro], **b** [prásino] + [áspro] + [kókino], **c** [mávro] +
[kókino] + [kítrino], **d** [kókino] + [áspro], **e** [ble] + [áspro] +
[kókino], **f** [kókino] + [kítrino]
3 **a** [moo arésoon i kathréftes], **b** [moo arésoon i kanapéTHes],
c [moo arésoon i karékles], **d** [moo arésoon i polithrónes], **e**
[moo arésoon ta bánia], **f** [moo arésoon ta krevátia]
4 **a** v, **b** iv, **c** i, **d** iii, **e** ii
5 **a** [mikró], **b** [oréo], **c** [THíkeo], **d** [lígo], **e** [áshimo], **f** [polí],
g [áTHiko], **h** [megálo], **i** [tetrágono]
6 e, b, d, a, f, c
7 **a** [praktikó], **b** [vévea], **c** [lootró], **d** [arésoon], **e** [kathréftis],
f [áspro], **g** [alá], **h** [THíkio]
8 **a** false, **b** true, **c** true, **d** false, **e** true
9 *Mary* I like Greece because it's small. *[elpíTHa]* I don't agree.
It's not very small. *Mary* I disagree but … I like the weather in
Greece. *[elpíTHa]* Here I agree with you. You are right. *Mary* Of
course, because I don't prefer the rain in London. *[elpíTHa]* You
are not wrong.

Mini test

a [áspro], [mávro], [mov], [ble], [prásino], [kítrino], [portokalí],
[kókino] **b** [antipathó], [THiafonó], [ého áTHiko] **c** [moo arési] or
[moo arésoon], [simfonó], [ého THíkio] **d** [antipathó], [THen
marési] **e** [karékla], [trapézi], [kanapés], [polithróna], [kreváti]
f [strongilós], [mikrós], [áspros] **g** [tetrágonos], [megálos], [mávros]

Θα σε δω εκεί! means 'I will see you there!'

Unit 8

The phrases correspond to the cartoons on page 93:
e, a, k, j, n, d, m, c, h, b, g, i, f, l
1 b, i, g, e, a, j, h, k, c, f, l, d
2 **a** *I arrive at work at 8:00.* **b** *I get up early.* **c** *I return home late.*
d *I go to bed late.* **e** *I go to work.* **f** *I have dinner at 9:00.* **g** *I
don't have [lit. eat] breakfast, only coffee.* **h** *I have lunch at
work.* **i** *I take a shower.* **j** *I have (lit. drink) a lot of coffee at
work.* **k** *I finish work at 6:00.* **l** *I watch some TV at 10:00.*
3 There are no correct or incorrect answers in this exercise. If you
have scored less than 200, you need to put in more effort! If you
have scored more than 400, then **[sinharitíria ke brávo]!**
4 **a** iii, **b** v, **c** i, **d** vi, **e** ii, **f** iv

5 **a** 8:05, **b** 8:30, **c** 10:30, **d** 1:45, **e** 11:45, **f** 7:05
6 **a** ii, **b** ii, **c** iv, **d** iii
7 **a** [óli], **b** [ksipnáo], **c** [tró-o], **d** [pérno], **e** [epistréfo], **f** [apó],
  g [méhri], **h** [tróte], **i** [yíro], **j** [ékso]

Mini test

a [ekató tésera] – [ekató ogTHónda tésera] – [THiakósia triánda
éna] – [tetrakósia penínda éksi] - [oktakósia íkosi eptá] – [eniakósia
penínda éna] – [hília] **b** [eftá ke íkosi], [októmisi], [eniá], [éndeka
ke tétarto], [miámisi], [téseris ke THéka], [éksi pará tétarto] **c**
[sikónome] – [ftáno] – [telióno] – [epistréfo] – [pérno] **d** **i** [pánda
sikónome stis eksímisi]. **ii** [poté THen ftáno sti THooliá norís].
iii [merikés forés telióno ti THooliá moo argá]. **iv** [spánia tró-o ékso].
v [sheTHón pánda pérno to tréno].

Unit 9

1 [THimítris] 1, 3, 6, 7 , [níkos] 2, 3, 4, [maría] 1, 2, 5, 6
2 **i** 3, **ii** 4, **iii** 6, **iv** 1, **v** 7, **vi** 2, **vii** 5
3 **a** i/ii/iv/v, **b** i/ii/iv/v, **c** i/ii/iv/v, **d** iii **e** i/ii/iv/v
4 **a** [vlépi], **b** [akoón], **c** [moo arésoon] or [mas arésoon],
  d [THiavázoome], **e** [sihénome], **f** [protimás] or [protimáte]
5 **a** Nick never watches TV. **b** Mary and James always listen to the
  radio. **c** I like pop and rock music. **d** We read many books in
  Greece. **e** I despise cigarettes. **f** Do you prefer the radio or the
  TV?
6 [ángelos] 1, 2, 4, 6, [THéspina] 2, 3, 5, 6, [ariána] 1, 3, 4, 5
7 **a** [marésoon], **b** [enTHiaféron], **c** [troháTHin], **d** [forés],
  e [piyéno], **f** [THiavázo], **g** [siníthos], **h** [istorías]

Mini test

a [laiká], [elafrolaiká], [rebétika] **b** [noovéles], [mithistorímata],
[astinomiká], [istoríes agápis], [peripéties] **c** [komoTHíes],
[THramatiká], [thríler], [astinomiká] **d** [ti kánis ton eléfthero hróno
soo]? and [pos pernás tis eléftheres óres soo]? **e** for example: [vlépo
tileórasi], [káno vóltes], [páo théatro], etc. **f** running, walks/rides,
interesting, usually, mainly **g** [pánda], [sheTHón pánda],
[sihénome] or [antipathó], [dramatiká]

Unit 10

1 **a** [banána], **b** [fráoola], **c** [yiarmás], **d** [stafíli], **e** [mílo], **f** [karpoózi],
  i [kolokitháki], **ii** [agoóri], **iii** [domáta], **iv** [karóto], **v** [ánithos],
  vi [maindanós]
2 **b** [i fráoola] – [i fráooles], **c** [o yiarmás] – [i yiarmáTHes],
  d [to stafíli] – [ta stafília], **e** [to mílo] – [ta míla], **f** [to karpoózi] –

[ta karpoózia], **ii** [to agoóri] - [ta agoória], **iii** [i domáta] -
[i domátes], **iv** [to karóto] - [ta karóta], **v** [o ánithos] - [i ánithi],
vi [o maindanós] - [i maindaní]

3 b η φράουλα – οι φράουλες, **c** ο γιαρμάς – οι γιαρμάδες,
d το σταφύλι – τα σταφύλια, **e** το μήλο – τα μήλα, **f** το
καρπούζι – τα καρπούζια, **i** το αγγούρι – τα αγγούρια,
ii η ντομάτα – οι ντομάτες, **iii** το καρότο – τα καρότα, **iv**
ο άνιθος – οι άνιθοι, **v** ο μαϊντανός – οι μαϊντανοί
4 b [i patátes], **c** [i domátes], **d** [to skórTHo], **ii** [to ahláTHi],
iii [ta stafília], **iv** [i fráooles]
5 a [penínda evró] πενήντα ευρώ, **b** [THekaeftá evró] δεκαεφτά
ευρώ, **c** [ekató evró] εκατό ευρώ, **d** [THóTHeka evró] δώδεκα
ευρώ, **e** [triánda tésera evró] τριάντα τέσσερα ευρώ,
f [evTHomínda evró] εβδομήντα ευρώ
6 a 5, **b** 3, **c** 6, **d** 2, **e** 4, **f** 1
7 i c, **ii** b, **iii** a, **iv** d, **v** e, **vi** f
8 a [marési na piyéno vóltes mazí soo]. **b** [thélo na páo sti laikí
agorá]. **c** [prépi na se THo]. **d** [boró na íme thimoménos]. **e** [borí
na tin léne eléni].
9 a [ipárhoon], **b** [portokália], **c** [epohí], **d** [fisiká], **e** [káto],
f [lahaniká], **g** [agoória], **h** [kiló]

Mini test

a [ananás], [hoormás], [yiarmás], [banána], [fráoola], [agriófrapa]
or [greípfroot], [stafíli], [pepóni], [roTHákino], [portokáli],
[karpoózi]
b [ánithos], [maintanós], [arakás] or [bizéli], [patáta], [domáta],
[melitzána], [karóto], [sélino], [kolokitháki], [maroóli], [agoóri]
c [eftihizménos], [pinazménos], [thimoménos], [THipsazménos],
[lipiménos], [taragménos], [ékpliktos], [koorazménos]; (the
masculine ending [-os] changes to [-i] for the feminine form).
d [tetrakósia penínda], [eksakósia evTHomínda], [hília THiakósia],
[tris hiliáTHes eniakósia], [pénde hiliáTHes], [eptá hiliáTHes
tetrakósia], [eniá hiliáTHes pendakósia], [THéka hiliáTHes]
e [aftí] with different spellings means (1) she (2) they (3) this. A
fourth word with the same sound is the word for 'ear'! The Greek
spellings respectively are: (1) αυτή, (2) αυτοί, (3) αυτή, (4) αυτί (n)
f [póso káni]? and [póso kánoon]?

Unit 11

1 a iii, **b** ii, **c** i, **d** ii, **e** i, **f** iii
2 a v, **b** viii, **c** i, **d** vii, **e** ii, **f** iii, **g** vi, **h** ix, **i** iv
3 a vi, **b** iv, **c** viii, **d** i, **e** vii, **f** iii, **g** v, **h** ii
4 i e, **ii** f, **iii** d, **iv** c, **v** h, **vi** g, **vii** a, **viii** b, **ix** i

5 a [thélo] [nalákso] [merikés taksiTHiotikés epitayés], **b** [íne se líres anglías], **c** [íme tiherós símera]. [marési aftó]. [oríste]!
6 a [nalákso], **b** [epitayés], **c** [nómizma], **d** [líra], **e** [léte], **f** [tahiTHromío], **g** [éfkolo], **h** [tahiTHromío] **i** [mólis]
7 You ticked numbers 1, 3, 4, 5, 6, 7
8 (1) **f**, (3) **e**, (4) **c**, (5) **d**, (6) **b**, (7) **a**

Mini test

a [tahiTHromío] ΤΑΧΥΔΡΟΜΕΙΟ, [trápeza] ΤΡΑΠΕΖΑ, [ksenoTHohío] ΞΕΝΟΔΟΧΕΙΟ, [moosío] [ΜΟΥΣΕΙΟ]
b [aristerá], [efthía], [ísia], [THeksiá] **c** [signómi], [me sinhoríte], [lipáme] **d** hospital, restaurant, car park, garage, petrol station, airport **e** [makriá], [THípla], [mínimarket] or [bakáliko], [THeksiá], [eTHó] **f** [mas léte] [póso éhi]…?, [ého] [merikés taksiTHiotikés epitayés]. [poo boró] [na tis alákso]?, [ého líres angliás ke amerikánika THolária].

Unit 12

1 a iv, **b** vi, **c** i, **d** v, **e** ii, **f** iii
2 e, b, f, c, a, d
3 i *Can I help you?* **ii** *Yes, I'd like to see this dress.* **iii** *What colour do you like?* **iv** *Light brown or beige.* **v** *Unfortunately, I've got only dark brown.* **vi** *I'm sorry. I dislike dark colours.*
4 i b, **ii** c, **iii** d, **iv** a
5 i *Mary wants to go to the bathroom.* **ii** *I have to buy a pair of glasses.* **iii** *I'd like to go for a walk now.* **iv** *Dimitris needs to go to the bathroom.*
6 a vi, **b** ii, **c** iii, **d** v, **e** iv, **f** i
7

Ε	Α	Ν	Ο	Ι	Κ	Τ	Ο
Κ	Ε	Α	Τ	Α	Τ	Α	Ш
Ε	Δ	Ω	Θ	Ν	Θ	Μ	Α
Ι	Ω	Σ	Θ	Τ	Κ	Ε	Ν
Γ	Π	Α	Σ	Ι	Δ	Α	Τ
Κ	Α	Ε	Ι	Σ	Τ	Θ	Α

8 a [timí], **b** [pookámiso], **c** [meséo], **d** [riyé], **e** [karó], **f** [perisótero], **g** [THokimáso], **h** [THokimastírio], **i** [péra]

Mini test

a If not more than half, revise again! **b** ΑΝΔΡΩΝ – Men, ΓΥΝΑΙΚΩΝ – Women **c** ΕΛΞΑΤΕ – Pull, ΩΘΗΣΑΤΕ – Push **d** No, it's not. Things are out of order... **e** ΕΞΟΔΟΣ – Exit, ΕΙΣΟΔΟΣ – Entrance **f** [leptó], [noómero], [galázio] or [skoóro ble], [áspro], [aniktó], [karékla] **g** Is that right? Do you agree with me? Is that so? **h** καφέ [kafé], ροζ [roz], μπεζ [bez], γαλάζιο [galázio] **i** Easy or fairly easy: Go directly to the next unit. Difficult: Revise once again before you go on to the next unit.

Unit 13

1 a [365 triakósies eksínda pénde iméres se éna hróno], **b** [12 mínes se éna hróno], **c** [52 evTHomáTHes se éna hróno], **d** [7 iméres se mía evTHomáTHa], **e** [2 evTHomáTHes se éna THekapenthímero], **f** [24 íkosi téseris óres se mía iméra], **g** [60 leptá se mía óra], **h** [100 hrónia se éna eóna].

2 a May 22, May 24, May 25, **b** [boró na se THo tin kiriakí] (21/5), [tin tríti], [tin paraskeví], [ke tin kiriakí] (28/5).

3 a 8 ΔΕΥΤΕΡΑ [THeftéra], 9 ΤΡΙΤΗ [tríti], 11 ΠΕΜΠΤΗ [pémpti], 12 ΠΑΡΑΣΚΕΥΗ [paraskeví], **b** 8 ΠΡΟΧΤΕΣ [prohtés], 9 ΕΧΤΕΣ [ehtés], 11 ΑΥΡΙΟ [ávrio], 12 ΜΕΘΑΥΡΙΟ [methávrio]

4 a iii, **b** iv, **c** i, **d** ii

5 a iv, **b** ii, **c** vi, **d** v, **e** iii, **f** i

6 a I never go to work by plane! **b** I like taking/going by train often. **c** Many times it is not easy (to find) a taxi in Athens. **d** There are usually many cars in my neighbourhood. **e** I sometimes go to school on foot. **f** I almost never take the bus.

7 a Ladies and Gentlemen... The Pet Shop Boys, Wednesday June 28 and Thursday June 29 at the Lycabettus Theatre. **b** Every day at 7:00

8 ΡΟΔΟΣ – ΤΡΙΤΗ, ΠΕΜΠΤΗ, ΣΑΒΒΑΤΟ, ΚΥΡΙΑΚΗ/ΣΑΝΤΟΡΙΝΗ – ΔΕΥΤΕΡΑ, ΤΡΙΤΗ, ΤΕΤΑΡΤΗ, ΠΑΡΑΣΚΕΥΗ/ΗΡΑΚΛΕΙΟ – ΤΡΙΤΗ, ΠΕΜΠΤΗ, ΣΑΒΒΑΤΟ

9 a [thélo merikés pliroforíes parakaló]. [ipárhoon plía yia tin éyina]?
b [pio íne to pio grígoro ke pio íne to pio fthinó]? [póte févyi to epómeno iptámeno THelfíni]? **d** [póso káni]? **e** [mepistrofí yia ména].

10a [petái], **b** [taksíTHi], **c** [ptísis], **d** [kéndro], **e** [leoforío], **f** [akóma], **g** [krátisi], **h** [amésos], i [as THoóme]

Mini test

a [tréno], [aeropláno], [aftokínito], [leoforío], [poTHílato], [taksí], [motosikléta], [metró], [várka], [plío] b [ipárhi taksiTHiotikó grafío eTHó kondá]? c [apló isitírio ke mepistrofí] d [krátisi], [thési], [pliroforíes] e [ti óra févyi]/[érhete]/[ftáni] f Information (Desk) g [hártis], [pínakas THromoloyíon], [telonío], [aposkevés], [valítsa], [THiavatírio]

Unit 14

1 i c, ii b, iii d, iv a
2 i b, c, e, f, h, ii a, c, d, g, h, iii a, b, d, e, g
3 a [mía méra], b [tris méres], c [téseris méres], d [éksi méres], e [mía evTHomáTHa], f [éna THekapenthímero]
4 [dooz], [sapoóni], [sampooán], [petséta], [tooaléta], [bánio]
5 i a b e, ii a c d, iii b c e
6 a [ne]! [mípos éhete THomátia]?, b [éna THíklino me bánio], c [boró na to THo]? [okéi], [tha to páro]. d [oríste]! [poo íne to asansér]?
7 a iv, b vi, c ii, d v, e i, f iii
8 a Δυστυχώς είμαστε γεμάτοι! [THistihós ímaste yemáti]! *Unfortunately, we're full!* b Καλή διαμονή! [kalí THiamoní]! *Have a nice stay!* c Πόσο καιρό θα μείνετε; [póso keró tha mínete]? *How long will you stay?* d Για έξι μέρες ή μία εβδομάδα; [yia éksi méres i mía evTHomáTHa]? *For six days or a week?* e Μπορείτε να συμπληρώσετε αυτό το έντυπο; [boríte na simlirósete aftó to éndipo]? *Can you fill in this form?* f Θέλουμε ένα δίκλινο, παρακαλώ! [théloome éna THíklino], [parakaló]! *We'd like a double room, please.*
9 a [théloome], b [krátisi], c [imerominía], d [tetárti], e [próvlima], f [théa]

Mini test

a [thélo éna monóklino]. [thélo éna THíklino]. b [thélo éna monóklino me bánio ke tileórasi]. c [thélo éna tríklino me théa tin thálasa]. d *Your room is on the third floor.* e [póso káni to THomátio] [tin ímera]? f e.g. [Krátisi], [THomátio], [éndipo], [monóklino], [bánio] g [lipáme], [poothená], [THíklino], [bánio], [élksate], [pithanós]–[borí], [isóyion]

Unit 15

1 a [éna tsái], b [éna kafé], c [éna gála], d [éna himó], e [mía bíra], f [mía retsína]/[éna krasí], g [éna bookáli neró]
2 a ένα: ένα τσάι, b δύο: ένα καφέ, c τρία: ένα γάλα,

d τέσσερα: ένα χυμό, **e** πέντε: μία μπύρα, **f** έξι: μία ρετσίνα – ένα κρασί, **g** επτά: ένα μπουκάλι νερό

3 a [flitzáni], **b** [piáto], **c** [mahéri], **d** [piroóni], **e** [kootáli], **f** [potíri], **g** [potíri bíras], **h** [potíri yia krasí]

4 a [mía horiátiki], [éna tzatzíki], [ke patátes tiganités]. **b** [arnáki ke patátes sto foórno]. **c** [mía meríTHa pastítsio] [ke mía yemistá].

5 a 303, **b** 383, **c** 391, **d** 881

6 a ΦΑΤΕ [fáte], **b** ΚΡΑΣΙ [krasí], **c** ΒΙΒΛΙΟ [vivlío], **d** ΝΕΡΟ [neró], **e** ΛΟΓΑΡΙΑΣΜΟ [logariazmó], **f** ΦΕΡΝΕΤΕ [férnete], **g** ΣΑΛΑΤΑ [saláta], vertical word: [tavérna]

7 i a, c, e, **ii** a, b, f, **iii** a, d, e

8 a [ítan], **b** [gliká], **c** [spitikó], **d** [epísis], **e** [ópos], **f** [skéto], **g** [glikó]

Mini test

a [moo férnete ton katálogo parakaló]?, [moo férnete ton logariazmó parakaló]? **b** [moo férnete], [moo THínete], [férte moo] **c** *I'll be right there!* **d** e.g. [lígo neró], [éna krasí], [mía bíra] **e** e.g. [éna moosaká], [mía saláta], [mía patátes] **f** [éna mahéri] [parakaló]!, [éna piroóni], [parakaló]!, [éna piáto], [parakaló]!, [éna potíri], [parakaló]!

g *appetizers, small dishes, fish, on the grill, cooked to order, desserts*

Revision test 1

1 **a** [kaliméra], **b** [hérete], **c** [kalispéra], **d** [kaliníhta],
   e [kaliníhta]

2 **a** [yiásas], **b** [yiásoo], **c** [pos íse]? **d** [kalá efharistó], [esí]?
   e [óhi áshima]/[kalá], [efharistó].

3 **a** [tría], [pénde], **b** [eptá], [THéka], **c** [éndeka], [THóTHeka],
   [THekatésera], **d** [THekaéksi], [THekaeniá], [íkosi]

4 **i** b, **ii** d, **iii** e, **iv** a, **v** c

5 **b** [hol], **c** [koozína], **d** [salóni], **e** [ipnoTHomátio],
   f [trapezaría], **g** [bánio]

6 **a** [amerikí], **b** [yermanía], **c** [galía], **d** [italía], **e** [eláTHa],
   i [angliká], **ii** [yermaniká], **iii** [galiká], **iv** [italiká], **v** [eliniká]

7 **a** ii, **b** i, **c** ii, **d** iii, **e** iii

8 **a** iii, **b** i, **c** ii, **d** ii, **e** i, **f** i

9 **a** [sigraféas], **b** [servitóra], **c** [athína], **d** [kaliméra], **e** [yiatrós],
   f [amerikí], **g** [moosikós], **h** [patéras], **i** [THoolévo], **j** [kondá],
   k [pianístas], **l** [THáskalos]

10 **a** [yiásoo maría]! [héro polí]! **b** [apó tin amerikí]. [apó tin néa
   iórki]. [esí]? **c** [ki'egó méno stin athína tóra]. [íme sigraféas
   peTHikón vivlíon].

Revision test 2

1 **a** v, **b** ii, **c** iv, **d** i, **e** vi, **f** iii

2 **a** *I work from 8:00 to 4:00.* **b** *Mary is at home from 9:30 to
   6:00.* **c** *I never eat from 12:30 to 9:00.* **d** *I am at work from
   7:00 to 4:00.* **e** *I don't like to work from 9:00 to 5:00.* **f** *George
   watches TV from 10:30 to 7:30.*

3 **a** iv, **b** ii, **c** i, **d** iii, **e** vi, **f** v

4 **a** *Mary is in the kitchen and is cooking.* **b** *John is outside the
   house.*

c *My mother watches TV a lot.* d *My father always reads the newspaper.* e *Kostas listens to music all day.* f *Helen is in the office from 9:00 to 1:00.*

5 a viii, b ii, c i, d ix, e iii, f iv, g x, h vi, i vii, j v

6 a *I take a shower.* b *I have breakfast.* c *I go to bed (lit. sleep).* d *I wake up at 7:00.* e *I read in bed.* f *I go to work.* g *I leave from work.* h *I get up from bed.* i *I get ready for work.* j *I get ready for sleep.*

7 a [ksipnáo stis eptá]. b [sikónome apó to kreváti]. c [páo sto bánio]. d [káno dooz]. e [tró-o proinó]. f [akoó-o ráTHio]. g [páo sti THooliá]. h [epistréfo spíti]. i [káno vraTHinó]. j [pérno tiléfono éna fílo]. k [vlépo tileórasi]. l [páo yia ípno].

8 a vii, b iii, c ix, d i, e x, f ii, g iv, h v, i vi, j viii

9

a	f	p	k	a	t	o
a	r	a	k	a	s	o
n	a	a	m	o	d	
a	o	a	l	e	l	a
n	o	t	o	r	a	k
a	l	a	t	oo	r	f
s	a	m	r	o	o	h

Revision test 3

1 a [tría tetrágona], b [tría tetrágona], c [tésera tetrágona], d [pénde tetrágona], e [pénde tetrágona]

2 i c, ii d, iii e, iv a, v b

3 a iii, b v, c i, d vi, e ii, f iv

4 a i, b iii, c v, d ii, e vi, f iv

5 a [ianooários], b [fevrooários], c [mártios], d [aprílios], e [máios], f [ioónios], g [ioólios], h [ávgoostos], i [septémvrios], j [októvrios], k [noémvrios], l [THekémvrios]

6 a [kiriakí], b [THeftéra], c [tríti], d [tetárti], e [pémpti], f [paraskeví], g [sávato]

7 *dishes à la minute, refreshments–soft drinks, beers–wines,* [kóka kóla], [spráit], [portokaláTHa], [sóTHa]

8 a [hília evró] χίλια ευρώ, b [THío hiliádes evró] δύο χιλιάδες ευρώ, c [THiakósia penínda evró] διακόσια πενήντα ευρώ, d [triakósia penínda evró] τριακόσια πενήντα ευρώ,

e [pendakósia evró] πεντάκοσια ευρώ.
9 **a** iv, **b** v, **c** iii, **d** i, **e** ii
10 **i** *Turn your radio on* (lit. open) – *station.* **ii** *Summer 2000 Eleftheroudakis Bookstore* **iii** *Ionian Bank* **iv** *Joker – the big game* **v** *Opening hours: Tuesday – Saturday 10:00 – 14:00, Sunday 11:00 – 14:00, Monday: closed*

taking it further

This section gives you many suggestions of sources to help you develop your interest in Greek language and culture. It also provides you with a number of email addresses and Internet sites which can give a different dimension to your search. Some of the sites listed are bilingual but others are only in Greek. Good luck!

Books

If you are in Athens, check out Eleftheroudakis bookshop at 16 Panepistimiou St. for the largest selection of books in English about Greek or Greece. Their website is **http://www.books.gr** and their email address is elebooks@hellasnet.gr. The National Book Centre of Greece issues a bi-monthly magazine promoting Greek books in translation abroad. They can be found at 76 Emmanuil Benaki St. or at **http://www.book.culture.gr**. The free *Travelling in Greece* brochure is very informative and available from any GNTO office in Greece or abroad. Their address is 2 Amerikis St. and their Internet address is below under the Travel heading. Check out **http://www.toubis.gr** for the largest selection of maps or travel books in English on Greece.

Cultural heritage

http://www.greece.gr is a sophisticated online magazine about Greece. **http://www.culture.gr** is the website of the Ministry of Culture and hosts many of the country's museums. **http://www.reconstructions.org** has fabulous 3-D models of the Parthenon. **http://www.fhr.gr** is the website of the Foundation of the Hellenic World. **http://www.pbs.org/empires/thegreeks** brings Ancient Greece alive. **http://www.sae.gr** is the site for the World Council of Hellenes Abroad.

Transport

http://www.gtp.gr gives ferry timetables. **http://www.ose.gr** offers train information. **http://www.ktel.gr** gives bus timetables and routes. **http://www.aia.gr** is the website for the new Athens airport. **http://www.olympic-airways.gr**, **http://www.airmanos.gr**, **http://www.cronus.gr**, or **http://www.airgreece.gr** offer flight information. **http://www.elit.gr** gives information about cruise ships.

Travel

http://www.greekholidays.com/cities_and_islands.html is a website about travel and holidays in Greece. The Greek National Tourism Organization can be found under **http://www.gnto.gr**. You can also access **http://www.travelling.gr** or **http://www.greekislands.gr** for travel agencies, tourist offices and tourist attractions. **http://www.ntua.gr/weather** offers frequently updated information on the weather. The site **http://www.allhotels.gr** offers hotel accommodation all over Greece. **http://www.travelplan.gr** is the largest travel agency in Greece.

Greek language

Information about online Greek language courses can be obtained from **http://www.polyglot24.com**. If you are interested in Greek poetry in English, send an e-mail to poetrygreece@hotmail.com. Writing to centre@greeklanguage.gr will connect you to the Greek Language Centre of the Ministry of Education which can offer valuable information about Greek classes or language examinations. **http://www.cyathens.org** is a study-abroad-programme of the College Year in Athens.

Miscellaneous

http://www.greekcuisine.com offers an extensive array of Greek recipes. **http://www.greekwine.gr** lists several Greek wines from all over Greece. There are two daily newspapers in English: **http://www.k-english.com** and **http://www.athensnews.dolnet.gr**. **http://www.in.gr** is the largest Greek portal on the web for Greek speakers. **http://www.athens.olympic.org** is an important site for everyone interested in the Olympic Games in Athens in 2004. Some sites for Greek music are: **http://www.babylon.gr**, **http://www.avpolis.gr**, or **http://www.mad.gr**. Online auctions can be found at **http://www.fleamarket.gr**. Greek comics can be purchased at **http://www.arkas.gr**.

English–Greek glossary

(Note: m = masculine, f = feminine, n = neuter)

a.m.	[pi-mi]	π.μ.
a/an/one	[énas], [mía], [éna]	ένας, μία, ένα
about/approximately	[perípoo]	περίπου
across/opposite	[apénandi]	απέναντι
adventure story/thriller	[peripétia]	περιπέτεια (f)
afterwards, later	[metá]	μετά
again	[páli]	πάλι
agree	[simfonó]	συμφωνώ
airplane	[aeropláno]	αεροπλάνο (n)
airport	[aeroTHrómio]	αεροδρόμιο (n)
almost	[sheTHón]	σχεδόν
along/together	[mazí]	μαζί
always	[pánda]	πάντα
America	[amerikí]	Αμερική (f)
and	[ke]	και
angry	[thimoménos, -i, -o]	θυμωμένος, -η -ο
another, more	[álos, -i, -o]	άλλος, -η, -ο
apartment building	[polikatikía]	πολυκατοικία (f)
apartment/flat	[THiamérizma]	διαμέρισμα (n)
appetizer, starter	[orektikó]	ορεκτικό (n)
April	[aprílios]	Απρίλιος (m)
architect	[arhitéktonas]	αρχιτέκτονας (m/f)
area	[hóros]	χώρος (m)
armchair	[poliTHróna]	πολυθρόνα (f)
around, about	[yíro], [perípoo]	γύρω, περίπου
arrive	[ftháno]	φθάνω
as	[ópos]	όπως
Athens	[athína]	Αθήνα (f)
August	[ávgoostos]	Αύγουστος (m)
Australia	[afstralía]	Αυστραλία (f)
autumn/fall	[fthinóporo]	φθινόπωρο (n)
availability	[THiathesimótita]	διαθεσιμότητα (f)

baby	[moró]	μωρό (n)
baby boy	[bébis]	μπέμπης (m)
baby girl	[béba]	μπέμπα (f)
balcony/porch	[balkóni]	μπαλκόνι (n)
banana	[banána]	μπανάνα (f)
bank	[trápeza]	τράπεζα (f)
basement	[ipóyion]	υπόγειον (n)
basketball	[básket]	μπάσκετ (n)
bass (fish)	[lavráki]	λαβράκι (n)
bathroom, bathtub	[bánio]	μπάνιο (n)
bathroom, toilet	[tooaléta]	τουαλέτα (f)
be	[íme]	είμαι
be able	[boró]	μπορώ
be glad	[hérome]	χαίρομαι
be happy	[héro]	χαίρω
be interested	[enTHiaférome]	ενδιαφέρομαι
be pleased	[héro]	χαίρω
beach	[plaz]	πλαζ (f)
bean	[fasóli]	φασόλι (n)
beautiful, nice	[oréos, -a, -o]	ωραίος, -α, -ο
bed	[kreváti]	κρεβάτι (n)
bedroom	[krevatokámara],	κρεβατοκάμαρα (f),
	[ipnoTHomátio]	υπνοδωμάτιο (n)
beef	[mosharísios, -a, -o]	μοσχαρίσιος, -α, -ο
beefsteak	[biftéki]	μπιφτέκι (n)
beer	[bíra]	μπύρα (f)
behind	[píso]	πίσω
beige	[bez]	μπεζ
bell	[kooTHoóni]	κουδούνι (n)
Berlin	[verolíno]	Βερολίνο (n)
between	[metaksí]	μεταξύ
beverage, drink	[potó]	ποτό (n)
big, large	[megálos, -i, -o]	μεγάλος, -η, -ο
bill	[logariazmós]	λογαριασμός (m)
black	[mávros, -i, -o]	μαύρος, -η, -ο
block	[tetrágono]	τετράγωνο (n)
blue	[ble]	μπλε
blues (music)	[blooz]	μπλουζ (n)
boat	[várka]	βάρκα (f)
book	[vivlío]	βιβλίο (n)
bookshop	[vivliopolío]	βιβλιοπωλείο (n)
booklet	[filáTHio]	φυλλάδιο (n)
bottle	[bookáli]	μπουκάλι (n)
bottled (mineral) water	[emfialoméno neró]	εμφιαλωμένο νερό (n)
boy	[agóri]	αγόρι (n)
bravo	[brávo]	μπράβο
bread	[psomí]	ψωμί (n)
breakfast	[proinó]	πρωινό (n)
bridge	[yéfira]	γέφυρα (f)

brother	[aTHelfós]	αδελφός (m)
brown	[kafé]	καφέ
bus	[leoforío]	λεωφορείο (n)
bus station	[stathmós leoforíon]	σταθμός λεωφορείων (m)
bus stop	[stási leoforíon]	στάση λεωφορείων (f)
busy	[apasholiménos, -i, -o]	απασχολημένος, -η, -ο
but	[alá], [ma]	αλλά, μα
butcher's shop	[kreopolíon]	κρεοπωλείο
butter	[voótiro]	βούτυρο (n)

café	[kafetéria]	καφετέρια (f)
can	[boró]	μπορώ
can/tin	[kootí]	κουτί (n)
car	[aftokínito]	αυτοκίνητο (n)
car park	[párkin]	πάρκιν (n)
card	[kárta]	κάρτα (f)
carrot	[karóto]	καρότο (n)
cash desk	[tamío]	ταμείο (n)
celery	[sélino]	σέλινο (n)
central	[kendrikós, -í, -ó]	κεντρικός, -ή, -ό
centre	[kéndro]	κέντρο (n)
century	[eónas]	αιώνας (m)
cereal	[dimitriaká]	δημητριακά (n/pl)
chair	[karékla]	καρέκλα (f)
changing room	[THokimastírio]	δοκιμαστήριο (n)
cheap	[fthinós, -í, -ó]	φθηνός, -ή, -ό
checked	[karó]	καρώ (m/f/n)
cheque	[epitayí]	επιταγή (f)
child	[peTHí]	παιδί (n)
church	[eklisía]	εκκλησία (f)
cigarette	[tsigáro]	τσιγάρο (n)
cinema	[sinemá]	σινεμά (n)
close to	[kondá]	κοντά
closed	[klistós, -í, -ó]	κλειστός, -ή, -ό
closet/wardrobe	[doolápa]	ντουλάπα (f)
coca cola	[kóka kóla]	κόκα κόλα (f)
coffee	[kafés]	καφές (m)
coffee house	[kafenío]	καφενείο (n)
coffee (medium sweet)	[métrios]	μέτριος (m)
coffee (sweet)	[glikós]	γλυκός (m)
coffee (without sugar)	[skétos]	σκέτος (m)
comedy	[komoTHía]	κωμωδία (f)
company	[etería]	εταιρεία (f)
computer	[kompioóter]	κομπιούτερ (n)
conservatory	[tzamaría]	τζαμαρία (f)
contrast, antithesis	[antíthesi]	αντίθεση (f)
cook	[mayirévo]	μαγειρεύω
cooked foods	[mayireftá]	μαγειρευτά (n/pl)
corner	[gonía]	γωνία (f)

counter	[pángos]	πάγκος (m)
courgette, zucchini	[kolokitháki]	κολοκυθάκι (n)
cousin	[(e)ksaTHélfi],	(ε)ξαδέλφη (f),
	[(e)ksáTHelfos]	(ε)ξάδελφος (m)
credit card	[pistotikí kárta]	πιστωτική κάρτα (f)
creme caramel	[krem karamelé]	κρεμ καραμελέ (n)
croissant	[krooasán]	κρουασάν (n)
cucumber	[agoóri]	αγγούρι (n)
cup	[flitzáni]	φλυτζάνι (n)
currency	[nómizma]	νόμισμα (n)
customs	[telonío]	τελωνείο (n)
cutlet	[brizóla]	μπριζόλα (f)

dark	[skoóros, -a, -o]	σκούρος, -α, -ο
date	[imerominía]	ημερομηνία (f)
daughter	[kóri]	κόρη (f)
day	[(i)méra]	(η)μέρα (f)
December	[THekémvrios]	Δεκέμβριος (m)
deposit, down payment	[prokatavolí]	προκαταβολή (f)
dessert	[glikó]	γλυκό (n)
dialogue	[THiálogos]	διάλογος (m)
difficult	[THískolos, -i, -o]	δύσκολος, -η, -ο
dill	[ánithos]	άνιθος (m)
dining room	[trapezaría]	τραπεζαρία
dinner	[vraTHinó]	βραδινό (n)
disagree	[THiafonó]	διαφωνώ
discotheque	[THiskothíki]	δισκοθήκη (f)
dislike	[antipathó]	αντιπαθώ
doctor	[yiatrós]	γιατρός (m/f)
door	[pórta]	πόρτα (f)
dorado or gilthead	[tsipoóra]	τσιπούρα (f)
double room	[THíklino]	δίκλινο (n)
down	[káto]	κάτω
dress	[fórema]	φόρεμα (n)
drink	[píno]	πίνω

early	[norís]	νωρίς
easy	[éfkolos, -i, -o]	εύκολος, -η, -ο
eat	[tró-o]	τρώω
eight	[októ]/[ohtó]	οκτώ/οχτώ
eight hundred	[oktakósia]/[ohtakósia]	οκτακόσια/οχτακόσια
eighteen	[THekaoktó]	δεκαοκτώ
eighty	[ogTHónda]	ογδόντα
eleven	[éndeka]	έντεκα
England	[anglía]	Αγγλία (f)
English (language)	[angliká]	Αγγλικά (n/pl)
entrance	[ísoTHos]	είσοδος (f)
envelope	[fákelos]	φάκελος (m)
Euro	[evró]	ευρώ

evening	[vráTHi]	βράδυ (n)
every	[káthe]	κάθε
everything/all	[óla]	όλα
everywhere	[pandoó]	παντού
exactly	[akrivós]	ακριβώς
excuse me, pardon me	[signómi], [me sinhoríte]	συγνώμη, με συγχωρείτε (pl/fml)
exit	[éksoTHos]	έξοδος (f)
fall (verb)	[péfto]	πέφτω
family	[ikoyénia]	οικογένεια (f)
father	[patéras]	πατέρας (m)
February	[fevrooários]	Φεβρουάριος (m)
ferryboat	[féribot]	φέρυμποτ (n)
fifteen	[THekapénde]	δεκαπέντε
fifth	[pémptos, -i, -o]	πέμπτος, -η, -ο
fifty	[penínda]	πενήντα
film	[érgo] [film]	έργο (n), φιλμ (n)
finally	[teliká]	τελικά
finish	[telióno]	τελειώνω
first	[prótos, -i, -o]	πρώτος, -η, -ο
fish	[psári]	ψάρι (n)
fish restaurant	[psarotavérna]	ψαροταβέρνα (f)
five	[pénde]	πέντε
five hundred	[pendakósia]	πεντακόσια
flat, apartment	[THiamérizma]	διαμέρισμα (n)
flight	[ptísi]	πτήση (f)
floor	[órofos]	όροφος (m)
flying dolphin, hydrofoil	[iptámeno]	ιπτάμενο (n)
food	[trofí]	τροφή (f)
food cooked in oil	[laTHerá]	λαδερά (n/pl)
foot	[póTHi]	πόδι (n)
football	[poTHósfero]	ποδόσφαιρο (n)
for	[yia]	για
fork	[piroóni]	πιρούνι (n)
fortnight	[THekapenthímero]	δεκαπενθήμερο (n)
forty	[saránda]	σαράντα
four	[téseris, -is, -a]	τέσσερις, -ις, -α
four hundred	[tetrakósia]	τετρακόσια
fourteen	[THekatéseris, -is, -a]	δεκατέσσερις, -ις, -α
fourth	[tétartos, -i, -o]	τέταρτος, -η, -ο
France	[galía]	Γαλλία (f)
free	[eléftheros, -i, -o]	ελεύθερος, -η, -ο
French (language)	[galiká]	γαλλικά (n/pl)
friend	[fílos] [fíli]	φίλος (m), φίλη (f)
from	[apó]	από
front	[brostá]	μπροστά
fruit	[froóto]	φρούτο (n)
fruit and vegetable market	[laikí agorá]	λαϊκή αγορά (f)

garage	[garáz]	γκαράζ (n)
garlic	[skórTHo]	σκόρδο (n)
German (language)	[yermaniká]	γερμανικά (n/pl)
Germany	[yermanía]	Γερμανία (f)
get up	[sikónome]	σηκώνομαι
girl	[korítsi]	κορίτσι (n)
glass	[potíri]	ποτήρι (n)
go	[páo]	πάω
go for a walk	[páo vólta]	πάω βόλτα
good evening	[kalispéra]	καλησπέρα
good morning	[kaliméra]	καλημέρα
goodnight	[kaliníhta]	καληνύχτα
grandchild	[egóni]	εγγόνι (n)
granddaughter	[egoní]	εγγονή (f)
grandfather	[papoós]	παππούς (m)
grandmother	[yiayiá]	γιαγιά (f)
grandson	[egonós]	εγγονός (m)
grape	[stafíli]	σταφύλι (n)
Greece	[eláTHa]	Ελλάδα (f)
Greek (language)	[eliniká]	ελληνικά (n/pl)
green	[prásinos, -i, -o]	πράσινος, -η, -ο
grilled foods	[psitá]	ψητά (n/pl)
ground floor	[isóyion]	ισόγειον (n)
hairdresser's	[komotírio]	κομμωτήριο
half	[misós, -í, -ó]	μισός, -ή, -ó
hallway	[hol]	χωλ (n)
hand	[héri]	χέρι (n)
hand basin	[niptíras]	νιπτήρας (m)
happy	[eftihizménos, -i, -o]	ευτυχισμένος, -η, -ο
have	[ého]	έχω
he	[aftós]	αυτός
heating	[thérmansi]	θέρμανση (f)
hello / goodbye (pl/fml)	[hérete]	χαίρετε
hello / goodbye (pl/fml)	[yiásas]	γεια σας
hello / see you (sing/infml)	[yiásoo]	γεια σου
her	[tis]	της
herb	[aromatikó fitó]	αρωματικό φυτό (n)
here	[eTHó]	εδώ
here you are!	[oríste]	ορίστε
hi	[yia]	γεια
his	[too]	του
hobby	[hóbi]	χόμπυ (n)
homemade	[spitikós, -í, -ó]	σπιτικός, -ή, -ό
hospital	[nosokomío]	νοσοκομείο (n)
hotel	[ksenoTHohío]	ξενοδοχείο (n)
house/home	[spíti]	σπίτι (n)
how/what	[pos]	πώς

hungry	[pinazménos, -i, -o]	πεινασμένος, -η, -ο
husband/wife, spouse	[sízigos]	σύζυγος (m/f)
I	[egó]	εγώ
iced coffee/frappé	[frapés]	φραπές (m)
idea	[iTHéa]	ιδέα (f)
immediately	[amésos]	αμέσως
in	[se]	σε
information (piece of)	[pliroforía]	πληροφορία (f)
instant coffee	[nes kafés]	νες καφές (m)
interested (I'm)	[enTHiaférome]	ενδιαφέρομαί
interesting	[enTHiaféron]	ενδιαφέρον
introduce	[sistíno]	συστήνω
Ireland	[irlanTHía]	Ιρλανδία (f)
island music	[nisiótika]	νησιώτικα (n/pl)
it	[aftó]	αυτό
Italian (language)	[italiká]	ιταλικά (n/pl)
Italy	[italía]	Ιταλία (f)
its	[too]	του
January	[ianooários]	Ιανουάριος (m)
jazz music	[tzaz]	τζαζ (f)
job/work	[THooliá]	δουλειά (f)
juice	[himós]	χυμός (m)
July	[ioólios]	Ιούλιος (m)
June	[ioónios]	Ιούνιος (m)
keys	[kliTHiá]	κλειδιά
kilo	[kiló]	κιλό (n)
kiosk	[períptero]	περίπτερο (n)
kitchen	[koozína]	κουζίνα (f)
knife	[mahéri]	μαχαίρι (n)
know	[kséro]	ξέρω
lamb	[arnáki]	αρνάκι (n)
late	[argá]	αργά
lawn/grass	[grasíTHi]	γρασίδι (n)
learn	[mathéno]	μαθαίνω
leave	[févgo]	φεύγω
left	[aristerá]	αριστερά
lemonade	[lemonáTHa]	λεμονάδα (f)
letter	[gráma]	γράμμα (n)
lettuce	[maroóli]	μαρούλι (n)
lift/elevator	[asansér]	ασανσέρ (n)
light (colour), open	[aniktós, -í, -ó]	ανοικτός, -ή, -ό
(I) like	[marési]	μ'αρέσει
likely, probably	[pithanós, -í, -ó]	πιθανός, -ή, -ό
little	[lígos, -i, -o]	λίγος, -η, -ο
live	[méno]	μένω

living room	[salóni]	σαλόνι (f)
London	[lonTHíno]	Λονδίνο (n)
love	[agápi]	αγάπη (f)
love story	[istoría agápis]	ιστορία αγάπης (f)
lucky	[tiherós, -í, -ó]	τυχερός, -ή, -ό
luggage	[aposkeví]	αποσκευή (f)
lunch	[mesimerianó]	μεσημεριανό (n)
lyre	[líra]	λύρα (f)
Madrid	[maTHríti]	Μαδρίτη (f)
mainly	[kiríos]	κυρίως
man/husband	[ándras]	άνδρας (m)
map	[hártis]	χάρτης (m)
March	[mártios]	Μάρτιος (m)
market	[agorá]	αγορά (f)
marmalade/jam	[marmeláTHa]	μαρμελάδα (f)
May	[máios]	Μάιος (m)
may/is possible to	[borí na]	μπορεί να
me (after a preposition)	[(e)ména]	(ε)μένα
me (before a verb)	[moo]	μου
medium, middle	[meséos, -a, -o]	μεσαίος, -α, -ο
melon	[pepóni]	πεπόνι (n)
mezzanine (floor)	[imiórofos]	ημιόροφος (m)
midday/afternoon	[mesiméri]	μεσημέρι (n)
milk	[gála]	γάλα (n)
minute	[leptó]	λεπτό (n)
mirror	[kathréftis]	καθρέφτης (m)
Miss	[THespiníTHa]	δεσποινίδα
moment	[stigmí]	στιγμή (f)
month	[mínas]	μήνας (m)
more	[pio]	πιο
more	[perisóteros, -i, -o]	περισσότερος, -η, -ο
morning	[proí]	πρωί (n)
mother	[mitéra]	μητέρα (f)
motorcycle	[motosikléta]	μοτοσυκλέτα (f)
mountain	[voonó]	βουνό (n)
Mr/Sir	[kírios]	κύριος (m)
Mrs/Madam	[kiría]	κυρία (f)
much/very	[polís, polí, polí]	πολύς, πολλή, πολύ
museum	[moosío]	μουσείο (n)
mushroom	[manitári]	μανιτάρι (n)
music	[moosikí]	μουσική (f)
musician	[moosikós]	μουσικός (m/f)
must / have to	[prépi na]	πρέπει να
my	[moo]	μου
name	[ónoma]	όνομα (n)
national	[ethnikós, -í, -ó]	εθνικός, -ή, -ό
naturally	[fisiká]	φυσικά

nought/zero	[miTHén]	μηδέν
near, close to	[kondá]	κοντά
need	[hriázome]	χρειάζομαι
neighbourhood	[yitoniá]	γειτονιά (f)
never	[poté]	ποτέ
New York	[néa iórki]	Νέα Υόρκη (f)
newspaper	[efimeríTHa]	εφημερίδα (f)
next to	[THípla]	δίπλα
nice, beautiful	[oréos, -a, -o],	ωραίος, -α, -ο,
	[ómorfos, -i, -o]	όμορφος, -η, -ο
nine	[enéa]/[eniá]	εννέα/εννιά
nine hundred	[eniakósia]	ενιακόσια
nineteen	[THekaeniá]	δεκαεννιά
ninety	[enenínda]	ενενήντα
no	[óhi]	όχι
not	[THen]	δεν
nothing	[típota]	τίποτα
novel	[noovéla],	νουβέλα (f),
	[mithistórima]	μυθιστόρημα (n)
November	[noémvrios]	Νοέμβριος (m)
now	[tóra]	τώρα
number, size (of clothes)	[noómero]	νούμερο (n)
nurse	[nosokóma],	νοσοκόμα (f),
	[nosokómos]	νοσοκόμος (m)
October	[októvrios]	Οκτώβριος (m)
of course, naturally	[vévea]	βέβαια
often	[sihná]	συχνά
oh	[ah]	αχ
OK, all right	[kalá], [endáksi]	καλά, εντάξει
Olympic Airways	[olimbiakí]	Ολυμπιακή (f)
one	[énas], [mía], [éna]	ένας, μία, ένα
one hundred	[ekató]	εκατό
one thousand	[hílies], [hílji],	χίλιες (f), χίλιοι (m)
	[hília]	χίλια (n)
one-family house	[monokatikía]	μονοκατοικία (f)
orange (colour)	[portokalí]	πορτοκαλί
orange (fruit)	[portokáli]]	πορτοκάλι (n)
orangeade	[portokaláTHa]	πορτοκαλάδα (f)
our	[mas]	μας
out, outside	[ékso]	έξω
oven	[foórnos]	φούρνος (m)
over	[péra]	πέρα
p.m.	[mi-mi]	μ.μ.
pair	[zevgári]	ζευγάρι (n)
Paris	[parísi]	Παρίσι (n)
parsley	[maindanós]	μαϊντανός (m)
passport	[THiavatírio]	διαβατήριο (n)

pear	[ahláTHi]	αχλάδι (n)
penthouse	[retiré]	ρετιρέ (n)
petrol/gas	[venzíni]	βενζίνη (f)
petrol/gas station	[pratírio venzínis]	πρατήριο βενζίνης (n)
pharmacy	[farmakío]	φαρμακείο (n)
phrase	[ékfrasi]	έκφραση
pianist	[i pianístria],	η πιανίστρια (f),
	[o pianístas]	ο πιανίστας (m)
pineapple	[ananás]	ανανάς (m)
pink	[roz]	ροζ
plate	[piáto]	πιάτο (n)
play	[pézo]	παίζω
please/you're welcome	[parakaló]	παρακαλώ
police	[astinomía]	αστυνομία (f)
pop music	[laiká]	λαϊκά (n/pl)
pork	[hirinó]	χοιρινό (n)
portion	[meríTHa]	μερίδα (f)
post office	[tahiTHromío]	ταχυδρομείο (n)
potato	[patáta]	πατάτα (f)
pound (sterling)	[líra]	λίρα (f)
practical	[praktikós, -í, -ó]	πρακτικός, ή, -ό
prefer	[protimó]	προτιμώ
prepare	[etimázo]	ετοιμάζω
price	[timí]	τιμή (f)
private	[iTHiotikós], [-í], [-ó]	ιδιωτικός, -ή, -ό
problem	[próvlima]	πρόβλημα (n)
prospectus	[prospéktoos]	προσπέκτους (n)
purple	[mov]	μωβ
question	[erótisi]	ερώτηση (f)
radio	[raTHiófono]	ραδιόφωνο (n)
rain	[vrohí]	βροχή (f)
rarely	[spánia]	σπάνια
read	[THiavázo]	διαβάζω
realize, see	[vlépo]	βλέπω
reception	[ipoTHohí]	υποδοχή (f)
red	[kókinos], [-i], [-o]	κόκκινος, -η, -ο
red mullet	[barboóni]	μπαρμπούνι (n)
reservation	[krátisi]	κράτηση (f)
residence	[katikía]	κατοικία (f)
restaurant	[estiatório]	εστιατόριο (n)
return	[epistréfo]	επιστρέφω
return/round trip	[meepistrofí]	μεεπιστροφή (f)
right (direction)	[THeksiá]	δεξιά
right (justice)	[THíkio]	δίκιο (n)
river	[potamós]	ποταμός (m)
rock music	[rok]	ροκ (n)
Rome	[rómi]	Ρώμη (f)

room	[kámara]/[THomátio]	κάμαρα (f) / δωμάτιο (n)
round (in shape)	[strongilós, -í, -ó]	στρογγυλός, ή, ό
running	[troháTHin]	τροχάδην (n)
sad	[lipiménos, -i, -o]	λυπημένος, -η, -ο
salad	[saláta]	σαλάτα (f)
sale/discount	[ékptosi]	έκπτωση (f)
same	[íTHios, -a, -o]	ίδιος, -α, -ο
Saturday	[sávato]	Σάββατο (n)
saucer	[piatáki]	πιατάκι (n)
school	[sholío]	σχολείο (n)
science fiction	[epistimonikí fantasía]	επιστημονική φαντασία (f)
Scotland	[skotía]	Σκωτία (f)
sea	[thálasa]	θάλασσα (f)
season	[epohí]	εποχή (f)
second (adjective)	[THéfteros, -i, -o]	δεύτερος, η-, -ο
second (with time)	[THefterólepto]	δευτερόλεπτο (n)
see	[vlépo]	βλέπω
see again	[ksanavlépo]	ξαναβλέπω
September	[septémvrios]	Σεπτέμβριος (m)
sesame bagel	[kooloóri]	κουλούρι (n)
seven	[eptá]/[eftá]	επτά/εφτά
seven hundred	[eptakósia]/[eftakósia]	επτακόσια/εφτακόσια
seventeen	[THekaeftá]	δεκαφτά
seventy	[evTHomínda]	εβδομήντα
shampoo	[sampooán]	σαμπουάν (n)
she	[aftí]	αυτή
ship	[plío]	πλοίο (n)
shirt	[pookámiso]	πουκάμισο (n)
shoe	[papoótsi]	παπούτσι (n)
shoe lace	[korTHóni]	κορδόνι (n)
shop window	[vitrína]	βιτρίνα (f)
shower	[dooz]	ντους (n)
side	[plevrá]	πλευρά (f)
single room	[monóklino]	μονόκλινο (n)
sister	[aTHelfí]	αδελφή (f)
sit	[káthome]	κάθομαι
sitting room	[kathistikó]	καθιστικό (n)
six	[éksi]	έξι
six hundred	[eksakósia]	εξακόσια
sixteen	[THekaéksi]	δεκαέξι
sixty	[eksínda]	εξήντα
size	[mégethos]	μέγεθος (n)
sky blue	[galázios, -a, -o]	γαλάζιος, -α, -ο
sleep	[kimáme]	κοιμάμαι
slip-ons (loafers)	[pandoflé]	παντοφλέ (n)
slipper	[pandófla]	παντόφλα (f)
small	[mikrós, -í, -ó]	μικρός, -ή, -ό

smoke	[kapnízo]	καπνίζω
smoking	[kápnizma]	κάπνισμα (n)
so	[étsi], [tósos, -i, -o]	έτσι, τόσος, -η, -ο
soap	[sapoóni]	σαπούνι (n)
soda water	[sóTHa]	σόδα (f)
sofa	[kanapés]	καναπές (m)
soft	[malakós, -iá, -ó]	μαλακός, -ιά, -ό
soft pop	[elafrolaiká]	ελαφρολαϊκά (n/pl)
son	[yios]	γιος (m)
sorry	[signómi]	συγνώμη (m)
soup spoon	[kootáli]	κουτάλι (n)
space, area	[hóros]	χώρος (m)
Spain	[ispanía]	Ισπανία (f)
Spanish (language)	[ispaniká]	ισπανικά (n/pl)
speak	[miláo]	μιλάω
sport	[spor]	σπορ (n)
spring	[ániksi]	άνοιξη (f)
stamp	[gramatósimo]	γραμματόσημο (n)
stay (verb)	[káthome]	κάθομαι
stay	[THiamoní], [paramoní]	διαμονή (f), παραμονή (f)
still/yet	[akóma]	ακόμα
stool	[skambó]	σκαμπό (n)
story/history	[istoría]	ιστορία (f)
straight	[efthía]	ευθεία
straight ahead	[efthía brostá], [ísia]	ευθεία μπροστα, ίσια
strawberry	[fráoola]	φράουλα (f)
striped	[riyé]	ριγέ (m/f/n)
studio/bedsit	[garsoniéra]	γκαρσονιέρα (f)
study (verb)	[THiavázo]	διαβάζω
stuffed peppers and tomatoes	[yemistá]	γεμιστά (n/pl)
suitcase	[valítsa]	βαλίτσα (f)
summer	[kalokéri]	καλοκαίρι (n)
Sunday	[kiriakí]	Κυριακή (f)
supermarket	[soópermarket]	σούπερμαρκετ (n)
sure!	[amé]!	αμέ!
surprised	[ékpliktos, -i, -o]	έκπληκτος, -η, -ο
sweet	[glikós, -iá, ó]	γλυκός, -ιά, -ό
swimming	[bánio]	μπάνιο (n)
Sydney	[síTHnei]	Σίδνεϋ (n)
table	[trapézi]	τραπέζι (n)
table tennis	[ping pong]	πίνκ πονκ (n)
take	[pérno]	παίρνω
taxi	[taksí]	ταξί (n)
tea	[tsái]	τσάι (n)
tea spoon	[kootaláki]	κουταλάκι (n)
teacher	[THaskála], [THáskalos]	δασκάλα (f), δάσκαλος (m)
telephone booth	[tilefonikós thálamos]	τηλεφωνικός θάλαμος (m)

television	[tileórasi]	τηλεόραση (f)
ten	[THéka]	δέκα
tennis	[ténis]	τένις (n)
thanks (lit. I thank you)	[efharistó]	ευχαριστώ
thanks (lit. we thank you)	[efharistoóme]	ευχαριστούμε
that / who (in statements)	[poo]	που
the	[o], [i], [to]	ο, η, το
theatre	[théatro]	θέατρο (n)
their	[toos]	τους
them	[aftoós, aftés]	αυτούς (m), αυτές (f)
then, afterwards	[metá]	μετά
then/after that/later	[épita]	έπειτα
there	[ekí]	εκεί
Thessaloniki	[thesaloníki]	Θεσσαλονίκη (f)
they (only females)	[aftés]	αυτές
they (males and females)	[aftí]	αυτοί
they (only things)	[aftá]	αυτά
think	[nomízo]	νομίζω
third	[trítos, -i, -o]	τρίτος, -η, -ο
thirsty	[THipsazménos, -i, -o]	διψασμένος, -η, -ο
thirteen	[THekatrís, -ís, -ía]	δεκατρείς, -είς, -ία
thirty	[triánda]	τριάντα
though, although	[ómos]	όμως
three	[tris, tris, tría]	τρεις, τρεις, τρία
three hundred	[trakósia]	τριακόσια
thriller/horror (film)	[thríler]	θρίλερ (n)
ticket	[isitírio]	εισιτήριο (n)
time	[óra], [hrónos]	ώρα (f), χρόνος (m)
timetable	[pínakas THromoloyíon]	πίνακας δρομολογίων (m)
tired	[koorazménos, -i, -o]	κουρασμένος, -η, -ο
tiring	[koorastikós, -í, -ó]	κουραστικός, ή, ό
to (used with verbs)	[na]	να
to/ in/at the	[ston], [stin], [sto]	στον, στην, στο
to, until	[méhri]	μέχρι
today	[símera]	σήμερα (n)
toilet	[tooaléta]	τουαλέτα (f)
tomato	¨[domáta]	ντομάτα (f)
toothbrush	[oTHondóvoortsa]	οδοντόβουρτσα (f)
toothpaste	[oTHondópasta]	οδοντόπαστα (f)
towel	[petséta]	πετσέτα (f)
town/city	[póli]	πόλη (f)
train	[tréno]	τρένο (n)
train station	[stathmós trénon]	σταθμός τρένων (m)
travel agency	[taksiTHiotikó grafío]	ταξιδιωτικό γραφείο (n)
trip	[taksíTHi]	ταξίδι (n)
triple room	[tríklino]	τρίκλινο (n)
trout	[péstrofa]	πέστροφα (f)
truth	[alíthia]	αλήθεια (f)
twelve	[THóTHeka]	δώδεκα

twenty	[íkosi]	είκοσι
two	[THío]	δύο
two hundred	[THiakósia]	διακόσια
underground	[metró]	μετρό (n)
understand	[katalavéno]	καταλαβαίνω
unfortunately	[THistihós]	δυστυχώς
until	[méhri], [óspoo]	μέχρι, ώσπου
up	[páno]	πάνω
upset	[taragménos, -i, -o]	ταραγμένος, -η, -ο
usually	[siníthos]	συνήθως
vegetable	[lahanikó]	λαχανικό (n)
view	[théa]	θέα (f)
volley ball	[vólei]	βόλεϋ (n)
WC	[vesé]	WC (no Greek script) (n)
wait	[periméno]	περιμένω
waiter	[servitóros]	σερβιτόρος
waitress	[servitóra]	σερβιτόρα
wake up	[ksipnáo]	ξυπνάω
Wales	[oo-alía]	Ουαλία (f)
walk	[perpató]	περπατώ
walk, stroll, car ride	[vólta]	βόλτα (f)
want	[thélo]	θέλω
watch	[vlépo]	βλέπω
water	[neró]	νερό (n)
we	[emís]	εμείς
weather	[kerós]	καιρός (m)
week	[evTHomáTHa]	εβδομάδα (f)
weekend	[savatokíriako]	Σαββατοκύριακο (n)
well (e.g. I'm well)	[kalá]	καλά
well (e.g. Well, what?)	[lipón]	λοιπόν
what/how	[ti]	τι
when (in questions)	[póte]	πότε
when (within a sentence)	[ótan]	όταν
where	[poo]	πού
white	[áspros, -i, -o]	άσπρος, -η, -ο
white wine	[áspro krasí]	άσπρο κρασί (n)
why	[yiatí]	γιατί
window	[paráthiro]	παράθυρο (n)
wine	[krasí]	κρασί (n)
winter	[himónas]	χειμώνας (m)
woman/wife	[yinéka]	γυναίκα (f)
word	[léksi]	λέξη (f)
work (verb)	[THoolévo]	δουλεύω
work (noun)	[THooliá]	δουλειά (f)
world	[kózmos]	κόσμος (m)
write	[gráfo]	γράφω

writer	[sigraféas]	συγγραφέας (m/f)
yard	[avlí]	αυλή (f)
year	[hrónos]	χρόνος (m)
yellow	[kítrinos, -i, -o]	κίτρινος, -η, -ο
yes	[ne]	ναι
Yes, sure! Of course!	[málista]	μάλιστα
you (pl/fml)	[esís]	εσείς
you (pl/fml) (e.g. to you)	[sas]	σας
you (sing/infml)	[esí]	εσύ
you're welcome	[parakaló]	παρακαλώ
your (pl/fml)	[sas]	σας
your (sing/infml)	[soo]	σου

teach
yourself

greek
aristarhos matsukas

- Do you want to cover the basics then progress fast?
- Do you want to communicate in a range of situations?
- Do you want to reach a high standard?

Greek starts with the basics but moves at a lively pace to give you a good level of understanding, speaking and writing. You will have lots of opportunity to practise the kind of language you will need to be able to communicate with confidence and understand Greek culture.

teach yourself®

From Advanced Sudoku to Zulu, you'll find everything you need in the **teach yourself** range, in books, on CD and on DVD.

Visit **www.teachyourself.co.uk** for more details.

Advanced Sudoku & Kakuro
Afrikaans
Alexander Technique
Algebra
Ancient Greek
Applied Psychology
Arabic
Aromatherapy
Art History
Astrology
Astronomy
AutoCAD 2004
AutoCAD 2007
Ayurveda
Baby Massage and Yoga
Baby Signing
Baby Sleep
Bach Flower Remedies
Backgammon
Ballroom Dancing
Basic Accounting
Basic Computer Skills
Basic Mathematics
Beauty
Beekeeping
Beginner's Arabic Script
Beginner's Chinese
Beginner's Chinese Script

Beginner's Dutch
Beginner's French
Beginner's German
Beginner's Greek
Beginner's Greek Script
Beginner's Hindi
Beginner's Italian
Beginner's Japanese
Beginner's Japanese Script
Beginner's Latin
Beginner's Portuguese
Beginner's Russian
Beginner's Russian Script
Beginner's Spanish
Beginner's Turkish
Beginner's Urdu Script
Bengali
Better Bridge
Better Chess
Better Driving
Better Handwriting
Biblical Hebrew
Biology
Birdwatching
Blogging
Body Language
Book Keeping
Brazilian Portuguese

Bridge
Buddhism
Bulgarian
Business Chinese
Business French
Business Japanese
Business Plans
Business Spanish
Business Studies
Buying a Home in France
Buying a Home in Italy
Buying a Home in Portugal
Buying a Home in Spain
C++
Calculus
Calligraphy
Cantonese
Car Buying and Maintenance
Card Games
Catalan
Chess
Chi Kung
Chinese Medicine
Chinese
Christianity
Classical Music
Coaching
Collecting
Computing for the Over 50s
Consulting
Copywriting
Correct English
Counselling
Creative Writing
Cricket
Croatian
Crystal Healing
CVs
Czech
Danish
Decluttering
Desktop Publishing
Detox
Digital Photography
Digital Home Movie Making

Dog Training
Drawing
Dream Interpretation
Dutch
Dutch Conversation
Dutch Dictionary
Dutch Grammar
Eastern Philosophy
Electronics
English as a Foreign Language
English for International
  Business
English Grammar
English Grammar as a Foreign
  Language
English Vocabulary
Entrepreneurship
Estonian
Ethics
Excel 2003
Feng Shui
Film Making
Film Studies
Finance for Non-Financial
  Managers
Finnish
Fitness
Flash 8
Flash MX
Flexible Working
Flirting
Flower Arranging
Franchising
French
French Conversation
French Dictionary
French Grammar
French Phrasebook
French Starter Kit
French Verbs
French Vocabulary
Freud
Gaelic
Gardening
Genetics

Geology
German
German Conversation
German Grammar
German Phrasebook
German Verbs
German Vocabulary
Globalization
Go
Golf
Good Study Skills
Great Sex
Greek
Greek Conversation
Greek Phrasebook
Growing Your Business
Guitar
Gulf Arabic
Hand Reflexology
Hausa
Herbal Medicine
Hieroglyphics
Hindi
Hinduism
Home PC Maintenance and
  Networking
How to DJ
How to Run a Marathon
How to Win at Casino Games
How to Win at Horse Racing
How to Win at Online Gambling
How To Win at Poker
How to Write a Blockbuster
Human Anatomy & Physiology
Hungarian
Icelandic
Improve Your French
Improve Your German
Improve Your Italian
Improve Your Spanish
Improving Your Employability
Indian Head Massage
Indonesian
Instant French
Instant German
Instant Greek

Instant Italian
Instant Japanese
Instant Portuguese
Instant Russian
Instant Spanish
Irish
Irish Conversation
Irish Grammar
Islam
Italian
Italian Conversation
Italian Grammar
Italian Phrasebook
Italian Starter Kit
Italian Verbs
Italian Vocabulary
Japanese
Japanese Conversation
Java
JavaScript
Jazz
Jewellery Making
Judaism
Jung
Keeping a Rabbit
Keeping Aquarium Fish
Keeping Pigs
Keeping Poultry
Knitting
Korean
Latin American Spanish
Latin
Latin Dictionary
Latin Grammar
Latvian
Letter Writing Skills
Life at 50: For Men
Life at 50: For Women
Life Coaching
Linguistics
LINUX
Lithuanian
Magic
Mahjong
Malay
Managing Stress

Managing Your Own Career
Mandarin Chinese Conversation
Marketing
Marx
Massage
Mathematics
Meditation
Modern China
Modern Hebrew
Modern Persian
Mosaics
Music Theory
Mussolini's Italy
Nazi Germany
Negotiating
Nepali
New Testament Greek
NLP
Norwegian
Norwegian Conversation
Old English
One-Day French
One-Day French – the DVD
One-Day German
One-Day Greek
One-Day Italian
One-Day Portuguese
One-Day Spanish
One-Day Spanish – the DVD
Origami
Owning a Cat
Owning a Horse
Panjabi
PC Networking for Small
  Businesses
Personal Safety and Self
  Defence
Philosophy
Philosophy of Mind
Philosophy of Religion
Photography
Photoshop
PHP with MySQL
Physics
Piano

Pilates
Planning Your Wedding
Polish
Polish Conversation
Politics
Portuguese
Portuguese Conversation
Portuguese Grammar
Portuguese Phrasebook
Postmodernism
Pottery
PowerPoint 2003
PR
Project Management
Psychology
Quick Fix French Grammar
Quick Fix German Grammar
Quick Fix Italian Grammar
Quick Fix Spanish Grammar
Quick Fix: Access 2002
Quick Fix: Excel 2000
Quick Fix: Excel 2002
Quick Fix: HTML
Quick Fix: Windows XP
Quick Fix: Word
Quilting
Recruitment
Reflexology
Reiki
Relaxation
Retaining Staff
Romanian
Running Your Own Business
Russian
Russian Conversation
Russian Grammar
Sage Line 50
Sanskrit
Screenwriting
Serbian
Setting Up a Small Business
Shorthand Pitman 2000
Sikhism
Singing
Slovene

Small Business Accounting
Small Business Health Check
Songwriting
Spanish
Spanish Conversation
Spanish Dictionary
Spanish Grammar
Spanish Phrasebook
Spanish Starter Kit
Spanish Verbs
Spanish Vocabulary
Speaking On Special Occasions
Speed Reading
Stalin's Russia
Stand Up Comedy
Statistics
Stop Smoking
Sudoku
Swahili
Swahili Dictionary
Swedish
Swedish Conversation
Tagalog
Tai Chi
Tantric Sex
Tap Dancing
Teaching English as a Foreign
    Language
Teams & Team Working
Thai
The British Empire
The British Monarchy from
    Henry VIII
The Cold War
The First World War
The History of Ireland
The Internet
The Kama Sutra
The Middle East Since 1945
The Second World War
Theatre
Time Management
Tracing Your Family History
Training
Travel Writing

Trigonometry
Turkish
Turkish Conversation
Twentieth Century USA
Typing
Ukrainian
Understanding Tax for Small
    Businesses
Understanding Terrorism
Urdu
Vietnamese
Visual Basic
Volcanoes
Watercolour Painting
Weight Control through Diet &
    Exercise
Welsh
Welsh Dictionary
Welsh Grammar
Wills & Probate
Windows XP
Wine Tasting
Winning at Job Interviews
Word 2003
World Cultures: China
World Cultures: England
World Cultures: Germany
World Cultures: Italy
World Cultures: Japan
World Cultures: Portugal
World Cultures: Russia
World Cultures: Spain
World Cultures: Wales
World Faiths
Writing a Novel
Writing Crime Fiction
Writing for Children
Writing for Magazines
Writing Poetry
Xhosa
Yiddish
Yoga
Zen
Zulu